Fido, Come!

Training Your Dog with Love and Understanding

by Liz Palika

Doral Publishing
Wilsonville, Oregon
1993

Published by Doral Publishing,
P.O. Box 596, Wilsonville OR 97070.
Printed in the United States of America.
Copyedited by Luana Luther
Cover Illustration by Pam Posey
Cover Design by Tara Lee Torburn

Library of Congress Number: 93-71334
ISBN: 0944875-29-7

Palika, Liz.
        Fido, come! / Liz Palika. — Wilsonville,
    Or. : Doral Pub., 1993

        p.   ; cm.

        Includes bibliographical references and
    index.
        ISBN: 0944875-29-7

        1. Dogs—Training.   I. Title.
    SF431.P   363.7'0887 dc20
                                    00-

Dedication

to my dad, Wray Stout, who taught me to say "I can" instead of "I can't."

to my husband, Paul Palika, for his unswerving love, support and patience.

to my friend, Eva Shaw, for her enthusiastic encouragement.

and to the dogs who have taught me so much, including how to give of myself; Watachie, Michi, Inu, Chocho, Care Bear and Ursa.

Acknowledgements

My thanks to all my students, both human and canine, who have taught me so much over the years. My thanks, too, to my friends and students who helped with this book:

Eva Shaw and *Zippy*, Welsh Terrier

Linda Abel and *Henry*, Giant Schnauzer

Pam Posey and *Gracie*, Basset Hound

Kim Fraley and *Miss Kali*, Doberman Pinscher

Miles Dupriest and *Cassie*, Australian Shepherd

Cameron Dupriest and *Desi*, Australian Shepherd

Jane Manion and *Wilma* and *Emily*, Weimeraners

Tony Castellano and *Jazzy*, Weimeraner

Katherine Cleary and *Junior*, Australian Shepherd

Joan and Wayne Hamilton and *Kodi*, Newfoundland and *DC*, Golden Retriever

Jeri and Ken Klosson and the Poodles; *Chica*, *Amiga* and *Topo*

Rachel Amada and *Sparky*, Dalmation

Bonnie Zobell and *Jupiter*, Golden Retriever

Paul Palika and *Ursa*, Australian Shepherd and *Chocho*, Papillon.

iv

Foreword

If you ask Liz Palika why she spends most of her day working with people and dogs, she'll tell you that her "primary motivation is to make the world a better place for both."

As with most of us who are deeply entrenched in the *doggy culture*, it all started with her own dog—and a demolished sofa. With the help of an obedience class, that dog was trained and Liz's multifaceted career in dogs was launched. As a regular columnist of *Dog Fancy* magazine, Liz's name was familiar to me, but we first began our working relationship several years ago as fellow board members of The National Association of Dog Obedience Instructors. I found Liz to be a good communicator who shares her knowledge with enthusiasm, laughter, warmth and patience.

Fido, Come! is the result of many years of work toward her ultimate goal, a method of obedience training that revolves around refining the communication skills between dogs and their people. Her theme throughout is that training, whether it be manners for the household pet or advanced exercises for the competition dog, can be an enjoyable experience for both people and dogs.

This is a one-stop, easy-to-follow, user-friendly book. It's a program designed to produce happy, compliant pets and gentle, stress-free owners. If you do nothing more than read the quotes that begin each chapter, you're bound to appreciate better that special bond between you and your dog.

Terry Ryan

Terry Ryan is the past president of the National Association of Dog Obedience Instructors, teacher of canine behavior at the College of Veterinary Medicine, Washington State University, and program coordinator of the university-based People-Pet Partnership

Table of Contents

PART I. FIDO

Dogs are good for us, both emotionally and physically. (Australian Shepherd puppy)

Chapter 1
Dogs, People and the Evolution of Dog Training

A dog, well-educated, will ever enjoy a wise man's sympathy.
Johann Wolfgang Goethe

Dogs Are Good for Us

We have always been social creatures. Our lives have eternally been intertwined with other people, domestic animals and nature. Because the dog is also a social animal and is so adaptable, the dog alone of our domesticated animals has been present in almost all of our varied and assorted cultures, both as a companion and as a working animal.

Dogs are good for us, physically and emotionally. Historically, we've known that a dog's friendship and presence are as important as the job the dog performed, but researchers have recently come to the same conclusion.

Dr. Boris Levinson, a noted professor of psychology and an advocate of animal assisted therapy, said: "Dogs are of particular help to those groups of people which our society forces into a marginal position—children without families, the aged, the mentally retarded and the emotionally disturbed, both in and out of institutions, as well as the inmates of correctional facilities. All of these people suffer from isolation, a scarcity of rewarding activities and a sense of rejection from the world around them. A pet can literally mean the difference between life and death for such people."

Benefits from simply owning a dog don't come automatically because dog ownership is much more than just buying or adopting a dog. From puppyhood, Fido must be taught what living with people is all about. He needs to learn that food on the table is off limits, housetraining means relieving himself outside, accepting a leash is good, and so on. Even though dogs have been associated with man for thousands of years, each puppy must bond with man and must be taught, just as every child also needs an education.

The benefits of dog ownership begin quickly, though. Taking care of a puppy teaches patience and responsibility. Training Fido requires persistence, the establishment of a routine, assertiveness, a strong sense of fair play and the ability to laugh.

1

Even the simple act of taking Fido for a walk can accomplish strong sense of fair play and the ability to laugh at both yourself and much more than simply getting some fresh air and exercise. Dogs are a wonderful social lubricant and just the act of walking a dog can ease boredom or loneliness. Rarely can I take Care Bear and Ursa, my Australian Shepherds, for a walk without being approached by people we meet in my neighborhood or on the street. People ask me what kind of dogs they are or if they're related and comment on how well trained they are. They tell me about the dogs they have now or dogs they have owned in the past. Dog owners love to talk about their dogs and many friendships have been forged with dogs acting as the social mediators.

The list of benefits of ownership is almost endless. Owning a dog can also provide for a more positive self image, especially if the owner has been a successful dog owner and can display a well-behaved, attractive, healthy dog. A protective dog can increase the owner's sense of safety and a dog's requirement for play and exercise can stimulate an owner into getting out of the recliner and moving around. Training a dog requires patience, persistence and perseverance. Dogs are great emotional buffers, too. They are nonjudgmental and never criticize. Taking care of a dog can fill leisure hours by fulfilling the dog's need for play, grooming, affection, training and care.

Best of all, dogs make us laugh. We smile when the dog is cute, giggle when he's playing and have a good belly laugh when he's acting the clown. We laugh at the dog's antics as he chases a ball and we laugh at ourselves when we join in the game. Dogs don't respect social standing or our own inflated egos, and they will embarrass the best of us at inopportune moments. If you don't laugh, you'll cry and laughter is much healthier.

Researchers have now proved that all pets are good for us. Stroking a purring cat or a happy dog lowers blood pressure. Watching a tank of tropical fish allows us to relax after a stressful day. Several studies have shown that heart attack victims who own pets have a much higher survival rate than people who do not own pets. One theory is that everyone wants to feel loved and needed and pet owners that have bonds with their pets feel those emotions. Their pets are dependent upon them for their care and well-being and are important parts of families.

Dog Training Throughout History

Dog obedience training probably first began 12,000 years ago when a wolf cub tried to steal his caveman master's dinner. When Dino grabbed the pterodactyl thighbone and played keep-away around the fire, Caveman Fred discovered that Dino needed to learn some manners. Although no written records exist back to caveman

2

times, we do know that dogs lived with people and were an important part of their lives. A grave recently unearthed revealed the skeleton of a young girl surrounded by the skeletons of four dogs, each facing away from her. We can only guess that her grieving parents wanted her to have protection and companionship in the afterlife.

Who's happier—
the dog or the owner?
(Toy Poodle)

Cave drawings and statuary show that dogs were used to aid in the hunt, to drive prey to the human hunters, to run down and track prey animals. Cave rock paintings at Hill Station, Sefar, Algeria, clearly show a hunter armed with a bow, arrow and quiver following a tracking dog. Other cave drawings in France and Niger show various hunting scenes with dogs running down wild oxen or other hoofed prey.

Dogs and people were of mutual benefit to each other and domestication was probably a two-way affair. Early man got a partner to help put food on the table, warn of dangers and provide a new type of companionship. Fido got food, a warm body to cuddle with on cold nights, shelter from the weather and he, too, was the recipient of friendship.

As civilization developed and art became a part of most societies, the dog was portrayed in art as perceived in each culture. A knife sheath in the Cairo Museum is dated 6,000 BC and is decorated with dogs. Also in Egypt, around 2,600 BC, dogs, especially Greyhounds,

Therapy dogs provide hospitalized people with nonjudgmental love and affection. The "Love on a Leash" therapy dog group from Oceanside, California regularly visits local Alzheimer's facilities.

were included in tomb decorations portraying hunting scenes. In Persia, the dog was considered to be the best of all animals because he was both the guardian of the flock and the defender of man and his position is reflected in many pieces of art. Throughout the Near East, the Sahara regions, Eastern Asia, Europe and Mexico, dogs are found in the artwork and tombs of early man.

Zendavesta, one of the oldest existing books, details the traditions, habits and moral and ethical laws of mankind thousands of years ago. One headline in the book reads: "Without the help of dog—no world." We can surmise that the headline might continue: "Without training—no dog."

Although cave drawings and ancient artwork do show the place dogs held in ancient societies, it's difficult to tell how dogs were trained. Leashes are seen in some works—a Persian statue shows a man and two leashed dogs by his side. Although instinct can account for much of what the dogs were used for, guardians of domesticated animals, tracking dogs, hunting dogs and so on, there also had to be some training so the dogs could live peacefully in the growing societies.

Europeans began formally training dogs as far back as 2,000 years before Christ. At one point, the early Germans were being defeated by the Romans' style of fighting, in which the soldiers carried large iron shields in front of them so that spears and arrows bounced off. In retaliation, the Germans, who had already trained dogs for other

4

purposes, trained their war dogs to attack the legs and feet of the Roman soldiers.

Sophisticated training was known as long ago as Christ's time. An artist's rendering of dogs leading the blind was found on the wall of a house in Pompeii that was buried by lava in 79 AD. A German king in 100 BC was reported by several sources to be the first to use a guide dog.

It was during the medieval era that the dog gradually began taking his place as part of the family. A closer companionship developed between dog and owner and training became more refined. During this era, man also began breeding the dog for specific attributes, such as size, temperament, looks and working instincts. Many of the breeds we know today originated during medieval times—the Papillon as a lap dog, the Rottweiler as a drover or draft dog and the Mastiff as a guard dog.

During the centuries that followed, the dog continued to aid his owner in the conquest of the world around him. The dog was a hunter, tracker, draft animal, war dog, shepherd, flock guardian, sled dog, protector and companion. The dog became more integrated into the changing world and history reflected it. Sculptures, paintings, songs and stories showed the dog's place in man's society.

Obedience competition can be both a challenge and a lot of fun, as Pam and Gracie can testify after a High in Trial award. (Basset Hound)

Dogs bring love and laughter, a warm body to hug and unconditional love. (Papillon)

Dog Training Comes of Age in the United States

Dog training was well known in the United States by the 1920s and '30s, but it was primarily limited to the traditional working breeds: German Shepherd Dogs and Doberman Pinschers. Helen Whitehouse Walker was the inspiration for modern dog training, and especially competition, in the United States.

She bred Standard Poodles under the kennel name Carillon Kennels and was developing a reputation for quality dogs. However, friends involved with other breeds often commented to her that Poodles were "sissy dogs." Mrs. Walker decided that the only way to convince everyone that the Poodle, despite its fancy appearance, was intelligent was to teach her Poodles a number of obedience exercises.

Mrs. Walker patterned her training after the tests held in England under the rules established by the Associated Sheep, Police, Army Dog Society (ASPADS). The first test was held at Mt. Kisco, New

York, in October 1933. The eight entries included Labrador Retrievers, Poodles, Springer Spaniels and German Shepherds.

The first American Kennel Club obedience trial held in conjunction with an all-breed show was held June 9, 1934, with the North Westchester Kennel Club. Ten dogs competed—three Cocker Spaniels, three Poodles, three Doberman Pinschers and one Newfoundland—and first place was awarded to a Poodle, Nunsoe Skagin of Carillon, owned and handled by Henry Whitehouse. In response to pleas from dog enthusiasts all over the country, Helen Walker and her good friend Blanche Saunders, plus three Standard Poodles, set out across the country in a 1936 Buick Sedan pulling a 21-foot Auto Cruiser house trailer. They gave obedience demonstrations throughout the nation, stopping in Pennsylvania, Ohio, Texas, California and innumerable places in between. Ten weeks and 10 thousand miles later, a new American sport was born.

The American Kennel Club (AKC) issued its first Obedience Regulations in April 1936. It set regulations for three titles, the Companion Dog (CD), Companion Dog Excellent (CDX) and Utility Dog (UD). The exercises and rules have been revised and changed over the years and additional classes and titles have been added, but the basic concept has remained the same: All dogs, not just working dogs, can be trained. Helen Walker was emphatic that obedience training would bring out the best in every dog.

Modern Dog Training

Dog training today has evolved in a number of different directions, encompassing working dogs, hunting dogs, herding dogs, dog sports and the home companion dog. There is, literally, something available for every dog and every owner.

Obedience training and competition have continued to grow since Helen Walker's and Blanche Saunders' time. The AKC's program has evolved and changed over the years and has grown in scope. The United Kennel Club (UKC) added obedience to its roster of activities in 1979. Many rare-breed clubs, including the enormous Australian Shepherd Club of America, offer obedience programs and titles.

First open only to purebred dogs, mixed-breed dogs can now earn obedience titles through several groups or registries. The largest of these is the Mixed Breed Dog Clubs of America (MBDCA). MBDCA offers obedience, tracking and retrieving titles and also has conformation competition. For more information, or a copy of the regulations, write to: Mixed Breed Dog Clubs of America, 512 Minahen Street, Napa, CA 94559.

A number of other obedience competitions are available outside of the different kennel club programs. There are national competitions, such as the Gaines Dog Obedience Championships that draw the top obedience dogs and handlers from all over the country for yearly regional and national competitions. Many areas offer obedience competitions for club teams, such as Southern California's Top Dog Competitions. Member clubs of the Southern California Obedience Council send teams made up of their best dogs and handlers to a once-a-year competition to choose, through competition, the best Novice Dog, Open Dog, Utility Dog and Best Team. The competition is fierce but always laced with good humor and sportsmanship.

Many dog sports have been developed and dog owners can play for fun and exercise or for competition; most of these activities are open to both purebred and mixed-breed dogs. Agility is a sport that combines a playground with a military obstacle course. Dogs must jump hurdles, go through tunnels, walk over different surfaces and are judged for both speed and accuracy.

Flyball is a sport that has relay teams run over a set of four hurdles, trigger a mechanism that tosses a tennis ball in the air and then turn and run back to the owner over the hurdles again. The fastest team wins. Scent hurdles racing is very similar except the dog must use his scenting ability to find his owner's dumbbell instead of catching a tennis ball.

Other dog sports include Frisbee catching, sledding, carting, weight pulling, lure coursing, terrier trials, retrieving trials, hunting tests, herding trials and much, much more. All of these dog sports can be played for fun or for competition. It's your choice. All you need is a dog with the instinct, attitude and physical capability to play the sport and your time, patience and training ability.

Dog training can be very serious, too. Sophisticated techniques are available to train top-notch dogs to serve the disabled, the blind, the hearing impaired, people with balance or other mobility problems, and even people with emotional disabilities.

Therapy dogs are being trained for work in hospitals and nursing homes to give love and affection in a natural, nonjudgmental manner. By doing so, these animals motivate people to enjoy life again and to aid in healing. Therapy dogs also work with children and the elderly, visiting public schools, special schools, retirement homes, Alzheimer's care facilities and senior centers.

The military, police, search and rescue units and the customs service would be seriously handicapped without their working dogs. The dogs aid in searches for lost people, suspected criminals, drugs, bombs, contraband and a variety of other things that can be identified by smell. The dogs also work with crowd control and with apprehensions. Most importantly, these working dogs help keep the peace. Just the presence of a police dog, coupled with the dog's image and reputation, especially the German Shepherd, Rottweiler and Doberman, helps defuse potential problems more than any uniformed officer.

Over thousands of years, dog owners have found that training, formal or informal, purposeful or accidental, taught Fido what was expected of him and what his limits were. Training taught the dog the meaning of certain words, commands and hand signals. In many cases, such as with a guard dog or herding dog, training controlled or guided the dog's instinctive actions.

Training also helped the dog fit into a human world. Training built the best relationship possible between dog and owner. When there is time spent together, learning from each other and sharing experiences, the bond grows stronger and the understanding deeper.

Once you have trained a dog, you will never again live with a dog that is not trained. In addition, as many dog owners have found out over the years, obedience training can be fun.

Dogs are social animals and friends always enjoy time to play.

Chapter Two

Setting the Stage for Success

In the beginning, God created man. But seeing him so feeble, He gave him the dog.
Toussenel

In the Beginning

Even though dogs and people have lived together for thousands of years, the bond that we have with dogs must be re-learned with each new puppy. The bond itself is not hereditary although the tendency and ability to bond are and can vary from dog to dog and breed to breed. The relationship between a dog and owner that makes owning a dog so special doesn't happen automatically. To understand when and how the bond develops, it's important to understand that a dog is a unique creature, not a person in a fuzzy dog costume.

Most researchers agree that thousands of years ago the first domesticated dogs were descended from wolves. Wolves are very social animals and live in an extended family pack. The group might consist of a mated couple who are the leaders or alpha male and female, one or two other adults, a couple of last year's pups and the newest litter. Contrary to Hollywood's perception of wolves, this is a very harmonious family. Each individual knows his or her place in the pack and most are very friendly and supportive of each other.

The only discord occurs when there is a change in the pack. When an adult dies, becomes disabled or leaves, or when another adult tries to join, then there may be some jockeying for status. If a pup stays with the pack, there may be some rearranging in the pack order as the pup matures. During these changes, most of the communication is accomplished through body postures, facial expressions and verbalizations—growls, barks and whines. In most situations, the alpha or dominant wolf can quell insubordination with a stern look. Wolves are expert communicators. There may occasionally be fights but rarely enough to cause bodily harm. After all, survival of the pack may depend on the number of sound, healthy adults available to hunt.

Many people feel that the dog has been able to adapt so well to human society because we live in family groups and our family can be compared to a wolf pack. It can be safely said that we are social

At nine weeks of age puppies are ready to go to new homes. (Australian Shepherd puppies.)

This nine-week-old litter of Australian Shepherds is being socialized to different people so that they will have a head start before going to their new homes.

creatures just as the dog is but comparing our families to wolf packs is taking it a little too far. Our families are much more chaotic than the typical wolf pack. For one thing, we are very confusing when communicating; we say one thing but our body language often says another. We tell "white lies" to spare feelings. Fido doesn't understand lies. We are also much less consistent with our social rules and discipline. Fido is allowed on the couch when he's clean but scolded if he jumps up with dirty feet. People are very complex, confusing creatures! We can use the two social groups as a comparison to explain dog behavior, but it is important to remember that in reality, our family is very different from a wolf pack.

Mom's Influence

For the first three weeks of a puppy's life, the family and the pack are unimportant as far as Fido is concerned. The only one of any significance is Momma dog. She is the key to Fido's survival and is the source of food, warmth and security.

At four weeks of age, Fido's basic needs still center on his mother but his littermates are becoming more important. Littermates provide security when Mom leaves the nest and are built-in playmates. During this period, Fido learns to use his senses to follow sounds and to focus his eyes. His curiosity about the world around him is developing now and he'll begin exploring the whelping box or nest.

Mom starts disciplining the pups at this age and her instinctive training is vitally important to the puppies' future acceptance of owner dominance, discipline and training. We can also learn a lot by watching Mom discipline her babies. Ebony, a tri-colored Australian Shepherd and the mother of my Care Bear, is a wonderful teacher. If a puppy bites her too hard, her correction is short, sharp, fair and firm:

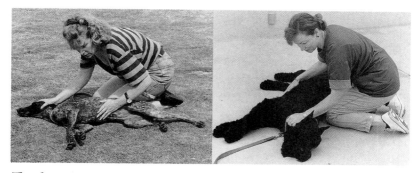

The dominance-down exercise teaches Fido to relax and accept your handling. (German Shorthaired Pointer, left, and Giant Schnauzer, right)

a growl and a muzzle bite that ceases as soon as the puppy reacts submissively. Every correction is always followed by love and affection, and she never holds a grudge.

During weeks five through seven, Fido is going through some tremendous changes, both mental and physical. He is gaining coordination and learning to walk without stumbling. He's learning to recognize people and is starting to respond to individual voices. Fido's littermates are becoming increasingly more important. The wrestling and scuffling with brothers and sisters teaches each puppy how to get along, how to play, when the play is too rough, when to be submissive and what to take seriously. Mom's discipline at this point teaches Fido to accept discipline, correction, training and affection.

The eighth week of Fido's life is a fearful time. Even though this is the traditional time for puppies to leave the breeder and go to a new home, they would benefit more by remaining with Mom for one more week. If Fido leaves Mom now, and is frightened on the car ride home—that one bad experience will have lasting repercussions. The same applies to the veterinarian's office, the introduction to the leash or the neighborhood. Anything that frightens Fido during this period could remain a fear for the rest of his life.

When You Bring Fido Home
At nine or ten weeks of age, Fido is ready to go to a new home. This is when he develops the ability to form permanent relationships. Take advantage of this important stage of growth and spend time with him. Play with him gently and cuddle him. Begin some very basic training. Teach Fido his name by repeating it in a high-pitched, happy tone of voice when he moves toward you. (Never use his name to scold him.) Encourage Fido to follow you by talking to him in a high-pitched tone of voice, clapping your hands and patting your leg.

The dictionary's definition of socialization,"To make fit or adapt to the needs of a common group," means that every puppy must learn to get along in a society that includes people of all varieties, dogs, cats, sheep, cars, trucks, motorcycles, airplanes, jackhammers, whistles, sirens and balloons. Today's dogs live in a noisy and potentially frightening place.

Socialization is an ongoing process throughout puppyhood but should begin in earnest now. Socialization is more than simply introducing Fido to other people and dogs and making noise around the puppy. It is making sure that Fido is not frightened by all these things and that he is introduced to them gradually, as he can handle them. For example, a trip to the pet store for dog food could include introducing Fido to the clerks, to some customers and to the store parrot. It could also include walking up three stairs, walking on a tile floor in the store and walking on an automatic door opener. All of these things, done gradually and repeated all over town, add up to a well-socialized, confidant puppy.

Fido's pack instincts are developing now, too, and you can use this stage of growth to help teach Fido his position in the family. Gently lay Fido on his side, feet away from you and restrain him with one hand on the scruff of the neck and one hand on the body. (See photo.) If Fido resists, give a verbal correction such as a deep-throated, growly "Acck!" or "That's enough!" Don't scream and yell; Fido will not understand and you will only cause him to panic.

Once Fido has relaxed under your hands, begin stroking him calmly and gently. Run your hands over his entire body and don't allow him to resist. This exercise helps establish Fido's place in the family—YOU are doing it to HIM—therefore, you are in charge. This exercise, called the dominance down, also helps calm Fido when he's over excited. Just keep him in the position until you feel him relax under your hands, then very casually let him up. Don't make a fuss over him, keep it matter of fact. The dominance down also teaches Fido that you must be able to touch his body so that you can take care of it, making grooming and veterinary care easier on everyone.

At 11 and 12 weeks of age, discipline becomes more important. Love, attention and security are vital, but Fido is ready for the establishment of some basic household rules. Don't allow Fido to do anything now, such as jumping on people, climbing on the furniture or eating off your plate, that you don't want him to do when he's full grown.

Begin retrieving games at this age. Throw a toy about six feet away and encourage Fido to chase it. When he grabs the toy, call him back to you. Praise him enthusiastically when he brings it back to you and allows you to take it from him. If he runs away from you and turns it into a keep-away game, stop playing. Don't chase him! Let him learn that he must play by your rules. Chasing a ball or soft Frisbee can be good exercise for the puppy and it sets the stage for a sound working relationship.

From 13 to 16 weeks of age, Fido begins testing his place in the family so the dominance exercises are very important. Consistency in enforcing the household rules is vital and everyone in the family should be doing things the same way. If Fido senses a soft heart or a weak link in the chain of command, he will take advantage of it.

At four months of age, Fido is past the most critical periods of development, but cannot be considered "grown up" either emotionally or physically. The dominance exercises and socialization should be continued and obedience training should become more important.

15

Even though she is five-years old, Ursa still has a crate. It is her bed at night, her refuge in stressful times and her own private den. (Australian Shepherd)

Joan uses a treat to draw DC's eyes up to her to teach him the "Watch Me."

Laura uses a treat to bring the puppy's head up, and a hand on the rump to make sure the puppy follows through and sits. (Australian Shepherd)

Steps for Success

Because Fido is living with a human family instead of a dog pack, there are times when he is going to be confused by the messages you are giving him—intentionally or unintentionally. There will also be plenty of times when you're going to shake your head and wonder why on earth he did what he did. After all, what purpose was served by shaking the stuffing out of the chaise lounge cushion? (Fido thinks it was a lot of fun!)

You can help alleviate some of this confusion by setting up some basic rules that everyone in the household should follow, even if you have to post them around the house. These rules will allow you to establish and reinforce Fido's place in the family without having to resort to hard-line training methods that might damage the relationship more that it could help it.

1. *Fido must have his own bed and must sleep there.* He's not to sleep in your bed or in the kids' beds. Even though you may enjoy having a warm, fuzzy foot warmer, that is not Fido's job. Get a cat to do that. When Fido sleeps in your bed, he starts thinking that perhaps he's your equal. Especially if he can push against you and cause you to move over while you're sleeping.

Fido's bed should be a crate. (See Chapter Five) His crate can take the place of your nightstand next to your bed, if you want. That way you can reach over and tap on the top of it if he starts making noise, and you can hear him if he needs to take a trip outside during the night.

Even if you don't put Fido's crate next to your bed, it should be in your bedroom. By putting it there, he gets eight uninterrupted hours of being close to you, listening to you snore or toss and turn, of smelling you and being comforted by your closeness. If Fido is made to sleep in the garage, laundry room or worse yet, back yard, he is going to suffer from loneliness and a variety of behavior problems could easily develop as a result. Just being near you is important, especially nowadays when people are so busy and have so little leisure time.

2. Practice the dominance down regularly. Use it as a training tool when Fido throws a temper tantrum or challenges you. Rather than jerking him around on the leash or arguing with him, simply put him down and sit there with him until he calms down.

Use the dominance down as a social handling tool so that you can groom him and care for him. Lay him down and when he is relaxed, go over his body from nose to tail, checking for burrs, foxtails, fleas, ticks, cuts, scrapes, lumps, bumps and bruises. This can turn into a very pleasurable puppy massage and teaches him that you must be able to touch and take care of his body.

The dominance down can also be used as a quiet time for bonding. When you're watching a show on the television, sit down on the floor and have Fido do a half hour dominance down in front of you while you give him a massage and do some social handling. Don't allow him to decide when to get up. Decide on a time before you put him down and stick to that time. If you're going to do a 15-minute or 30-minute down, don't let him up after 10 minutes just because he's restless.

3. Watch me! Many dogs get into trouble, both in the home and out in public, because they have never been taught to focus on and really look at their owners. When you teach Fido to look at you on command and to look to you for guidance, you are reinforcing your position as his leader. You are also eliminating a lot of trouble that he might have otherwise discovered on his own.

Have Fido sitting in front of you. (See Chapter Four) With a treat in your right hand, take the treat from Fido's nose to your face, drawing his eyes up to yours, as you tell him, "Fido, watch me!" As soon as he makes eye contact with you, smile and praise him, "Good boy!" and pop the treat in his mouth. Your timing is very important because you want to make sure that you're praising the eye contact, not looking at the treat.

After a few days of practice, start using it around the house. If Fido is in the room with you, simply tell him, "Fido, watch me!" Dur-

The bond we have with dogs is renewed with each puppy and is strengthened through training and understanding. (Australian Shepherd)

ing this stage of training make sure that you have some treats and ALWAYS use them. Right now we want the "Watch me" to be a very exciting command for the dog and your happy smile, verbal praise and the treat will help make that happen.

4. *Does Fido nudge you when he wants attention?* Does he nudge you when he wants you to throw the ball? Does he paw you when he wants a treat? Do you do what he wants? If you do, then Fido has trained you well and has you responding to his wishes. That makes him the dominant dog in his eyes or at least equal to you.

To change that attitude, have Fido sit for everything that he wants: Have him sit before you scratch his ears; have him sit before you toss the ball; and have him sit before you give him a treat, or before you put down the dinner bowl; and, have him sit before going outside or coming in. By doing this, you are having Fido do something for you before you do something that he wants; therefore, you are maintaining control of the situation. If he refuses to sit, nothing happens—no treat, no ball, no petting.

If Fido willingly sits for everything and still becomes a pest demanding petting or the ball, don't allow him to set the rules as to how much time you must spend catering to him. If you want to read the newspaper and Fido is being a pest, make him lie down and be still. (See Chapter Four, *Building a Sound Foundation.*)

5. *Make sure that some very simple things you do don't give Fido the wrong idea.* When you go up stairs, have you noticed that Fido charges up to the top and then turns around and waits for you? Well, in reality he's not waiting. He's savoring being the top dog as you follow slowly BEHIND him with LOWERED eyes (looking at the stairs) as a properly submissive dog would do.

Put Fido on the leash and teach him that he cannot charge up the stairs and that he must wait for you. If he tries to go past you, brace yourself so that you don't fall and snap the leash, telling him "Fido, NO! Get back!" and position him behind you on the stairs. You will have to repeat it again and again because he's not going to easily give up, especially if he's been doing this a while.

The same thing might be happening at your doors. Does Fido charge through any door as soon as it's opened? As far as Fido is concerned, the dominant dog always goes first. You can teach him to wait for you just as you did on the stairs, using the leash. If Fido is off the leash, simply close the door in his face, turn around and walk away. After a few repetitions, Fido is going to start watching you instead of the door because he's going to be confused: "What happened to the fun game?"

Teach Fido to wait behind you at all doors, even the door to the bedroom. If he tries to charge past, close the door, block him with your leg or snap the leash. If he does get past you, DON'T follow him through the door or into the room. Turn away. If you need something from that room, wait until Fido comes back out looking for you, then try again.

6. *Set up some household rules and require that everyone in the house abides by them, consistently.* Don't allow Fido to do anything as a puppy that you are going to dislike when he's full grown. Do you want him up on the furniture? Do you want him to beg in the kitchen? Or under the dining room table? Do you want him to steal things from the closet? Carrying around a slipper might be funny now but what are you going to think when he's carted out all of your shoes?

7. *Always feed Fido AFTER you have eaten.* If he eats in the morning, eat breakfast first. If he eats in the evening, eat dinner first. The Alpha dog ALWAYS eats first. This seems like a very simple thing but food is one of the dog's strongest survival instincts and eating is very important to most dogs. This simple rule will make a big impression on Fido.

Living with Fido and training Fido are much easier when you understand his heritage, how his mother started his training and how he views living with us. Never feel guilty about making Fido behave and observing some rules. As a social animal, he needs rules and limits, a feeling of usefulness, a job to do, companionship and a strong, caring leader—you!

We are, dogs and people, really made for each other and the relationship that we have is unique in the world. Although we have relationships with cats, horses, monkeys, rats and other domesticated animals, even the best of those relationships can't begin to measure up to what we share with dogs. Understanding Fido only makes that relationship better.

Chapter Three

How Fido Learns

But now ask the beasts, and they shall teach thee.

Job 12:7

Can Fido Think? And Reason?

Aristotle said that the primary difference between man and animals was that although animals could learn and remember, man was the only animal capable of reason. Webster's *New World Dictionary* defines reason as the ability to think, draw conclusions and to use sound thought.

Whether they knew Aristotle or not, most dog owners will vehemently disagree that dogs are incapable of reasoning. They get a great deal of enjoyment seeing their dogs think and puzzle out problems. The challenge might be as simple as figuring how to get a bone from the other side of a fence or as complicated as opening a door with a round door knob.

Dogs do think and reason differently from the way we do. Obviously, Fido's instincts are not the same as ours, which is the basis for how he reacts to what happens around him. He is a dog with four feet on the ground and equipped with senses that are similar, but yet unlike our own. For example, Fido's sense of smell is thousands of times more sensitive than ours, as is his hearing. Our eyesight is more important to us compared to Fido's, as is our sense of touch. We live in the same world but perceive it differently.

The most essential deviation is due to language. Dogs have a complex language comprised of verbalizations, facial expressions and body postures. It is rich in meaning and is vital to Fido's relationships with people and other dogs.

Fido has a variety of vocalizations, each of which has its own meaning. A deeper bark with a growl indicates a footstep outside. A volley of deep barks means a stranger is at the door while a barrage of higher pitched barks welcomes home a family member. Groans and moans while you are cuddling Fido or scratching his tummy obviously show his happiness, trust and relaxation.

Fido's body language is just as expressive as his vocalizations. His tail conveys happiness, excitement, fear, worry, unhappiness and submission. When combined with other body postures, his language becomes easy to understand. When Fido bows, with front end lowered and rear end high, he's inviting play. The bow is often accompanied by smiles, quick high-pitched barks and is always topped off with a wagging tail.

Man's language gives us a decided advantage. Spoken and written words convey thoughts, dreams, facts, events, abstracts, lies and much, much more. Just try to think without using words. It's almost impossible! Our language and ability to formulate a language is what separates us from the rest of the animal kingdom.

Fido will never be fluent in our spoken language. Tone of voice, facial expressions and body language will always be more important to his understanding. These methods of communication are natural to him and more like his own means of communicating. This is why your smile and petting work as well, if not better, than any spoken words. Fido can, however, learn to recognize many of our spoken words.

My Australian Shepherd, Care Bear, understands and responds to about 250 different words and phrases. The words start with the basic obedience commands: heel, sit, down, stay and come, and extend to more advanced obedience commands. He also understands commands for sheep herding, tracking, therapy dog work, agility and carting. Then, there are a number of different commands and phrases that I use around the house. Care Bear is, of course, special to me but most dogs can learn to understand an extensive vocabulary.

Dogs also learn by experience and are good at putting two and two together. If Fido discovers you have left the gate open as you take the trash cans out to the street, he might try to take advantage and

The herding instincts and prey drive (the instinct to chase moving things) are very close. (Bearded Collie)

24

dash out. Now, if he gets away from you and has a good time running around the neighborhood, you may have a hard time breaking him of that habit. It was self-rewarding and he'll remember! However, if you see him begin to come through the gate, slam the metal trash can lid to the driveway as you run for the gate, Fido may turn around and run back into the yard. He thinks it's noisy and dangerous outside the gate. He'll remember that, too!

I like to think that if Aristotle had been a dog owner, more people would appreciate that Fido is obviously capable of learning, remembering and reasoning. We must keep in mind when we are teaching Fido that he is a dog, not a person in a fuzzy dog costume. It's our job to figure out how to communicate with him and to teach him; however, we can learn from the behaviors he instinctively knows to help the process.

Influences on Learning

Instincts. Fido has some very primeval instincts that were passed down to him from his ancestors. The first and most important instinct is to eat. If a puppy doesn't eat, he will die. The strength of this instinct can be used later to assist you in your training.

The "fight-or-flight" instinct is what governs Fido's reactions to danger. Some dogs have a very strong flight response and will try to run away from anything that is strange or frightening. Jupiter is a handsome Golden Retriever. Even though he is very well trained and was well socialized as a puppy, he has a very strong flight instinct and a tendency to avoid or run away from anything he doesn't understand.

Other dogs have a stronger fight reaction and will stand their ground even in the face of danger. This could cause them to react aggressively to anything or anyone new. On the other hand, a dog with a strong flight instinct may try to run away from anything evenly remotely scary, including an agility obstacle, a jump or even a sheet blowing on the clothesline. Both extremes can cause training problems.

The prey drive, or chase instinct, is another survival instinct. Fido's ancestors needed to hunt for their food and were keyed to respond to anything that moved. This instinct is why dogs chase moving cars, birds that fly over the yard or rabbits flushed in the field. This instinct is also why dogs that live peaceably with cats will often chase a stray cat that runs through the garden.

The urge to reproduce is a very strong instinct. A female dog in season is extremely emotional. The intact male who knows she's around can become uncontrollable. Survival of the species is dependent on reproducing. Fido doesn't realize that there is a severe

Wilma has a strong prey drive and when she doesn't have birds to work, a tennis ball will do fine. (Weimaraner)

pet overpopulation problem, he is simply following his instinctive drives.

For most families, either a spayed bitch or a neutered dog is the best choice for a family companion dog. With the sexual hormones significantly reduced after spaying or neutering, behaviors associated with reproduction are diminished. Mounting, leg lifting, dog aggression and roaming, to name just a few, are eliminated, or if not eliminated at least controllable. Spayed and neutered dogs are often more bonded to their owners, too, and are, as a general rule, more affectionate.

Spaying or neutering does not change the dog's personality; it simply removes the sexual hormones and hence, the urge to reproduce. Spayed and neutered dogs can compete in obedience trials and other performance events. They are barred only from conformation competition.

There are a number of other instincts that explain many of Fido's actions but these four are the most important to us right now.

Breed Characteristics. Fido's breed can have great bearing on his behavior and how he learns. Each breed today was developed for a specific reason; rarely was a breed continued simply because someone liked it. Before modern times, men were too poor to have luxury animals. Instead, the dog was needed for tracking game or for pointing, flushing or retrieving game birds. He hunted and killed vermin, guarded against trespassers, or herded sheep. Fido had a valuable job.

The breed's originators combined characteristics that were beneficial to those jobs. If a herding dog had to handle rough terrain yet be gentle on the sheep, those characteristics were looked for in the breeding stock. If a dog couldn't do the job or had a number of unfavorable traits, then that dog wasn't bred. Thus each breed, and sometimes groups of breeds, became known for some very specific things. Herding dogs that are used to gather sheep like to run in circles and will often circle together children, groups of people or even the family cats. However, herding dogs that are used to drive cattle are known to be heel nippers. That's how they move cattle and they don't understand that it's not appreciated by soft-skinned people. Sighthounds are incredibly fleet-footed hunters who find and track their prey visually. This trait is sometimes triggered by a running cat or rabbit. Sled dogs were bred to pull loads and run all day long in rugged conditions. Beagles were bred to use their noses to hunt and to bay while hunting. Terriers dig out their prey and often have a hard time understanding why the petunia bed is off limits. And the list goes on! All of these characteristics must be taken into account during the dog's training and learning process.

Body Sensitivity. Does Fido cry every time he gets a vaccination or is he the stoic kind? Body sensitivity can be seen in several forms, one of which is Fido's pain threshold. Dogs that have a very low pain tolerance will react to day-to-day life, as well as training, very differently from the dog that has a high pain threshold.

Fido will also demonstrate his body sensitivity when you pet him. My youngest Australian Shepherd, Ursa, is not very body sensitive. To pet her so that she enjoys it, I thump on her rib cage and scratch (hard!) down her back. On the other hand, some dogs can't handle a lot of physical praise (hands-on petting) because the petting over-stimulates them. As a result, they become very active, spinning in circles, jumping, sometimes even biting. Gretchen is a lovely Doberman Pinscher. Her only petting during training session is a soft ear rub because any more than that is too stimulating. This sensitivity can obviously affect your approach to training the dog.

How We Affect Our Dogs

Physical Characteristics. When people began selectively breeding dogs for specific physical traits rather than the function for which the breed was originally designed, many breeds began to deviate from the "norm." They developed exaggerated characteristics: short legs, long backs, heavy bodies, extra heavy coat, extreme angulation, short muzzles, wrinkled skin, poor feet. These can all affect the dog's health, physical stamina and ability to handle training.

Genetic Health. Indiscriminate breeding or injudicious breeding has unfortunately produced generation upon generation of unhealthy dogs. Diseases are prevalent that can incapacitate a dog. Today, hip dysplasia is common in many breeds of all sizes, not just large dogs, and is crippling. Elbow dysplasia is seen more and more frequently in large and medium-sized breeds. Thyroid problems, bleeding disorders, allergies, blindness and deafness are just the tip of the iceberg concerning genetic problems.

Home Environment. Fido's home environment plays a large part in his emotional and physical well being and his ability to learn. He needs a secure place to live, a regular routine, good food, exercise, health care, regular vaccinations, protection from parasites and most important, time with you.

Any disruptions at home, such as a new baby, a child going to college, a divorce or marriage, new furniture, new working hours, and especially, a move to a new house, can upset Fido's sense of routine. Many dogs get into trouble when these disruptive things occur. In these situations, Fido is not being bad when he chews on the lawnchair; instead, he's reacting in the only way he can to the birth of the new baby and the fact that he's spending more time outside, alone. (For more information, see Chapter Five, *Problem Prevention and Problem Solving.*)

Your Behavior. Fido doesn't understand a personality changed by drugs or alcohol. Never try to train Fido when you have been indulging. He doesn't cope well with extremes of emotion, either. If you've had a hard day at work, don't take it out on Fido! It's not his fault.

Your Ability to Communicate. When you are teaching Fido anything new, keep in mind that he wasn't born understanding English, French, Spanish or any other human language. As a comparison, think what you would feel like if you were dropped in the middle of a *Martian* city. You wouldn't know the spoken or written language,

This nine-week-old puppy is learning to navigate the agility dog walk, motivated by food treats, steady hands and verbal encouragement. (Australian Shepherd)

body language, customs or anything else. How confusing, frustrating and scary that would be.

It's your job to communicate with Fido and to teach him a verbal language. It's not his job to make you understand, although he does that pretty well. He brings you a ball when he wants to play and brings you his leash when he wants to go for a walk. What are you doing to communicate with him?

Teaching Fido

Positive Reinforcement. Most of us work much better with praise than criticism. If you put a lot of effort into a project and your boss tells you what a good job you did (perhaps with a small token of appreciation in your paycheck), you will be motivated to continue your hard work. And you will work much harder than if your effort goes unnoticed or is taken for granted.

Driving to work one day, I saw a wonderful saying on a freeway billboard, author unknown: "Anything that is praised or rewarded will be repeated." As a society, we are quick to complain or criticize, especially if we receive poor service or an inferior product. Unfortunately, we are very slow to praise. If we receive excellent service, we are less likely to praise the establishment or clerk than we would be to complain should the service be poor. This is too bad because we all work better for praise than we do criticism.

When teaching Fido, we use as much positive reinforcement as possible because it works. Positive reinforcement tells Fido that what he did was good. It encourages him when he's unsure but is trying. Most importantly, positive reinforcement gives Fido the incentive to try to do these things for us. "Sit," has no meaning for Fido. Even once he's learned what the word means, he doesn't know why we want him to assume this position. By using positive reinforcement, we give Fido the motivation to work for us.

Positive reinforcement also puts both Fido and you in a better frame of mind about training. It becomes a more positive thing rather than a series of negative things. The positive reinforcements that we will use will vary from dog to dog, depending on the dog's response. The most common reinforcements include: verbal praise, petting, food treats or toys and a combination of some or all.

The verbal praise should be in a high-pitched tone of voice and sound really happy. The tone of voice you used as a kid when you screamed "Ice Cream!" is just about right. Please don't scream at Fido, however. You don't need to be loud and really shouldn't be. Simply use a joyful tone. Now, when Fido does something extra special, then yes, use your voice to reward him and then a happier, higher pitched, slightly louder voice is fine.

The amount of verbal praise depends on the individual dog and the situation. A good sit might be rewarded with a "Good boy, Fido." However, if you and Fido have been working on a difficult exercise and Fido suddenly makes a breakthrough and the light bulb goes off in his head, then reward him with more extravagant praise, a jackpot: "Thank you! What a good boy, Fido! Super!"

When Fido is learning a new exercise, verbal praise should always be given as he does what you asked him to do. When you say sit, praise should happen as his rump hits the ground. Timing is very important for if you delay the praise, he might think he's being praised for holding still, not sitting on command. Later, when you are working with exercises that Fido already knows, the praise can be given at the end of an exercise. Even then, if Fido tries extra hard or does something very well, you will praise during the exercise, too.

Delayed praise or reward is difficult for Fido to comprehend and even harder for you to make sure you are rewarding what you want to reinforce. Are you rewarding the sit, as in his rump hitting the ground? Or are you rewarding the speed of the sit? Or the position in regard to you? Don't be afraid to reward exactly what you like, when Fido does it.

The petting or physical praise includes ear scratches, chest rubs, hugs or anything else that gives both you and Fido pleasure. If Fido is very body sensitive, as we talked about earlier, then physical praise should be limited to the amount that Fido can handle without getting over-stimulated. Maybe just a scratch behind the ear. Dancer, a Golden Retriever, is very body sensitive and petting during training consists of gentle finger scratches behind the ear or on the top of his head. Any more than that and he can't control himself and forgets what he's supposed to be doing.

Physical praise or petting should always be accompanied by verbal praise. Your voice is your most important training tool and during training there will be many times when you will only use your voice to praise Fido and that may be his only positive reinforcement for that moment. However, all other positive reinforcements, food treats, toys or petting, are never given alone and are always given with verbal praise.

Using food treats to train is a controversial subject. Some trainers abhor using food, others swear by it. In reality, food is a training tool, just like the leash and collar or praise and petting. The desire for food is a basic survival instinct and is the easiest way to capture Fido's attention.

We'll use food in two different ways: one, to help Fido position himself, and two, as a reward. For example, in Chapter Four we will teach Fido to lie down on command. With one of the methods, you will hold a food treat in your right hand. Letting Fido see and smell it and as you tell him "Fido, down!" move your hand and the treat to the floor in front of Fido so that he follows it and lies down. Up to this point, the treat is a training tool just like your leash. The treat is a very tiny piece of something Fido wants, so he is motivated to work for it. When Fido lies down and you praise him, you will also give him the treat. Now the treat becomes part of your positive reinforcement—a reward, a motivator.

Again, just like petting, food treats should always be accompanied by verbal praise. As the dog becomes proficient in an exercise, decrease the food treats and award them on a random basis. Reward the best performance, or extra effort, or simply give one every now and then. But the verbal praise will remain constant and up beat.

The food treat you use depends on your dog's tastes. A tiny piece of dog beef jerky is good, or a bit of hot dog, or cheese. Whatever you use should be easily and quickly eaten by the dog without much chewing. It should also be cut into tiny pieces. We don't want the dog to get full, we just want to tempt him.

There are some dogs that will not or cannot work for food treats. If the dog does not regard food as something worth putting out extra effort for, then obviously, the treat is not going to be any kind of a motivator. Or if Fido is on a strict diet, food treats will add calories. For these dogs, something else is needed. How about a tennis ball? Or a racket ball for a smaller dog? Or a pocket Frisbee? A foxtail toy? Or a squeaky toy? You need something that the dog loves and goes crazy about, so that it will work as a motivator. Allow the dog to have it only as a reward during training sessions. Keep it special.

Negative Reinforcement

Interruptions. Negative reinforcements are used both as an interruption and as a correction. An interruption is exactly that—a means to stop something that Fido is doing that you don't want to continue. Remember earlier in this chapter, we talked about Fido learning by experience. Fido tried to dash out the open gate and you dropped the metal trash can lid as you ran to intercept him. But making a lot of noise the trash can lid acted as an interruption. It stopped Fido's dash out the gate and instilled in him a respect for the gate. He reasoned: "Something loud and scary happens if I try to run out the gate without permission."

An interruption is useful in many situations. If Fido is barking at something on the other side of the fence, a "throw can" (soda can containing a dozen pennies) tossed towards, but not at, Fido startles him and interrupts the barking. When he stops barking, you then reward the quiet with a "Good boy to be quiet." (Chapter Five, *Problem Prevention and Problem Solving* has more detailed information on how to go about problem solving.)

Interruptions can be brought about by just about anything that gets Fido's attention, especially if he's intent on misbehavior. A firm, authoritative "Acck! Leave it!" might be enough to cause some dogs to drop a forbidden item. A squirt bottle filled with a solution of vinegar and water, half and half, is often useful for a barking dog within squirt-gun range. The squirt gun is good for heel nippers, too.

What is used for causing the interruptions isn't as crucial as what you do after interrupting the behavior. If the dog is barking, praise the quiet. If he was stealing something, praise him for dropping it.

Corrections. A correction is used when Fido already knows what is expected of him and does not do it. However, do not correct what Fido does not yet know and understand. When you're teaching Fido to sit, for example, you will help him to do it in the beginning so that there is no confusion. During this stage, you will not correct Fido if he doesn't sit. Instead you will help position him in the sit. Later, when he has been sitting on his own when you give the command and you know he understands, then if he refuses, correct him.

Verbal corrections are given in a firm, authoritative, growly tone of voice. Don't scream, yell or lose your temper. Other corrections

Tony praises Jazzy, using a happy tone of voice, a good chest scratch and happy eye contact. Jazzy reacts to the praise with a big smile. (Weimaraner)

include a scruff shake or a snap and release of the leash, both accompanied by a verbal correction.

Each correction should be firm enough to get Fido's attention but no harder. On the other hand, the corrections should not be nagging, either. One firm correction is much better than a dozen little yanking ones. A general rule of thumb is that the correction should get Fido's attention. He shouldn't ignore it and continue the unwanted behavior and yet the correction should not be so hard that Fido is cowed or intimidated.

Just as with positive reinforcement, the timing of interruptions and corrections is very important. An interruption will not work if Fido has already stopped barking on his own by the time you toss out the throw can. You must interrupt or correct the unwanted behavior as it is happening.

33

Jane uses Wilma's strong prey drive and love of the tennis ball to help motivate her obedience work. The tennis ball is Wilma's motivator. (Weimaraner)

Using a combination of positive and negative reinforcements offers a number of training alternatives. You can vary the amount and intensity of both the positive and negative reinforcements depending upon how Fido reacts.

Training Tools. Building a foundation requires tools and just as a carpenter or mason requires certain tools to do the job properly, so does a dog trainer. The different kinds of positive and negative reinforcements that we use are some our tools, but there are also different collars that can be a part of our tool chest.

Choosing the right collar to use depends upon you, your training philosophy and your dog. None of the tools listed below are right or wrong if used properly and your dog reacts in a positive manner.

The most common training tool available is a training collar or choke chain. This is a length of chain with a ring at each end. Used properly, with a snap and release motion, it can be used as an interruption or as a correction. Fido should never be allowed to pull this

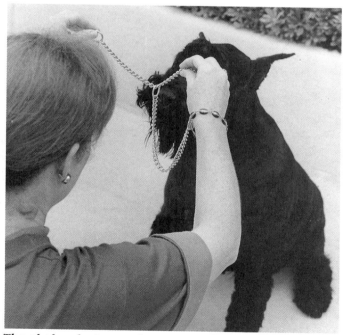

The choke chain can be a very effective training tool when used properly, but can kill Fido if left on him when unattended. Use this collar carefully, and always take it off when you are not directly supervising him. (Giant Schnauzer)

Left: The nylon/chain combination is a very nice training collar for many dogs. Right: The prong collar can be a very effective collar for some dogs, but can give a severe correction to a body-sensitive dog. (Left, Australian Shepherd; Rignt, Golden Retriever)

There are a number of different makes of head halters on the market, and all can be useful. (Fox Terrier mix)

collar tight because it can choke him, and as a result, if used improperly, can cause neck damage. This collar can kill a dog so it should never be left on the dog while unsupervised.

There are also two kinds of nylon slip collars that work in the same manner as a choke chain. The first is a round nylon cord with a ring at each end. This gives a very similar correction but without the noise of a chain. The second collar is a wide nylon strap with a D ring at one end that moves and allows a slip correction. This collar, because of the width of the strap, gives a milder correction.

A snap around slip collar is very similar to a choke collar except that it can be fitted so that it rides higher up on the neck of the dog. This is my favorite training collar for most dogs. It should be used with the same reservations as the choke chain.

A buckle collar is a wide nylon or leather collar that has no choking or slip action and either buckles or snaps around the dog's neck. Most puppies begin on this collar but by adolescence graduate to a more traditional training collar. However, if Fido is listening and responding to commands without pulling into the collar, there is absolutely no reason why he must change. This is a good collar for Fido to wear everyday with his identification tags attached.

Every training tool has its benefits and shortcomings. Some of the commonly available tools are, from upper left: prong collar, nylon strap partial slip collar, fine link choke chain, medium weight choke chain, nylon strap/chain combination, in the middle a snap around slip collar and on the bottom a head halter.

A prong collar looks like a medieval torture device, but when used properly on the right dog, it can be a very humane and effective training tool. This collar is recommended for dogs who use their strength against their owners and know that they are stronger than their owners. It is also recommended for dogs who are not body sensitive, who pull into a choke chain or cough when a slip collar is used. This collar must be used with a snap and release motion and Fido should never be allowed to push into the collar. Always take this collar off when Fido is unsupervised.

A chain/buckle combination is a collar that is, for three quarters around the dog's neck, a wide nylon strap and the other quarter a slip chain. This collar is especially good for a pre-trained dog because the dog can react to the noise of a chain correction yet the collar gives the soft correction of a nylon buckle collar.

A head halter is very similar to the halter on a horse. As many horse trainers say, "Where the head goes the body will follow." The halter is very effective for dogs that have neck damage and cannot wear a traditional collar, or for dogs that will not respond to a traditional collar correction. The halter should not be used with a snap and release but should instead be used with a gentle guiding motion.

When deciding what training collar to use with your dog, try a variety of different tools and look at your dog's reactions. Is he still working happily? Or did he cry at the correction? Did he urinate? Or did he react aggressively when you corrected him? When training, you want to use only as much force as necessary to accomplish your objectives AND NO MORE! More is not better. Use a training tool that will allow both you and Fido to be happy.

Training Success

The success of any training program, this one included, is measured in direct proportion to the diligence, determination, attitude and interest of the dog's owner. The best program in the world will not succeed if the dog's owner does not use it at home.

Release. Fido needs to learn a command that means "You're done. You can move about freely." You'll use the release command to let Fido know that he can play with his toy, eat his treat, bounce around or stretch his legs. The release command gives Fido a break from the stress of learning and concentrating. (See Chapter Four,

Building a Sound Foundation for more information on how to teach Fido what the release word means.)

Training Steps. There are several things you can do to ensure your success as a teacher. First of all, set Fido up for success rather than failure. Each time you teach him something new, break it into small steps and teach each step thoroughly before going on to the next step. Work on only one new thing per step. These steps allow you to organize Fido's training in a logical, progressive manner and eliminate the more usual haphazard approach to training. This way, too, you always know what you will be teaching Fido next in case he makes a sudden leap forward in understanding. By using steps set forth in a progressive manner, you can build very complicated routines with a minimum of confusion.

Let's use the sit as an example. The steps might be as follows, with the new variance in each step capitalized:

Step 1. Give sit command (Fido, Sit!") and let him sniff the motivator (a treat or toy). With the motivator in your hand, move your hand from Fido's nose back over his head towards his shoulders so that his head follows you up and back. He will sit to be more comfortable. Praise him.

Step 2. Give command, and start the hand signal BUT AS SOON AS HIS HIPS START MOVING TOWARD THE GROUND, STOP MOVING THE SIGNAL TOWARD HIS BACK BUT INSTEAD MOVE ITUPWARDS,FINISHING IN A DIAGONAL ACROSS YOUR CHEST. Praise him for sitting.

Step 3. And so on. The complete instructions for teaching the sit are in Chapter Four, *Building a Sound Foundation.* The key is making sure the steps are small enough so that the dog can learn and succeed.

Don't try to teach Fido too much at a time. If you are trying to teach Fido to sit on command, to sit in the proper position to you, and with his legs folded under him just so, when you praise him what are you praising? His position? The quickness of his response? His leg position? How is Fido to know what you are praising? It can be very confusing. Work on one thing at a time, break it down into small training steps, reinforce it following the training sequence and schedule then go on to something else. The training sequence (TS) uses repetition to give Fido a chance to learn without allowing him to get bored. The repeated positive reinforcement and releases keep his motivation level high. By using a set schedule, the training sequence makes sure that you are following a logical approach to your training.

The training sequence is as follows:

- One repetition of a training step, followed by praise.
- Second repetition of the same step, followed by praise.
- Third repetition followed by praise, a release (Fido, Release! Good Boy!) and a reward with verbal praise, petting and the motivator.

Using the sit again as an example:
Step One.
One repetition: "Fido, sit" (signal, command, show, help Fido sit) "Good boy!" (praise, scratch ear) Take a couple of steps forward.
Second repetition: Exactly the same as the first.
Third repetition: Exactly the same except after Fido sits, praise him "Good Boy!" then release him from the exercise "Fido, Release!" (encourage him to get up and move around, reward with praise, petting and his motivator—food treat or toy.)

The entire routine, of three repetitions, is considered one training sequence (TS).

Training Schedule. The training schedule is as follows:

1. Do each step a minimum of 3 Training Sequences
2. If the third TS has no mistakes, Fido does the exercise correctly, is not fighting or resisting and does not act at all confused, go on to the next step.
3. If Fido is having problems, go back one step and repeat the TS at that step, working back up to former step.
4. If Fido is still confused, go back several steps, working back up.

Helping Fido Learn

When Fido is learning something new, don't be afraid to help him. Praise him for succeeding with each small step. Don't make him feel bad about making mistakes, just help him do it correctly and then praise him.

Never, ever skip steps, even if you think Fido is a canine Einstein. If he is, he'll breeze through each exercise. However, if he has trouble, just go back a step or two or three and review what he's already learned. It might be clearer to him the second or third time through. If he still doesn't understand, look at what he's doing and what you are trying to communicate to him. Where is the misunderstanding? What doesn't he understand? What can you do to help him?

When you're adding something new, relax your criteria on what he already knows. Then once he understands, tighten the old ones up again. Remember, training can be stressful; alleviate that stress as much as you can.

Time-outs are an important part of the learning process. If Fido has hit the proverbial wall and is having trouble understanding something, back up a step or two so that you can end your training session on a high note and quit for the day. Then, at your next training session, start a couple of steps back from where he was having trouble and work back up. Sometimes having a day or two off allows Fido to assimilate the new information. Now, I'm not saying that he is actually thinking about what he was having trouble with—he might be, I don't know—but I do know that having some time away from the problem often makes approaching it again much easier.

Keep the training sessions short and sweet. Care Bear learns very well in a 10-minute session, following the training repetitions and steps with releases in between to relieve the stress. Kato, a Bearded Collie, gets bored after five minutes. So her training sessions are five minutes long, adding 30 seconds here and there to help lengthen her attention span.

As has been mentioned before, always stop the training session on a high note, even if you have to manufacture one. Don't fake it by praising something enthusiastically that wasn't deserving of extravagant praise. Fido knows the difference. Instead, have him do something that you know he can do and do well. Then praise and release him and end the training session. "Good boy, Fido!"

Jane uses the tennis ball for Wilma's release. She lets her catch it and have fun between training sessions. (Weimaraner)

Chapter 4

Building a Sound Foundation

Everything should be made as simple as possible, but not simpler.
Albert Einstein

The Seven Basic Commands

There are seven basic commands that are the foundation for all obedience training. These commands are: release, sit, down, stay, walk on leash, come and retrieve. With a good foundation of these exercises, you and Fido can do just about anything.

In this chapter, we will introduce each of the seven exercises to Fido and start building a good, solid base for his later training. These exercises can be taught to puppies, young dogs and even older dogs just as they are presented. The key to making them work for you is to follow the training steps and sequences as they are given. Don't be in a hurry and skip steps. Training requires patience, persistence, consistency and repetition.

Teaching the Release

Self control is difficult, ask any dieter, and it's just as hard for Fido. During much of his training, you will be asking Fido to control his own actions and in many cases this will be very difficult. To help ease his stress during training, allow Fido to hop around, stretch and just act like a regular dog when he's given the release command. To help motivate Fido to continue his training, give him his motivator during the release. The motivator is exactly that—something to help Fido put forth more effort into the training, such as a ball, a pocket Frisbee or a treat.

We will use the word "Release!" to teach Fido that we mean, "Okay, the pressure's off." Release will be used at the end of every training sequence and will always be used with verbal praise and Fido's motivator. At the end of each training sequence, tell Fido, "Release!" in an ice cream tone of voice, and at the same time throw your hands in the air, praise Fido and encourage him to hop around. Give him his treat or toy and play with him. Let him know exactly how special he is!

Each release from training should be one minute, no shorter.

Joan uses DC's motivator to teach him the release command. (Golden Retriever)

Time it if you have to but make sure you don't short-change Fido because this is his reward for working for you. These releases help keep his motivation level high.

As a side benefit, these releases can help you, too. While Fido is rolling around, enjoying the fresh grass or is chewing on his toy, you can be reviewing the next training steps or joining Fido in some relaxation.

Before you begin training, keep these things in mind:

1. Don't scream and shout at Fido. He can hear you just fine.
2. Never train Fido when you are angry, drunk, stoned or sick.
3. Be consistent. Be patient.
4. Keep the training sessions short and sweet. Train for short periods of time, 10 to 15 minutes. Five minutes, several times a day is better yet.
5. Always, ALWAYS, end your training session on a high note.

Teaching the Sit

In Chapter Two, we talked about the importance of Fido learning to work for you and learning to enjoy it. One of the most important things we discussed was teaching Fido to sit for everything that he wanted. He was to sit before you threw his ball or toy. He must sit for a treat, for petting and for dinner. The sit is a very simple but important building block command.

When you tell Fido to sit, you want him to understand that sit means *lower your hips to the ground, keeping your front end up, and be still*. Sit does not mean assume the position and then pop back up again. There are two different ways to teach Fido the sit. Try both methods and use the one that is most comfortable for you and Fido, or if both methods work for you, practice both interchangeably.

Shaping Method. With this method, you will use your hands to help position Fido in the sit while you teach him the command.

Step 1. With Fido standing by your left side, gather up the excess leash in your right hand. With that same hand, take hold of the front of Fido's collar and push slightly up and back as you slide your left hand down Fido's back, around his hips, to tuck his back legs under him, as you say, "Fido, sit." Keeping your right hand on the collar under his chin, pet him with the left hand as you praise him, "Good boy to sit!" If he tries to pop back up, you have your right hand in position,

Inducive Sit, Step 2. Ken praises Chica verbally for sitting as he follows through with the sit signal. (Standard Poodle)

simply re-sit him with a verbal interruption, "Acck!" and praise him again when he's sitting.

Follow the training sequence and schedule and go on to the next step when Fido is ready. The new portion of each step is capitalized.

Step 2. Give the sit command, hold the collar in front with the right hand, and slide the left hand down Fido's back BUT DON'T TUCK HIS BACK LEGS UNDER. Continue to keep the right hand on the collar and pet with the left hand after Fido sits. Praise. Follow the training sequence and schedule.

Step 3. Give the sit command, hold the collar in front with the right hand, and KEEP YOUR LEFT HAND OFF THE DOG WHILE HE SITS. Keep the right hand on the collar and pet with the left hand after Fido sits. Praise. Follow the training sequence and schedule.

Step 4. Give the sit command, HOLD THE LEASH CLOSE IN THE RIGHT HAND BUT WITHOUT TOUCHING THE COLLAR. Again, keep the left hand off the dog while he's sitting. Pet and praise after sit. Follow training sequence and schedule.

Step 5. Give the sit command, with both hands off the dog, FROM ABOUT TWO STEPS AWAY. Pet and praise after the sit. Follow the training sequence and schedule.

NOTE: Don't be in a hurry to get your hand off of Fido's collar. If he's antsy and is trying to get up from the sit, keep your hand on his collar and don't move on to the next step until he is ready. It is not a failure to go back and repeat steps. Instead it's a smart trainer who recognizes when Fido needs extra work and waits until the dog is ready to move on.

Inducement Method. This method allows Fido to position himself as you again teach him the command.

Step 1. With Fido's motivator in your left hand (either his treat or his toy) gather up his leash in your right hand so that the leash is close to Fido but not tight. Let Fido sniff or see his motivator, and then as you tell him, "Fido, sit!" take your left hand (with the motivator) over Fido's head, from his nose straight back toward his shoulders. Don't allow him to step back or turn around. As his head goes up to follow the motivator, he will lower his hips to the ground to be more comfortable. Praise him as soon as his hips touch the ground. Tell him

"OK!" when you are ready for him to move. Follow the training sequence and schedule.

If you're having trouble getting Fido's attention, go back to Chapter Two and review the section discussing the "Watch me!" Use the Watch me command to get Fido focused on you, then continue. If Fido is still ignoring you, try another motivator. Perhaps what you're using is not important or exciting enough.

Step 2. Give Fido the command with your hands the same as in Step 1, then start your hand signal BUT AS SOON AS HIS HIPS START MOVING TOWARD THE GROUND, STOP MOVING THE SIGNAL TOWARD HIS SHOULDER AND INSTEAD MOVE IT UPWARDS, FINISHING IN A DIAGONAL ACROSS YOUR CHEST. (See photo) Praise him for sitting. Follow training sequence and schedule.

Step 3. Give the sit command with the motivator in the left hand, and HOLD THE LEASH LOOSELY IN THE RIGHT ABOUT TWO STEPS AWAY. Start the sit signal at Fido's nose, finishing with the signal across your chest. Praise. Follow the training sequence and schedule.

NOTE: Never tell Fido to sit and let him ignore you. Don't stand there and repeat, "Fido, sit. Sit. SIT!" Which command is he supposed to listen to? The third? Or fourth? Tell him *sit* one time, give him a second to start to respond and then help him do it by either shaping him into the position during the learning steps or by snapping the leash as you position him once he already understands the command.

Teaching the Down

You want Fido to understand that *down* means "Lie down and be still." It does not mean lie down and crawl, or lie down and wrestle. Just as with the sit command, there are two different methods of teaching the down.

Shaping Method. This method allows you to shape the down position as you teach Fido to lie down.

Step 1. Have Fido sit by your left side. Sit or kneel next to Fido and reach over his shoulders with your left arm. Take hold of his left front leg with your left hand and his right front leg with your right hand. As you tell him, "Fido, down," lift both front legs slightly, pull them forward and gently lay Fido down on the ground. Transfer your left hand to his shoulder so that if he tries to pop up, you can prevent it. Praise him. When you're ready for him to get up, pat him lightly on the

Shaping the down, Step 1. Kim scoops Kali's front legs forward and down, gently lowering her to the ground. (Doberman Pinscher)

ribcage and telling him "OK!" and "Fido, sit!" Follow the training sequence and schedule.

Step 2. With Fido in a sit by your left side, reach over with your left hand and arm as in Step 1 and pull the left leg out as you tell him, "Fido, down." YOUR RIGHT HAND WILL BE GIVING FIDO A SIGNAL MEANING TO LIE DOWN, GOING FROM FIDO'S NOSE TO THE GROUND, AS YOU GIVE THE DOWN COMMAND. Put your left hand on Fido's shoulder to prevent movement, as in Step 1. Praise the down. Follow the training sequence and schedule.

Step 3. With Fido in a sit, give Fido the down command and at the same time, the down signal with your right hand. INSTEAD OF REACHING OVER FIDO WITH THE LEFT HAND, PUT YOUR LEFT HAND ON FIDO'S SHOULDER. DON'T PUSH DOWN, SIMPLY REST IT THERE. Praise Fido for going down. Follow the training sequence and schedule.

Step 4. With Fido in a sit, give the down command and signal, KEEPING THE LEFT HAND OFF FIDO ENTIRELY. Praise Fido for going down. Follow the training sequence and schedule.

NOTE: Interrupt any crawling or sniffing with a scruff shake or leash snap and an appropriate verbal interruption, "Acck! No sniff!" Follow the interruption with praise, "Good boy to be still." The down

Laura uses a food treat to shape the puppy into a down position. Her left hand on the puppy's shoulder makes sure the pup doesn't get up before she tells him that he can. (Australian Shepherd)

Left: Desi was taught the down with a treat and now that he knows and understands the command, Cameron can give a signal without the treat. (Australian Shepherd) Right: Bonnie tells Jupiter to "stay" and gives him a very obvious signal, palm toward him, hand wide open. (Golden Retriever)

is to mean lie down and be still. Fido doesn't have to be a statue, but he should remember what he's doing. When he's sniffing the grass or crawling around the yard, he's obviously not holding still or paying attention to you.

Inducement Method. This method allows Fido to position himself as he learns to lie down on command.

Step 1. With Fido in a sit by your left side, with your left hand on his shoulder, allow Fido to see or sniff his motivator in your right hand. Tell him "Fido, down!" as you take the motivator from his nose straight down to the ground, slowly, to a spot just a few inches in front of his front feet. When his nose follows the motivator down, then move the motivator away from Fido so that he lays down to reach it. You will be making an "L" shape with the motivator. Praise him. Tell him "OK! Fido, sit." when you're ready to let him get up. Follow the training sequence and schedule.

Step 2. Start with Fido in a sit by your left side, with the motivator in your right hand. Give him the down command and signal as before except KEEP YOUR LEFT HAND OFF FIDO'S SHOULDER. Praise Fido for going down. Follow the training sequence and schedule.

Step 3. Follow Step 2, except MAKE A STRAIGHT SIGNAL DOWN, INSTEAD OF AN "L." Praise and follow the training sequence and schedule.

NOTE: If Fido doesn't immediately follow your hand to the ground in Step 1, tap the ground with the motivator or your fingers so that the sound and movement will also work to get his attention.

Teaching the Stay

You want Fido to understand that the command *stay* means to "Hold still, don't get up and move around until I return to you and tell you that you can move." This exercise can be difficult for many dogs because it requires that they concentrate on holding still and that in itself is hard. However, this is a very important command, not just because Fido learns to hold still but because it also allows you to control Fido's actions. With a good sit or down stay, you can open the front door and know that Fido isn't going to dash out into the street. You can get the groceries out of the car, telling Fido to stay in the back seat and know that he won't jump out before you release him. There are dozens of other practical uses for the stay and that's not taking into account the fact that it is a foundation exercise for many advanced obedience commands.

Step 1. Start with Fido sitting on your left side. Hold the leash in your left hand close to his collar. Don't hold the leash tight. Tell Fido, "Stay!" as you give him the stay hand signal. With your hand open, palm toward Fido, move your hand up and down about three inches in front of him, as if you were building an invisible wall in front of his nose. Pivot toward the front of Fido, no more than a step away from him. Count to three, then step back to Fido and praise him, then tell him "OK."

If Fido moves from the sit before you tell him, "OK!" give him a quick "Acck!" and reposition him into the sit. If he jumps up from the sit while you are praising him but before you have released him, again, give him a verbal interruption "Acck!" and re-sit him.

In the beginning, make sure that you make him hold the stay for no longer than a count of three. Not a long, stretched-out count of three but a *one Mississippi, two Mississippi, three*. You want Fido to be able to succeed and part of setting him up for success is building the steps of the exercise so that he CAN do it. If you ask him to hold the stay too long too soon, he will make mistakes too often. Follow the training sequence and schedule after each step.

Step 2. Have Fido sit by your left side, tell him "Stay" as you give him the stay signal and move away one step. Count 10 SECONDS, then return to him and praise him.

Step 3. Continue the sit/stay for 10 seconds but move THREE STEPS AWAY FROM FIDO.

Step 4. INCREASE THE SIT/STAY TO 20 SECONDS, but do not increase the distance beyond three steps away.

Step 5. Continue the sit/stay at 20 seconds, but move SIX STEPS AWAY FROM FIDO.

Step 6. INCREASE THE SIT/STAY TO 40 SECONDS, but do not increase the distance beyond six steps away.

Step 7. Continue the sit/stay at 40 seconds, but move 10 STEPS AWAY FROM FIDO.

Step 8. INCREASE THE SIT/STAY TO ONE FULL MINUTE, but do not increase the distance beyond 10 steps away.

Sit/stay, Step 3. Bonnie is about three steps, or six feet, away from Chang. (Akita)

NOTE: The down/stay is taught using the same schedule. You can alternate training sequences using the sit/stay one training sequence and the down/stay on another but make sure you go through all the steps with both the sit and the down.

Keep in mind that stays are very difficult and require a great deal of self control on Fido's part. Do two or three training sequences, with an enthusiastic release after each one, and then go on to something else. Don't do a lot of stays one after another.

If Fido is making a number of mistakes, go back a couple of steps and repeat them. If Fido is having trouble following this schedule, feel free to decrease the time period or distance so that Fido can succeed. However, don't be in a hurry to get away from Fido too fast or leave him for an extended time. If you rush him, he'll make mistakes. Set Fido up for success rather than failure. These exercises are your foundation, be patient and build it strong.

Teaching the Walk on Lead

You want Fido to understand that the leash is not something to fight, but that it is an umbilical cord between you and him and is fragile. YOU can tighten it when the need arises but HE is never to fight

Bonnie understands that the stays are hard for Chang and rewards him with enthusiatic praise and petting. (Akita)

or tighten the leash. There are a couple of different ways to work with Fido and the leash. Practice all of them.

Leash Awareness.

Step 1. Let Fido have the entire length of a six-foot leash. Back away from him. If he looks at you, praise him.

If he follows you, praise him even more. If he looks away from you, back up quickly and lightly snap the leash (just enough to get his attention) commenting to him in a high-pitched, surprised tone of voice, "Wow! What happened?" following up with praise when he reacts to the snap and your voice.

Step 2. Continue backing up in an erratic, zig-zag manner. If Fido starts watching you out of the corner of his eye as he continues to sniff or look around, USE A VERBAL INTERRUPTION as well as a snap of the leash. Make sure you praise him when he looks at you and follows you.

Step 3. If Fido catches on to this game and is trotting with you, face-to-face with you as you back away, STOP AND HAVE HIM SIT IN FRONT OF YOU and praise him enthusiastically! That is exactly what you want him to do.

Review the Watch Me. In Chapter Two, we talked about some of Fido's basic rules and the steps to achieve them. One of the exercises was the Watch Me. The Watch Me teaches Fido to pay attention to you. This might seem overly simple but if Fido doesn't pay attention to you, your alternative is a correction. If he doesn't pay attention to you, he'll miss commands or signals, he'll forget what he's doing or he'll ignore you. So review the Watch Me and use it as an exercise in its own right and incorporate it into the rest of your training.

Step 1. With Fido sitting in front of you, facing you, hold the leash in one hand, gathering up the slack. With a treat in the other hand, let Fido see the treat and sniff it. Take the treat from his nose to your face as you tell him, "Fido, Watch me!" As soon as his eyes flick to you give him verbal praise "Yeah! Thank you! Good boy!" and then pop the treat in his mouth. Follow the training sequence and schedule.

NOTE: Always give the verbal praise first, for two reasons. First, eventually, Fido will be working for your voice alone. Second, your timing is much better with your verbal praise than it is with your

Joan uses DC's motivator to bring him up to the heel position. (Golden Retriever)

hands. If you give him a "Good boy" as soon as you see his eyes move to your face you are rewarding him looking at you. However, by the time you get your hand with the treat to his mouth, he may have already looked away again. What are you rewarding then?

Step 2. With Fido sitting in front of you, tell him, "Watch Me," and BEGIN BACKING AWAY FROM HIM. Encourage him to follow you, praise him for the Watch Me and move the treat between you and Fido a couple of times if he gets distracted. Take only a few steps, then stop and have him sit and repeat the Watch Me and reward him. Follow the training sequence and schedule.

Step 3. Repeat as in Step 2, EXCEPT INCREASE YOUR BACKING AWAY with Fido following you. Back in a zig-zag pattern, a few steps this way, a few steps that way. Use your voice to encourage Fido. Then stop and have Fido sit in front of you and reward him. Follow the training sequence and schedule.

Step 4. HAVE FIDO SIT BY YOUR LEFT SIDE, HIS SHOULDER BY YOUR LEFT LEG. Bend around slightly so that Fido can see your face and do the Watch Me in this position. Follow the training sequence and schedule.

Beginning the Heel. You want Fido to understand that *heel* means "Walk by my left side, with your neck and shoulder by my left leg. Pay attention to me and don't move from this position in relation to me." That's a pretty complicated definition and it can be hard for Fido, too. However, you will incorporate the Watch Me command and that will make it much easier.

Step 1. Make sure that Fido is doing Steps 3 and 4 of the Watch Me. Repeat Step 3 of the Watch Me and then, AS YOU ARE BACKING UP FROM FIDO, TURN WHILE YOU ARE WALKING SO THAT YOU END UP FACING STRAIGHT AHEAD AND FIDO MOVES UP TOWARD YOUR LEFT SIDE. As he moves into position, tell him "Fido, Heel! Watch Me! Good boy!" Use your voice and Fido's motivator to encourage him to keep that position and to continue watching you. After six to ten feet, stop, have him sit, and praise him. Follow the training sequence and schedule.

Step 2. Repeat as in Step 1, except WALK ABOUT 15 TO 20 FEET before stopping and sitting Fido.

Step 3. Repeat as above, except ADD LEFT TURNS AND RIGHT TURNS to your walking pattern.

NOTE: This is one of the most important steps for teaching a good, enthusiastic heel. Don't rush this one. If Fido doesn't understand or is fighting the leash or you, don't get impatient.

Teaching the Come
Fido needs to learn that *come* means "Drop everything you're doing and come directly to me as fast as you can." He needs to ignore the cat on the back fence, the ball that rolled into the street and the dog barking behind the alley fence. A good, responsive, fast come could literally save Fido's life.

To teach Fido to come quickly every time you call, there are a couple of rules that everyone in the household needs to follow. First of all, never call Fido to come and then punish him. If he chewed up the chaise lounge cover when you left him in the back yard and went to work, don't come home from work, see the damage and then call him to you to punish him. He's not going to associate the punishment with the act of chewing up the chaise lounge cover. He will, however, associate the punishment with the last thing that happened and that was you coming home and calling him.

Second, never call him to come and do something nasty to him. Don't call him to come and flea spray him. Don't call him to come and give him a bath. This works just like the punishment does.

When Fido is Off Leash. When Fido is running around the back yard, off leash and you need to call him to you, you need to make sure that you can back up your come command. If Fido learns that he doesn't have to come when you call, then you've got a problem.

Step 1. Take your box of doggy treats and go out in the backyard with Fido. Shake the box so that Fido hears the noise it makes and simply hand him a cookie. Follow the training sequence and schedule. (Yes, even for something this simple. We want Fido to know that the sound of the box means a treat.)

Step 2. When Fido is in the back of the house or in a far corner of the yard, shake the box and ask him in a very positive tone of voice, "Fido, do you want a cookie?" and as soon as he starts towards you, CALL HIM TO COME! "Fido, cookie? Fido come! Good Boy!" As soon as he reaches you, pop a cookie in his mouth and praise him. Follow the training sequence and schedule.

Step 3. Step outside and CALL HIM TO COME THEN SHAKE THE BOX. Follow the training sequence and schedule.

Step 4. Continue step 3 above, except WHEN FIDO REACHES YOU, HAVE HIM SIT, THEN GIVE HIM THE COOKIE. Follow the training sequence and schedule.

NOTE: This technique also works for the instances when Fido sneaks out the open gate or front door and is taking off down the street. Simply shake the box and ask him if he wants a cookie. Reward him and pop a cookie in his mouth when he comes to you. Don't correct him. Keep it positive.

When Fido is on Leash. Think of the leash as an umbilical

cord between you and Fido. It's a connection that transmits your thoughts and feelings, therefore, think of it as a positive connection. Even though the leash ensures that Fido comes when you call him, use the leash to help Fido come to you and come quickly. Keep in mind that Fido learns much faster when he does something on his own rather than is forced to do it.

Step 1. With Fido on the leash, simply back away from him and call him to come. "Fido, come! Good boy!" Back up about 10 feet or so, as quickly as you can without tripping or falling down. Praise Fido as he follows you. Give him a treat. Follow the training sequence and schedule.

Step 2. Repeat Step 1 above except WHEN YOU STOP, HAVE FIDO SIT IN FRONT OF YOU. Praise and reward Fido. Follow the training sequence and schedule.

NOTE: If Fido at any time does not follow you, snap the leash, but only as hard as you need to interrupt whatever he is doing, and continue to back away from him, encouraging him to follow you. DO NOT correct him hard, snap his head off or jerk him off his feet. Keep the come as positive as humanly possible.

Teaching the Retrieve

Retrieving is an excellent form of exercise. It is good for the dog's attitude toward you and is also a basis for many of the advanced obedience exercises. Many of the common day-to- day problems that people have with their dogs are based on boredom and lack of exercise. Retrieving games give Fido a chance to work off some of that excess energy. Frisbees, balls and retrieving "dummies" are great motivators, too, especially once Fido has become enthusiastic about retrieving.

Retrieving games are under your direction, playing when you allow the game to continue and stopping when you call it quits. If Fido really enjoys it and pesters you by throwing the ball at you, or plopping it in your lap, have him do a couple of exercises first. Have Fido sit, down, and sit again then throw the ball for him.

Natural Retrievers. A natural retriever is a dog that will chase anything that is thrown. These dogs can be any breed, although the sporting breeds, especially those bred to be retrievers, are naturally very good at it. Many dogs belonging to the herding breeds are also natural retrievers. Most natural retrievers need very little encouragement to chase a ball or Frisbee. These dogs only need encouragement and a chance to learn the basic commands associated with retrieving to become good, reliable retrievers.

Zippy is a retrieve-a-holic. If there were a Retrievers Anonymous, Zippy would need to go. A spunky little Welsh Terrier, Zippy will literally chase her ball until she's exhausted. But this has its advantages, too. The ball is a great motivator for her, and retrieving games ensure that she always has her exercise.

Not-so-Natural Retrievers. Is Fido hesitant about chasing a ball? Does he just watch it as it's thrown? Does he run after it but not pick it up? If so, you need to teach him that this new game can be fun and exciting.

Chocho is a seven-pound Papillon who was sure that retrieving was for sporting dogs only. He was sure that a dog of his caliber shouldn't pick up a dirty, gooey ball! However, after a few training sessions, some good treats and some time spent watching the other dogs get attention when they played ball, he decided to give it a try. Now he's an avid retriever and will even initiate retrieving games on his own.

Teaching the Retrieve.

Step 1. Acquaint him with the toy. If you're using a ball, smear a tiny bit of peanut butter on the ball and then set it on the ground. Encourage Fido to investigate. "What's this? Take it!" and point at the ball.

Care Bear is a natural retriever and will bring back anything. Retrieving is good exercise and is a necessary obedience skill as well. (Australian Shepherd)

When Fido smells it, praise him. When he licks it, praise him more. If he picks it up, tell him, "Good boy to take it!" Follow the training sequence and schedule.

NOTE: When he spits out the ball to take the treat you're offering him, tell him, "Give! Good boy!" so that he learns a word that means give me the ball.

Step 2. Take the peanut-butter-scented ball and ROLL IT ALONG THE FLOOR as you tell Fido, "What's that? Take it!" Follow the ball, encouraging Fido to chase it. Point at the ball if you need to. When he catches the ball, praise any interest at all—sniffing, pawing, licking. Exuberantly praise Fido if he picks up the ball.

NOTE: Don't worry if Fido doesn't immediately pick up the ball on his own. Encourage him and give him a chance. Don't force him by putting it in his mouth. That will teach him to hate the ball and to resist you, or that *take it* means "Allow my owner to pry my jaws apart and place the ball in my mouth."

Step 3. START LOBBING THE BALL just a few feet instead of rolling it, but continue following the ball with Fido, encouraging him to chase it. Follow the training sequence and schedule.

Step 4. Continue as in Step 4, except FOLLOW FIDO JUST A FEW FEET AND THEN WHEN HE'S CHASING THE BALL, slow down and fall behind. If he hesitates, step toward him again but only enough to get him to the ball. Follow the training sequence and schedule.

Step 5. Continue as in Step 5, except that when Fido has the ball ENCOURAGE HIM BACK TO YOU. Call him—not with a come—but with a "Bring it here! Good boy!" Clap your hands, pat your legs, open your arms to him and praise him when he comes back to you. As he begins to walk back to you with the ball, walk toward him and meet him half way. Praise him. Follow the training sequence and schedule.

Step 6. Continue as in Step 5, except DON'T WALK FORWARD TO MEET HIM. Back away from Fido as he's coming toward you, and encourage him to catch up with you. Praise him. Follow the training sequence and schedule.

Step 7. START THROWING THE BALL, very gradually increasing the distance of the throws. If Fido has any problems with following the ball or bringing it back, review the basics again.

NOTE: Remember, even though you may get faster results initially when you try to force Fido to do something, HE, himself, learns much faster when he does something on his own. So take your time, teach him what you want or encourage his natural instincts, and remember to keep it fun!

A Sound Foundation

These seven commands: the release, sit, down, stay, come, walk on leash and retrieve, are the foundation for all the commands around around the house, for fun activities and for advanced obedience work. Don't rush Fido while he's learning these. Make sure he understands these before you go on to anything else.

Chapter Five

Problem Prevention and Solving

It is common sense to take a method and try it. If it fails, admit it frankly and try another. But above all, try something.

Franklin D. Roosevelt

Why Fido Gets into Trouble

Very few dogs are intentionally bad. The dog that is trying to dig up your landscaped yard is not saying to himself, "Ha! I'll get him for going to work everyday and leaving me here at home alone!" Even though you might believe that he's muttering it under his breath, he's not. Really!

Unfortunately, the number one reason why dogs are given up by their owners is because of things that they consider problems. Barking, digging, chewing, jumping on people, dashing out the gate or door, tearing up plants and having housetraining accidents are all very common problems.

Most dogs get into trouble for a number of reasons. First, most young dogs don't get enough exercise. When there is energy to spare, it has to be expressed in some manner and when Fido is alone and unsupervised for several hours, he'll use his energy to amuse himself. That amusement may be destroying your pool cover, uprooting your landscaping bushes or tearing the clean clothes off the line. He doesn't think about what might happen when you come home eight hours later and find the mess. That's beyond his mental capabilities.

Regular exercise can use up some of that excess energy. Every young, healthy dog needs exercise daily. A fast-paced, vigorous two-mile walk might suit the needs of a Basset Hound but a Labrador Retriever or German Shepherd is going to need a good run or a stimulating game of Frisbee. Exercise is just as important for your dog as it is for you. It works the body, uses up excess energy, relieves stress and clears the mind. If your dog has any physical limitations or if you have doubts about your dog's exercise needs, talk to your veterinarian.

Nutrition also plays an important part in problem behavior. A dog with a poor diet that doesn't digest well may crave vitamins or minerals, or he might simply be hungry. Even a dog on an excellent diet can crave certain nutrients if his body isn't digesting his food well.

These dogs will begin to chew, either plants, dirt, rocks or wallboard, trying to satisfy their nutritional needs. A high-quality diet and something to aid the digestion can help. If you have questions, please ask your veterinarian.

Some dogs also need more than a dry kibble food. Dynamite, a Rottweiler, craved fruits and vegetables so much that she would raid her owner's garden. When her owner started adding small amounts of leftover "veggies" or a couple of strawberries to Dyna's dinner, she stopped snitching from the garden. Remember, dogs are not strict carnivores. Wolves, coyotes and foxes will all eat fallen fruit, wild berries and fresh spring grass.

On the other hand, some dogs who eat a high-calorie, high-fat diet will develop a type of hyperactivity. Other dogs are sensitive (even allergic) to foods containing sugar, beef or red dyes. If you feel that your dog might not be doing as well as he should on a particular diet or if you see your dog described above, talk to your veterinarian about some of the various foods available.

Training plays a big part in eliminating problem behavior. A fair, firm but very positive training program can be both fun and educational for you and Fido. Training should let Fido know that you are in control, that he is below you in dominance, and should reinforce his concept of you as a kind, calm, caring leader. Training also teaches respect. Fido should respect you but you should also respect him. It's a two-way street.

Play is also important. Fido needs time to catch a ball or Frisbee and time to chase squirrels or rabbits. A roll in the grass, while you and Fido mimic each other and make noises and funny faces at each other, is a better stress reliever than anything else on earth. The time spent with you, while you throw the ball or walk through the woods with Fido, is irreplaceable. Play is a wonderful time for bonding and getting to know each other.

Dogs are creatures of habit and are secure in a routine. If you train a specific time each day, you will find that Fido will begin anticipating that session. As the time nears to go outside, he will begin to whine or pace, and even stare at the leash. If you drive to training class, you'll notice that Fido will recognize your route or freeway off ramp. When the normal routine changes, stress can result with problem behavior following.

It's also important to remember that many of the things that we consider problems are not problems to the dog. Fido digs to get to cooler dirt in hot weather. He digs because there is a gopher and his instincts tell him to get it. He barks to warn of real or imagined intruders. He barks because he's bored. He digs up your rose bushes because he saw you digging in the garden. He jumps on you to greet

A friend can help relieve the stress of lonliness and boredom. Ursa relaxes with her best friend Squirt. (Australian Shepherd)

you, face to face. And so on. We, as dog owners, consider these things problems because we don't like them, but we must also keep in mind that they ARE natural behaviors. In order to live compatibly with a dog, we must have realistic expectations.

Because so many of these things are natural to Fido, we must try to prevent them from happening as much as possible when we are not around to supervise. That means puppy-proofing the yard or house, picking up the trash cans, fencing off the garden and coiling up the hose. Puppy-proofing doesn't mean picking up what looks attractive to you, but rather what is attractive to Fido. Get down on your hands and knees and crawl around the house or yard. "Hmm, let's see, the nut bowl is right at nose level. The bathroom trash can is overflowing and, again, is right at nose level." There is a very different view of the world from Fido's perspective and that must be kept in mind when you are puppy proofing.

When we can keep an eye on Fido, we can teach him what is allowed and what isn't. This is done by praising him when he's occupying himself with his chewbone or toys and interrupting him when he touches something that you don't want him to destroy. When you interrupt him, use your voice "Acck!" or use something else that can get his attention quickly. A throw can (soda can with five or six pennies inside) tossed towards but not at Fido works very well if Fido is misbehaving outside. A squirt bottle filled with a solution of half water and half vinegar will stop many of Fido's misbehaviors in the house.

Fido will not stop all his problem behavior as a result of corrections, though, he also needs to learn what to do. For example, if when you let him in the house, he dashes down the hallway, bounces on the bed, jumps over the coffee table and lands on the sofa. You can chase him down, throw him off the bed and yell at him to quiet down but unless you also show him what he is supposed to do, he won't be able to change. His bouncing around is very natural for him. Instead, put the leash on Fido when he comes inside, have him lie down at your feet and give him a rawhide. Teach him what you want him to do. Make sure that when you're teaching Fido, you remember to praise him when he's being good—don't rely upon your interruptions alone to teach him.

Love and affection are also a vital part of your relationship with Fido. He won't be good just because you love him, however the relationship is much easier to shape and mold if there is a strong bond of love and affection between dog and owner. Some people seem to be afraid to admit that they love their dog. A gruff gentleman in one of my training classes obviously loved his Doberman Pinscher, Gretchen, but he couldn't admit it in words. He responded to any question about his dog with an off hand answer: "Ah, she's just a dog. She digs and she jumps on my wife. She's just a dog." But I could see through that charade. He always looked at Gretchen with love in his eyes and he always had a hand on her, stroking her head, fondling her ears or rubbing her chest. When the gentleman thought no one was looking, he would whisper to her.

Fido CAN live in peace with rose bushes and can learn to bring you your slippers without shredding them, but it will take patience, perseverance and commitment on your part. Listed below are some specific solutions to some of the most common problems.

The Landscape Artist. The Landscape Artist needs to be prevented from digging up your lawn and tearing up your plants until you're home to teach him. That means building a run for Fido if he stays outside. Make sure the run is, at minimum, wider than Fido's body is long and long enough so that Fido can break into a trot. There should be shade available at all times of the day somewhere in the run. His water should be in an unspillable container and he should have shelter from bad weather. Toss some toys in with him, leave a radio on a soft music station and he's set for the day.

When you get home from work, Fido will need your attention and time. This is when you can do some training—throw the ball, brush him and let him have free run of the back yard. Watch him closely and when he sticks his nose in a hole he has previously dug, interrupt him. Use either the throw can or your voice or both, "Acck! What do you think you're doing! Bad!"

You can prevent re-digging of existing holes by filling the already dug holes with his feces, covered by a layer of dirt. If Fido has been digging near or under a fence, fill the hole with concrete blocks, good-sized rocks or crumpled chicken wire. Then fill it in with dirt. In both cases, you will have taken all the fun out of the digging.

If Fido insists that he must dig, especially if he's a breed that was bred to dig, such as many of the Terrier breeds, give him a spot where he can dig to his heart's content. In essence, make him a sandbox. In an out of the way spot, maybe next to the garage, dig up a six-

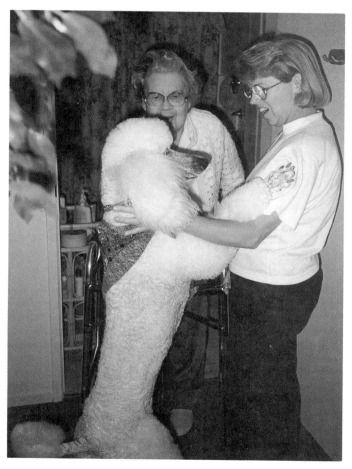

A dog that jumps on people does so for attention but can hurt people or even knock them down. (Standard Poodle)

by-six-foot plot. Break up the dirt clumps so that you have a nice, soft sandbox. Then while Fido is watching, bury some of his toys and a couple of bones. Encourage Fido to dig for them by saying "Where are they? Find your bone?" while you point to the tip of a partially buried bone or toy. Over the next few weeks, bury something daily so that Fido will keep returning to this spot.

Puppies imitate each other and their owners and many garden-related problems begin with watching the owner dig, pull up plants and sample the fruits of all the hard work. I learned this the hard way with Ursa, a pretty, tri-colored Australian Shepherd, who has always been motivated by her stomach. One day, when she was six months old, Ursa was lying in the shade watching me weed the garden. As I worked, I checked the strawberries, tasting a few and mentally marking the place of a few that could be picked the next day. Before I finished, I went over to our apricot tree and picked a couple for lunch. I then went in the house, leaving Ursa outside.

I should have noticed when Ursa didn't want to come inside with me, but I wasn't paying attention. Later, when I walked by the window, I saw Ursa with her head in the strawberry patch eating. She then walked over to the apricot tree, sniffed around and picked a fruit off a low-hanging branch. She promptly ate it, carefully chewing the fruit off the pit. I know she learned by watching me.

Will Fido Live out His Life With You?

Unfortunately, less than 30 percent of all dogs live out their lives with their original owners. Most are taken to Humane Societies, pounds or shelters because of unrealistic expectations of their owners or because of behavior problems. Those dogs are destroyed—killed at the rate of about one dog every four seconds, nationwide.

If Fido's owner understands his dog and what makes him tick, the chances of that relationship succeeding are that much greater. If Fido and his owner can form a strong, affectionate bond, the chances of the dog living out his life with his owner increase even more.

And finally, Fido's owner needs to make a commitment to Fido, that this relationship is for life, Fido's life. It is not to be tossed aside because of moves or transfers, because of destroyed property or because of bother. Instead, the relationship must be looked upon as a commitment.

Dog proofing your house means looking at the attractions in your house from the dog's point of view. (Papillon)

Exercise and diet are important to controlling a landscape artist. Exercise works off any excess energy that might otherwise be used destructively.

The Landscape Artist that seems to enjoy or need fruits and vegetables, like Ursa, may need those items added to the daily diet. Keep in mind that many canids are carnivores by scientific classification, but are omnivores as far as eating habits go.

The Landscape Artist needs to be taught what is acceptable and what is unwanted. That means you must be there to watch and observe him and then can either praise good behavior or interrupt unwanted actions. When you're not there, Fido must be prevented from getting into trouble.

The Home Demolition Crew. The dog that destroys the house, chewing furniture, scratching at walls or doors, stealing shoes and eating trash needs to be treated the same as a Landscape Artist. Allow Fido to be free in the house when you're at home with him, can watch him and teach him. Shut bedroom doors, put a baby gate across the hallway or attach his leash to your belt so that he can't sneak off down

All dogs need to know that they are loved, but they won't behave just because you love them. Fido also needs to respect you. (Australian Shepherd)

the hall and get into trouble. Restrict his access when you are not available to supervise him. Either crate him (See the section on Housetraining at the end of this chapter) or put him in a run outside. This problem is often caused by loneliness, boredom or lack of exercise.

The Neighborhood Choir. In a survey of the nation's mayors during a mayoral conference several years ago, barking dogs were the number three complaint received by mayors' offices, right behind crime and drugs. That's very sad. But barking dogs can be irritating, can interrupt your sleep and can create gigantic rifts in neighborhood relations.

Fido barks because he's bored, hears other dogs barking, hears a siren or alarm or because he has an over-developed sense of protectiveness. Remember, Fido doesn't understand our property lines. We know that the gentleman walking down the other side of the street is not on our property but Fido can see him, smell him and hear him. Therefore, he needs to warn him off.

You can teach Fido when you're home by interrupting the barking and then praising him when he's quiet. If Fido is out at the side gate, barking, toss out the throw can towards but not at him and at the instant after the can hits the ground, tell Fido, "Quiet!" in a firm, no-nonsense voice. Wait a few seconds and then praise him in a higher pitched tone of voice, "Good boy to be quiet!" If he remains quiet, go back out in a few minutes and again praise the quiet.

If Fido barks in the house, a squirt bottle works well as an interruption. Fill it with a solution of half water and half vinegar. When Fido lets loose with a volley at the front door and there is no reason for it, squirt at him and give your *quiet* command and then follow the same teaching techniques as you would outside.

If Fido is only barking excessively when you are not at home and you don't have a kind, caring neighbor that you would trust to work with Fido, then you might want to try one of the no-bark electronic collars. Two different kinds are available. One gives a high-pitched, ultra sonic sound as an interruption or deterrent and one gives an electric shock. Try the ultra sonic collar first. The electronic collars can be very severe for a soft or body-sensitive dog.

The Official Greeter. Does Fido insist on greeting everyone by jumping on them? You need to teach Fido that he can greet people and he can get the attention he wants but only when he sits. He can't both sit and jump on people at the same time so sitting works as a replacement action.

When Fido is not on a lead and tries to jump on you, grab him by the loose skin around his neck and as you tell him, "Acck! No jump!" and then shape him into a sit in front of you. Keep your hands on him so that you can forestall any additional jumps and pet and praise him while he's sitting. "Good boy to sit!" Remember, he's jumping on you for attention and it's up to you to satisfy that need while he's sitting. If you don't, he will continue to try to jump.

Jumping on guests is another matter entirely. Your guests, even good friends, will not correct him effectively and consistently. Before you let guests in the house, put Fido on a leash. Have Fido sit by your left side. If he tries to jump on the guests, correct him with a snap of the leash and a verbal "Acck! No jump!" and put him back into the sitting position. When he's holding the sit, even if he's sitting there quivering, allow the guests to greet him.

Be consistent with a jumping dog. Don't allow him to jump on you when you're in grubby clothes and then get mad when he trashes your work clothes.

The Dasher. Does Fido try to dash through any opening—garage door, gate or front door? Some dogs don't even know what's on the other side, they just want to get through that opening. This problem can be caused by dominance: Fido might feel that he is more important and should go through the door first. The problem can also be learned. Fido might have discovered by accident that he could dash through the door and could explore new territories and you couldn't catch him.

Teach Fido that every door is a barrier and that he is to wait for permission to go through. On leash, sit Fido in front of the closed door. Open the door and correct any forward movement from Fido with a snap and a verbal correction. Close the door and praise him. Follow the training sequence and schedule. Repeat at all openings to the outside world—the garage door, gate, front door or side door.

When Fido is off leash around the house, teach him that he must wait for you to follow you through doors. Re-read Chapter Two, the section "Steps for Success" step number 5.

The Mysteries of Housetraining

With all the conflicting advice and misinformation about housetraining that bombards the new puppy owner, it's amazing that so many dogs do eventually become dependable in the house. However, housetraining doesn't have to be a mystery. By understanding Fido's instincts to keep his bed clean, limiting his freedom, teaching him what you want, establishing a schedule, and by practicing patience, Fido can become reliable in the house.

It's a Crate Not a Jail. By about five weeks of age, most pups are toddling away from their beds to relieve themselves in a far corner of the whelping box or nest. You can use this instinct to keep the nest clean and start housetraining as soon as Fido joins your household. This is best done with a crate.

A crate is a plastic or wire travel cage that you can use as Fido's bed. A variety of makes and models are available. The crate should be big enough for Fido to stand up, turn around and stretch out but no larger. (You may have to get a couple crates of increasing sizes as he grows.) If the crate is too large, it will give Fido enough room to eliminate far enough away from the bed and he won't learn to hold his bladder or bowels.

Many new puppy owners shudder at the thought of putting their new puppy in a crate. "I would NEVER do that," the owner of a new Labrador Retriever puppy told me, "It would be like putting my children in jail!" A puppy is not a child, however, and has different instincts. Fido's instincts to keep his bed clean and a place of security, a den, can be a very useful tool for the new puppy owner.

The crate, used as Fido's bed, will also become a place of refuge for when he's tired, doesn't feel good or simply wants to chew on a toy in peace. Because the crate also confines him, it prevents other unwanted behaviors, such as chewing on electrical cords, destroying slippers and so on.

Because very few puppies will voluntarily soil their beds, the crate teaches Fido to hold his eliminations for increasing periods of time. YOU are responsible for making sure that he is not left in the crate for too long.

When Fido first joins your household, introduce the crate by propping open the crate door and tossing a toy or cookie inside, as you tell Fido "Go to bed!" Let Fido investigate the crate on his own and go in and out freely. When he is no longer afraid of the crate, feed him his next meal inside the crate with the door still propped open, letting him go in and out as he pleases. When Fido is going in and out of the crate easily, offer him a treat for going in and start closing the door behind him, briefly at first and then for gradually longer periods of time.

Never let Fido out of the crate when he's fighting the crate, screaming, howling or chewing on the bars. If you do, you will teach him that those unpleasant behaviors work because you let him out when he demanded it. Instead, let him out when you are ready to do so and when Fido is quiet.

Freedom is Not Always Good. A young puppy should never be allowed to roam the house unsupervised. Many times it's too easy for Fido to have an accident in a bedroom rather than go all the way to the back door. And he may repeat it a number of times before it's discovered, thus setting a pattern.

73

Contrary to what many puppy owners believe, a puppy does not need freedom. Instead, puppies need a structured environment with obvious limits. These limits help teach good habits and prevent the bad habits that might develop if the puppy runs free and chews on the television remote control, destroys the morning paper, raids the clothes' basket, steals knick knacks and any number of other appealing (to a puppy) occupations. By limiting the puppy's freedom to specific SUPERVISED areas, trouble can be averted before it begins.

When Fido is being supervised—actively supervised—he can run free in the house. The person watching the puppy should make sure that there is a baby gate across any hallways, that doors are closed and that Fido stays nearby.

Teaching so that Fido Understands. Even though the puppy's instincts tell him to relieve himself away from his bed and you try to use those instincts by utilizing a crate, the puppy still doesn't understand what you mean by housetraining. You need to teach the puppy exactly what you want him to do. That means you need to go outside with Fido, take him to the area where you want him to relieve himself, give him a command, "Go potty," "Find a place" (or whatever phrase you wish to use) and then when he does happen to go, praise him enthusiastically for doing so. You will need to repeat this over and over for quite a while.

If you try to teach Fido by scolding the accidents that happen in the house by rubbing his nose in his mess (the most commonly used correction) or sharply scolding him, you will confuse him more than you will teach him. Remember, the act of relieving himself is not what is wrong, it is only WHERE he relieved himself that was wrong.

Successful teaching is based upon setting the puppy up for success, and not allowing any accidents to happen and then praising that success.

The Myths of Papertraining. One of the most common methods of housetraining puppies, along with rubbing the dog's nose in his mess, is papertraining. The puppy is taught to relieve himself on newspaper and then at some point is taught to go outside.

Papertraining teaches the dog to relieve himself inside in the house on newspaper. Is that really where you want the dog to go? What happens when you drop the Sunday paper to the floor? To the papertrained dog, that is an invitation.

If you live in a small apartment and have a toy dog that you are willing to clean up after several times a day, then go ahead and papertrain your puppy. However, if your goal is to have your dog relieve himself outside, then teach him to go outside in the beginning.

Setting up a Schedule. Every baby needs a schedule and a puppy is no different. Housetraining the pup is much easier if the

Fence off the garden so that the Landscape Artist doesn't have easy access.

owner and the pup are both comfortable with the schedule for eating, eliminating, playing, walking and sleeping. A workable schedule might look like this:

6:30 a.m. Take Fido outside immediately to his run or potty area. After he relieves himself and is praised for doing so, Dad fixes Fido's breakfast, offers water and takes Fido back outside. Junior goes out in the backyard and plays with Fido for 10 minutes before getting ready for school.

7:00 a.m. Mom comes out and gives Fido some affection before getting ready for work. As she leaves, she brings Fido inside and puts him in his crate with a treat.

11:00 a.m. A dog-loving neighbor comes over and takes Fido outside to go potty. After praising Fido for eliminating, the neighbor plays with him, tossing the tennis ball. When he's tired, the neighbor cuddles the puppy for a few minutes and then puts him back in his crate with a couple of bites of food.

3:00 p.m. Junior gets home from school and lets Fido out in the backyard. After changing into play clothes, Junior and Fido go for a walk and then come back home. Junior leaves Fido in the backyard.

6:00 p.m. Mom feeds Fido dinner and then takes him back outside. After praising him for eliminating, Mom lets Fido come inside with the rest of the family.

8:00 p.m. Mom tells Junior to take Fido outside to relieve himself after the boy and puppy were playing.

11:00 p.m. Dad takes Fido outside for one last trip. He praises the pup and then crates him for the night.

The schedule for your family and your puppy will have to be able to work with your home and work schedules, but keep a few things in mind when making the schedule. First, the puppy should not remain in his crate for longer than four hours at a time except at night. Second, the puppy will need to relieve himself at some very specific times, including after eating, drinking, waking up from a nap and after exercise. Third, the puppy needs supervised activities with the family, both in the house and outside, even if you need to schedule those times.

Practicing Patience. New puppy owners seem to invite advice. Everyone has a method of housetraining that works so much better, faster and is more reliable than anyone else's method. Ignore your well-meaning friends. Every puppy is an individual and will progress at his own pace.

My Australian Shepherd, Care Bear, was reliable in the house very quickly. I was able to set up a schedule that suited him and he had one accident in the house during his entire puppyhood. However, his sister Ursa had a much harder time. I had more trouble finding a schedule that worked for her, and she had a harder time learning (or developing) bladder control. That didn't mean that Ursa was stupid, or bad or anything else except that this was hard for her. I had to practice patience.

All puppies need time to grow up and to develop bladder control. Don't assume that because Fido is having accidents the training method doesn't work. If you keep changing schedules or techniques, you and the puppy will both be frustrated and confused. Just establish a schedule that seems to work for you and Fido and then stick with it.

On the other hand, just because the puppy seems to be doing well, don't let up, allow too much freedom or stop your supervision of the puppy. If your pup isn't having any accidents in the house, it doesn't necessarily mean that the pup is housetrained. Instead it means that you have a good schedule that is working well for the puppy. Every pup needs time and maturity before he can be considered trustworthy. If you let up too soon, the puppy will backslide, sneaking off to make mistakes, and these mistakes can easily become habits.

A schedule that is comfortable for both you and your puppy, along with careful supervision and lots of patience, will work. Puppies do grow up and all your effort will be rewarded by a well-housetrained, reliable pet.

Patience, Persistence and Understanding

Fido can learn to live with you by your rules as long as you are patient and persistent with your training and you try to understand why Fido does what he does. Look at your world from Fido's perspective and keep that view in mind while you are teaching him. If you do, both you and Fido will have a much easier time and your training will be successful.

PART II. THE EXERCISES

Linda beams after Henry wins a medallion.
(Giant Schnauzer)

Chapter Six

Obedience Competition

People are always blaming their circumstances for what they are. I don't believe in circumstances. The people who get on in this world are the people who get up and look for what they want, and if they can't find it, make it.

George Bernard Shaw

What is Obedience Competition?

Obedience competition is an opportunity for dog owners to show off their dogs' training. Competition is also a showcase for demonstrating the teamwork between dog and owner. Each dog/owner team competes against a judge's vision of a perfect performance, as stated by the published obedience regulations, and also competes against the other dog/owner teams entered.

But obedience competition is more than performing in the ring. To produce a nice showing in the ring, Fido needs to be well trained, not just for the exercise to be tested but also to be around other people, other dogs, in different places and different circumstances. The goal is a well-behaved companion animal that is reliable all the time, no matter what you do and where you go with him.

The American Kennel Club (AKC) Obedience Regulations state: "The Purpose of Obedience Trials is to demonstrate the usefulness of the pure-bred dog as a companion of man, not merely the dog's ability to follow specified routines in the obedience ring...the basic objective of obedience trials is to produce dogs that have been trained and conditioned to behave in the home, in public places, and in the presence of other dogs, in a manner that will reflect credit on the sport of obedience."

The United Kennel Club (UKC), Australian Shepherd Club of America (ASCA), Mixed Breed Dog Clubs of America (MBDCA) and the other registries that license or sponsor shows and trials have all patterned their obedience programs with similar goals in mind. The only difference is that the Mixed Breed Dog Clubs of America and the other registries for mixed-breed dogs are promoting well-behaved, mixed-breed dogs rather than purebred dogs.

There are several different types of competition available for dog owners. The obedience trial is the standard for all competition. An obedience trial is held by a licensed club, either through the AKC,

Three friends share the spotlight after a successful obedience trial. (Australian Shepherds)

UKC, ASCA or MBDCA, and a qualifying score (passing) counts toward an obedience title.

A fun or practice match is held under the same guidelines as a trial except that it is for practice. Often, depending upon the club's guidelines, praise and corrections are allowed in the ring whereas in a trial, they are not allowed during competition. A match does not count toward an obedience title.

Special competitions and tournaments are held occasionally for advanced competition. In Southern California, the Southern California Dog Obedience Council sponsors a yearly Top Dog competition. Each member club sends a team of dogs and owners to compete. Awards are given for best overall team scores and for outstanding individual scores. Top Dog tournaments are so well thought of within the obedience community that the competition is fierce between club members just to get a spot on the club team to compete in the tournament.

Nationally, the Gaines Dog Obedience Regional and Classic competitions are, literally, the best of the best. To enter, the dogs must have earned very specific high scores and the dogs and owners that win are very, very good.

Basically, obedience competition can be what you want it to be. If you enjoy competition and winning trophies, ribbons and awards, you can train seriously and go for the gusto. If you are more relaxed and just enjoy training your dog, you can do that too, and use fun matches as social events. Neither approach is right or wrong—the sport is for you to enjoy.

The Obedience Regulations

The obedience regulations are published by the regulating registries. The most popular registries sponsoring obedience are the AKC, the UKC, ASCA and MBDCA. Each club has published a booklet that provides exhibitors with all the rules and regulations pertaining to competition, including what dogs are eligible, what the classes are, how the classes should be run and so forth.

These regulations give exhibitors the chance to make sure they are training their dogs properly to ensure that they won't be surprised by something in the ring. Each registry provides judges with guidelines so that although there are always variations due to individual personalities, for the most part the judging is standardized.

Copies of the guidelines may be obtained by writing to the various registries and requesting copies of the obedience regulations:

American Kennel Club, 51 Madison Ave., New York, NY 10010.

United Kennel Club, 100 East Kilgore Road, Kalamazoo, MI 49001-5598.

Mixed Breed Dog Clubs of America, 512 Minahen Street, Napa, CA 94559.

Australian Shepherd Club of America, 1706-E East 29th Street, Bryan, TX 77803.

What are Obedience Titles?

Obedience titles are offered as a reward for a certain expertise in competition. The first title offered is the Companion Dog title, or CD. Fido and Jane (or Jack) compete in the Novice class for this title. They must earn three scores of 170 or more points (out of 200 available in each class), plus passing each exercise with over half of the points available, under three different judges. Once the registry is notified by the show-giving club of these scores, the exhibitor is mailed a certificate notifying success and the dog can be officially listed as "Fido, CD." The title from the United Kennel Club is U-CD.

The second title available is the Companion Dog Excellent, or CDX. Fido and Jane must compete in the Open class for this title and the requirements are the same: three scores of 170 or better, passing in all exercises and under three different judges.

The third title is the Utility Dog, or UD. Jane and Fido will compete in the Utility class and again, the requirements are the same.

The goal of many trainers is the ultimate title—Obedience Trial Champion or OTCh. Dogs that have earned their UDs may compete for Obedience Trial Champion and will do so by competing in both Open and Utility classes. To earn an OTCh, the dog must win a first place in a Utility class, a first place in an Open class and a third first place in either Open or Utility. Plus, those first places must be earned under three different judges. Along the way, the dog must amass a total of 100 points. The points are earned by placing either first or second in a class, and are based upon the number of other dogs competing. If there are 20 dogs in Open and Fido places first, he would earn 6 points. If he placed second, he would earn 2 points.

Other obedience classes are available for competitors, however these classes do not have titles to be won. The first class is for practice to get ready for competition and that is the beginners novice class or as it is sometimes called, subnovice. This class has the same exercises as novice, except heel off lead and all the exercises are performed on leash. This is a good class for young dogs that are not yet ready for off-lead work in public.

The other nonregular classes include Graduate Novice, which is for dogs that have their CDs but are not yet ready for Open, and Veterans, which is for dogs over the age of seven years. There is also a brace class in which one handler works two dogs together and a team class in which four dogs and four owners perform at the same time. More information about these classes is available in the obedience regulations.

Other titles are available to dogs that are proficient in tracking, herding, retrieving or field work. (See Chapter Fifteen, *More to do with Fido.*)

Dog Clubs

Whenever there are people around with like interests, they will form a club and dog people are no different. There are clubs that specialize in specific breeds and clubs that promote a single sport, like obedience or agility. There are kennel clubs that promote all breeds and perhaps sponsor one or two shows a year. Clubs are a wonderful chance to share your interest in dogs and to exchange ideas and information.

Defining a Match or a Trial

Titles are earned at trials. Trials are held by licensed member clubs and are closely supervised to make sure they follow the rules and

The following pages contain samples of forms used by the American and United Kennel Clubs for obedience competition.

OFFICIAL AMERICAN KENNEL CLUB ENTRY FORM

ALL BREED DOG SHOW & OBEDIENCE TRIAL of the   EVENT #92099702

CONEJO KENNEL CLUB, INC. (A)
(Licensed by the American Kennel Club)
Newbury Park High School
456 N. Reino Road
Newbury Park, California (B)
Saturday October 17, 1992

MAIL ENTRIES WITH FEES TO: JACK BRADSHAW, Supt., P.O. Box 7303, Los Angeles, CA 90022 MAKE ALL ENTRY FEE CHECKS payable to JACK BRADSHAW. FAX (213) 727-2949. ENTRIES must be received by the Superintendent not later than NOON, WEDNESDAY SEPTEMBER 30, 1992. FIRST ENTRY of a dog at this show $14.00 (includes 50¢ AKC recording fee). Each additional entry of the same dog $6.00. Puppy Class $5.00. Junior Showmanship only $5.00. Junior Showmanship as an additional class $5.00 ENTRY MUST BE SIGNED at the bottom by the owner or owner's duly authorized agent, otherwise entry cannot be accepted. (C)
I ENCLOSE $ _____ for entry fees

BREED PAPILLON (1)	VARIETY [1] NONE	SEX M (2)
DOG [2] [3] SHOW CLASS NONE (3)	CLASS [3] DIVISION Weight color etc N/A (4)	
ADDITIONAL CLASSES NONE (5)	OBEDIENCE TRIAL CLASS OPEN (6)	JR. SHOWMANSHIP CLASS N/A (7)
NAME OF (See Back) JUNIOR HANDLER (if any) N/A (8)	J.R.'s AKC NO.	

FULL NAME OF DOG CH ELMAC'S WATACHIE CHOCHO DES CDX, CGC (9)

AKC REG NO. ☒ / AKC LITTER NO. ☐ / ILP NO. ☐ / FOREIGN REG. NO & COUNTRY ☐   Enter number here TC120922 (10)

DATE OF BIRTH Dec 18, 1932 (11)

PLACE OF BIRTH ☒ U.S.A ☐ Canada ☐ Foreign Do not print the above in Catalog

BREEDER B. E. McDONALD (12)

SIRE CH ELMAC'S GYMNOCLADUS CD (13)

DAM CH ELMAC'S MAHONI OF BONRICH CD (14)

ACTUAL OWNER(S) LIZ PALIKA (15) (Please Print)

OWNER'S ADDRESS 3809 PLAZA DR. #107-309

CITY Oceanside   STATE CA   ZIP 92057

NAME OF OWNER'S AGENT NONE (IF ANY) AT THE SHOW

I CERTIFY that I am the actual owner of the dog, or that I am the duly authorized agent of the actual owner whose name I have entered above. In consideration of the acceptance of this entry I (we) agree to abide by the rules and regulations of The American Kennel Club in effect at the time of this show or obedience trial, and by any additional rules and regulations appearing in the premium list for this show or obedience trial or both, and further agree to be bound by the "Agreement" printed on the reverse side of this entry form. I (we) certify and represent that the dog entered is not a hazard to persons or other dogs. This entry is submitted for acceptance on the foregoing representation and agreement.

SIGNATURE of owner or his agent duly authorized to make this entry (16)

TELEPHONE #

A. Name of kennel club hosting the show.

B. Date of show.

C. Where to send entry and amount of entry.

1. Breed of dog.

2. Male or female.

3. Conformation class. (Breed show class)

4. N/A for obedience.

5. If entered in more than one class, second class listed here.

6. Obedience class.

7. If dog handled by a junior handler in conformation class.

8. Same as #7.

9. Registered name of dog

10. Registration number.

11. Date of birth.

12. Breeder's name.

13. Sire (dog's father)

14. Dam (Dog's mother)

15. Your name and address.

16. Your signature.

OBEDIENCE JUDGE'S WORKSHEET
For Judge's Use ONLY - Not to be distributed or shown to exhibitors

DATE .... NOVICE ...... CLASS .... DOG NO. ......

SHOW .... (A or B) BREED ....

EXERCISE	NON QUALIFYING ZERO	QUALIFYING SUBSTANTIAL / MINOR		Maximum Points	Points Lost	NET SCORE
HEEL ON LEASH AND FIGURE 8	Unmanageable...........☐ Unqualified Heeling.......☐ Handler continually adapts pace to dog .....☐ Constant tugging on leash or guiding.......☐		**Heeling** / **Fig. 8** ☐ ..No change of pace ☐ Fast ☐ Slow ☐ ..Improper heel position.................☐ / ☐ ☐ ..Occasional tight leash.................☐ / ☐ ☐ ..Forging .. ☐ Crowding handler........☐ / ☐ ☐ ..Lagging ... ☐ ..☐ Sniffing..............☐ / ☐ ☐ ..Extra command to heel / ☐ ☐ ..Heeling wide ☐ Turns ☐ Abouts ☐ / ☐ ☐ ..No sits ..... ☐ Poor sits ☐ ..Brisk pace ....☐ / ☐ ☐ ..Handler error.................☐ / ☐	**40**		
STAND FOR EXAMINATION	Sits or lies down before or during examination...☐ Growl or snaps ....☐ Moves away before or during examination...☐ Shows shyness or resentment.............☐		☐ ..Moving Slightly Before or During ☐ ..Moves Feet ....☐ ☐ ..Moving after examination ....☐ ☐ ..Sits after exam ....☐ ☐ ..Heel Position ....☐ ☐ ..Extra Signal or Command ....☐ ☐ ..Handler error ....☐	**30**		
HEEL FREE	Unmanageable.............☐ Unqualified heeling ....☐ Handler continually adapts pace to dog .....☐ Leaving handler............☐		☐ ..No change of pace ☐ Fast ☐ Slow..........☐ ☐ ..Improper hand position ....☐ ☐ ..Forging .. ☐ Crowding handler ....☐ ☐ ..Lagging .. ☐ Sniffing ....☐ ☐ ..Extra command to heel ....☐ ☐ ..Heeling wide ☐ Turns ☐ Abouts ☐ ☐ ..No sits .... Poor sits ....☐ ☐ ..Brisk pace ....☐ ☐ ..Handler error.......................☐	**40**		
RECALL	Didn't come on first command or signal..............☐ Anticipated.................☐ Extra command or signal to stay............☐ Moved from position ......☐ Sat out of reach...........☐ Leaving handler............☐		☐ ..Stood or lay down ☐ ..Slow response Touched handler☐ ☐ ..No sit in front Sat between feet☐ ☐ ..No finish Poor sit☐ ☐ ..Failure to come directly to handler Poor finish☐ ☐ ..Failure to come at a brisk trot or gallop ☐ ..Handler arms not at side ☐ ..Handler error.......................☐	**30**		
	ZERO	MAX SUB-TOTAL		**140**		
LONG SIT (1 Minute)	Did not remain in place ....☐ Goes to another dog....................☐ Repeated whines or barks.................☐ Changes its position....☐		☐ ..Stood or lay down after handler returns to heel position ☐ ..Minor move before handler returns ☐ ..Minor whine or bark ☐ ..Forced into position ☐ ..Handler error ....☐	**30**		
LONG DOWN (3 Minutes)	Did not remain in place ....☐ Goes to another dog....................☐ Repeated whines or barks.................☐ Changes its position........☐		☐ ..Stood or Sat Down after handler returns to heel position ☐ ..Minor move before handler returns ☐ ..Minor whine or bark ☐ ..Forced into position ☐ ..Handler error.......................☐	**30**		
		MAX. POINTS ➜		**200**		

☐ H Disciplining ☐ Shows Fear ☐ Fouling Ring ☐ Disqualified ☐ Expelled ☐ Excused ☐ Physical Correction

Less penalty for Unusual Behavior ➜

EXPLANATION OF PENALTY

TOTAL NET SCORE ➜

OBEDIENCE JUDGE'S WORKSHEET
For Judge's Use ONLY - Not to be distributed or shown to exhibitors

DATE ....

SHOW ....

OPEN ...... CLASS
(A or B)

BREED ....

DOG NO. ......

HEIGHT .... JUMPS ......
at withers

EXERCISE	NON QUALIFYING ZERO		QUALIFYING SUBSTANTIAL	MINOR		Maximum Points	Points Lost	NET SCORE
HEEL FREE AND FIGURE 8	Unmanageable ....☐ Unqualified Heeling ....☐	Handler continually adapts pace to dog ....☐	☐ ..Improper hand position.............☐ ☐ Forging ☐ Crowding handler.............☐ ☐ Lagging .... ☐ Sniffing ....☐ ☐ .Extra command to heel.............☐ ☐ ..Heeling wide ☐ Turns ☐ Abouts ☐ ☐ No change of pace ☐ fast ☐ slow ☐ .No sits ..... Poor sits.............☐ ☐ .Lacks naturalness smoothness...........☐ ☐ Heel at brisk pace.............☐ ☐ Handler error.............☐	Heeling Fig. 8	40		
DROP ON RECALL	Does not come on first command or signal ....☐ Does not drop on first command or signal ....☐ Extra com. or sig. to stay after handler leaves............☐	Moved from place left............☐ Anticipated Recall............☐ Drop............☐ Come in............☐ Sat out of reach............☐	☐ Handler error............. ☐ Stood or lay down............. ☐ Finish............. ☐ Slow response Touching handler.......☐ ☐ Failure to Come Briskly Sat between feet.......☐ ☐ Slow drop Poor Sit............☐ ☐ No sit in front Poor finish..........☐ ☐ No finish ☐ Arms not at side		30		
RETRIEVE ON FLAT	Fails to go out on first command or signal ....☐ Fails to retrieve............☐ Goes before command or signal ....☐	Extra command or signal............☐ Sat out of reach............☐	☐ .Slow .... ☐ Going .. ☐ Returning ☐ Mouthing .... ☐ Dropping ☐ .Directly to dumbbell .. ☐ Poor Delivery ☐ No sit .... Poor sit............☐ ☐ Anticipate finish............☐ ☐ Arms not at side ☐ .No finish ☐ Poor finish............☐ ☐ .Handler error............☐ ☐ Touched Handler............☐		20		
RETRIEVE OVER HIGH JUMP	Fails to go out on first command or signal ....☐ Fails to jump going or returning............☐ Fails to retrieve............☐ Goes before command or signal............☐	Jumps only one direction............☐ Sat out of reach............☐ Extra command or signal............☐ Climbing jump............☐	☐ Slow .... ☐ Going .. ☐ Returning ☐ Mouthing .... ☐ Dropping ☐ .Directly to dumbbell .. ☐ Poor Delivery ☐ No sit .... Poor sit............☐ ☐ Anticipate finish............☐ ☐ Touches jump............☐ ☐ Arms not at side ☐ .Pause. Hesitation or reluctance at jump....☐ ☐ No finish .... ☐ Poor finish............☐ ☐ .Handler error............☐ ☐ .Touched Handler............☐		30		
BROAD JUMP	Refuses to jump on first command or signal............☐	Goes before command or signal............☐ Does not clear jump............☐ Sat out of reach............☐	☐ Poor return Touching handler............☐ ☐ No sit in front Sat between feet............☐ ☐ Anticipate finish Poor sit............☐ ☐ No finish Poor finish............☐ ☐ Hesitation. Pause or Reluctance to jump...☐ ☐ Touches jump ☐ Arms not at side ☐ Handler error............☐		20		
	ZERO		MAX SUB-TOTAL			140		
LONG SIT (3 Minutes)	Did not remain in place ....☐ Goes to another dog............☐	Stood or lay down before handler returns....☐ Repeated whines or barks............☐	☐ Forced into position Changes Position after ☐ Minor move before handler returns handler returns to heel position............☐ ☐ Minor whine or bark ☐ Handler error............☐		30		
LONG DOWN (5 Minutes)	Did not remain in place ....☐ Goes to another dog............☐	Stood or sat before handler returns....☐ Repeated whines or barks............☐	☐ Forced into position Changes Position after ☐ Minor move before handler returns handler returns to heel position............☐ ☐ Minor whine or bark ☐ Handler error............☐		30		
			MAXIMUM POINTS ➔			200		

☐ H. Disciplining ☐ Shows Fear ☐ Fouling Ring ☐ Disqualified ☐ Expelled ☐ Excused ☐ Physical Correction

Less penalty for Unusual Behavior ➔

EXPLANATION OF PENALTY

TOTAL NET SCORE ➔

87

OBEDIENCE JUDGE'S WORKSHEET
For Judge's Use ONLY - Not to be distributed or shown to exhibitors

DATE...

SHOW...

ARTICLES NO ....

UTILITY ...... CLASS
(A or B)

BREED...

DOG NO. ......

HEIGHT...........JUMPS...........
at withers

EXERCISE	NON QUALIFYING — ZERO			QUALIFYING — SUBSTANTIAL / MINOR	Maxiumum Points	Points Lost	NET SCORE
SIGNAL EXERCISE	Audible command or Failure on first signal to: Stand □ / Stay □ / Drop □ / Sit □ / Come □ / Anticipated □ / Sat out of reach □ Handler adapting self to dog pace □ / Unmanageable □ / Unqualified Heeling □			□ ..Forging . . □ Crowding handler............□ □ ..Lagging . . □ Sniffing.........................□ □ No change of pace □ Fast □ Slow.......□ □ ..Heeling wide - on turns - abouts..........□ □ ..Extra command to heel□ □ .. Holding signals..................................□ Slow response to signal to □ Stand . Down . Sit . Come . Touching handler..□ □ Walk Forward Sat between feet............□ □ No sit front-finish Poor sits.............□ □ Anticipate finish Poor finish..............□ □ Handler error	40		
SCENT DISCRIMI-NATION	No go out 1st comm. □L □M / No retrieve □L □M / Wrong article □L □M **LEATHER** Anticipated □ / Extra command □ / Sat out of reach □ **METAL** Anticipated □ / Extra command □ / Sat out of reach □			I M ... L M □ □.. Handler Turn in place □ □.. Directly to articles....................□ □ □ □.. Slow Going & Returning...........□ □ □ □.. Doesn't work continuously........□ □ □ □.. Dropping article on return........□ □ Mouthing □ □ Dropping Article Touched handler..□ □ □ □ Slow response Sat between feet..□ □ □ □ No sit in front Poor sit.............□ □ Poor finish.............□ □ □ □ Handler error............□ □ No finish..□ □	**LEATHER** 30 **METAL** 30		
DIRECTED RETRIEVE	Does Not: Go out on command ....□ Go directly to glove.............................□ Retrieve right article.............................□ Fails to retrieve ....□ Anticipated..........................□ Extra signal..........................□ Sat out of reach ....□			□ Facing Glove □ ..Touching dog sending.....................□ □ ..Excessive Motions..........................□ □ ..Slow response to command.............□ □ ..Mouthing . □ Playing □ □ ..Slow Going & Returning..................□ □ Dropping article Touching handler....□ □ Poor delivery Sat between feet......□ □ No sit in front Poor sit.............□ □ No finish Poor finish..............□ □ Turn in place................................□ □ Handler error................................□	30		
MOVING STAND AND EXAMIN-ATION	□ Sat out of reach □ Displays Fear or Resentment □ Sitting □ Lying down □ Growling or snapping □ Repeated whining or barking Failure to: Heel □ / Stand and stay □ / Accept examination □ / Return to handler □			□ ..Forging . . □ Lagging □ Wide □ ..Moves Slightly on stand..................□ □ ..Handler Hesitates or Pauses............□ □ ..Fails to return briskly....................□ □ ..Poor sit..□ □ ..Return to Heel position...................□ □ ..Slow response..............................□ □ ..Handler error................................□ □ ..Poor finish...................................□	30		
DIRECTED JUMPING	HIGH JUMP Does Not: Leave on order ....□ Stop on command ...□ Jump as directed ...□ Climbing jump .....□ □ ..Anticipated command □ ..Does not go at least 10' beyond jumps ..□ BAR JUMP Does Not: Leave on order....□ Stop on command ....□ Jump as directed ....□ Knocking bar off............□			□ ..Holding signals.............................□ □ ..Slow response to directions.............□ □ ..Slightly off direction......................□ □ ..Not back far enough......................□ □ ..Anticipated □ Turn □ Stop □ Sit □ ..Does not sit on command □ ..Hesitation or reluctance to jump.......□ □ No sit in front Touched handler.......□ □ Anticipate Finish Sat between feet...□ □ No finish Poor sits ....□ .Poor finishes.......□ □ .. Handler error.............................□	40		
				MAXIMUM POINTS ➡	200		

□ H. Disciplining □ Shows Fear □ Fouling Ring □ Disqualified □ Expelled □ Excused □ Physical Correction   Less penalty for Unusual Behavior ➡

EXPLANATION OF PENALTY   TOTAL NET SCORE ➡

88

UNITED KENNEL CLUB, INC.

100 EAST KILGORE RD. • KALAMAZOO, MI 49001-5593 • 616-343-9020

1992 OBEDIENCE TRIAL SCORE BREAKDOWN
U.K.C. COMPANION DOG (U-CD)
Rules effective January, 1979
Revised January, 1992

Date _____

Judge _____

Host Club _____

Dog No. _____

Honor Dog No. _____

Breed _____

Novice _____

(A or B)

Height at Withers _____

Jumps _____ High

EXERCISE	NON-QUALIFYING		QUALIFYING (OVER 50%)		Max. Pts.	Pts. Lost	Net Score
	ZERO	LESS THAN 50%	Major (4 pts.)	Minor (½ - 2 pts.)			
HONORING	Return to Handler ....□ Interfered with working dog or Handler ....□ Dog leaves ring ....□	Did not remain in place ....□ Sat up ....□ Barked or whined repeatedly ....□	□ ....Whined ....□ □ ....Sits when Handler returns ....□ □ .... Minor move when handler returns ...□ □ ....Forced into position ....□ □ ....Leaves ring between exercises		35		
HEEL ON LEASH & Figure 8 (On leash) (Release Honor Dog)	Unqualified Heeling ....□ Uncontrollable ....□ Dog leaves ring ......□	Constant guiding or tight leash ....□ Handler continually adapts pace to dog ....□ Constant jerking on leash ....□	□ ..Extra command or signals **Fig. 8** □ ...Improper heel position □ □ □ ..Lagging □ □ □ ..Forging □ □ □ ..Crowding handler □ □ □ ..Sniffing □ □ □ ..No change of pace □ fast □ slow □ ..Occasional tight leash □ □ □ ..Heeling wide □ □ □ ..About Turn □ □ □ ..Lacks natural smoothness □ □ □ ..No Sit...□ Poor sits □ □ □ ..Leaves ring between exercises		35		
STANDING FOR EXAMINATION (Off Leash)	Growls or snaps ......□ Sits before or during examination ....□ Dog leaves ring ......□	Moves away before or during exam..........□ Shows shyness or resentment ....□ Extra command after leaving ....□	□ ..Resistance to handler posing ....□ □ ..Moving feet ....□ □ ..Moves after examination completed ......□ □ ..Sits as handler returns ....□ □ ..Handler error....................□ □ ..Lack of natural smoothness ....□ □ ..Leaves ring during exercises............□		30		
HEEL OFF LEASH	Unqualified Heeling ....□ Uncontrollable ....□ Dog leaves ring ......□	Dog leaves handler.............□ Handler continually adapts pace to dog................□	□ ..Extra command or signal ....□ □ ..Improper heel position ....□ □ ..Forging ....□ □ ..Lagging ....□ □ ..Crowding handler ....□ □ ..Heeling wide ....□ □ ..About turns ....□ □ ..No change of pace □ fast □ slow □ ..Lack of natural smoothness..........□ □ ..Poor sits...□..No Sit □ ..Leaves ring between exercises ....□		35		

RECALL OVER JUMP (Place Stewards At Jump)	Doesn't come on first command or signal ....□
	 Refused to jump ......□
	 Handler steps over jump............□
	 Sits too far away ......□
	 Dog leaves ring ....□
		Moved from position ....□
		 Extra command or signal to stay ....□
		 Anticipated recall ....□
		 Went around jump...............□
		 Climbs jump ....□
			□ ..Lay down or stood Poor sit..□
			    Poor finish..□
			 □ ..Slow response Touched handler..□
			    Sat between feet..□
			 □ ..Lack of natural smoothness ....□
			 □ ..Touching jump
			 □ ..No sit in front
			 □ ..No finish
			 □ ..Leaves ring between exercises
					35		

SUB TOTAL					170		
LONG SIT (Group Exercise) (1 minute)	Did not remain in place ....□ Disturbed other dog.................□ Dog leaves ring ......□	Repeatedly whined or barked ....□ Stood or lay down before handler returns to heel position ....□	Minor move before Minor move after handler returns to handler returns to heel position...□ heel position...□ □ ..Forcing into Minor whine position or barks...□ □ ..Rough treatment Handler error...□ □ ..Leaves ring between exercises		30		
				MAX. POINTS	200		

□ ..H. Disciplining   □ ..Shows Fear   □ ..Fouling Ring   □ ..Disqualified   □ ..Expelled   □ ..Excused

Less penalty for Unusual Behavior

Explanation of Penalty

TOTAL NET SCORE

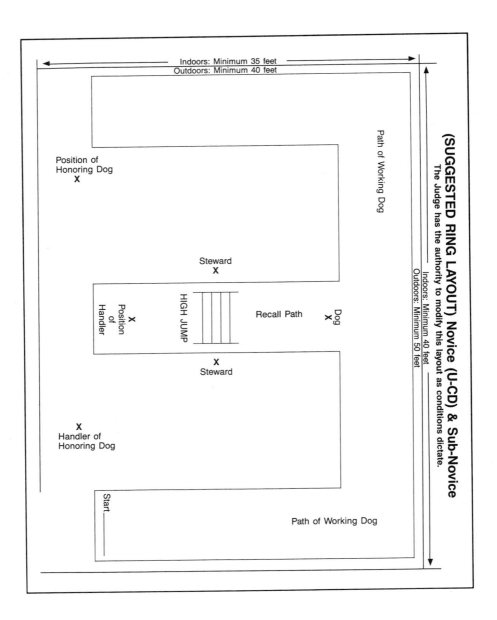

(SUGGESTED RING LAYOUT) Novice (U-CD) & Sub-Novice

The Judge has the authority to modify this layout as conditions dictate.

Indoors: Minimum 35 feet
Outdoors: Minimum 40 feet

Indoors: Minimum 40 feet
Outdoors: Minimum 50 feet

Path of Working Dog

Position of
Honoring Dog
X

Steward
X

X
Position
of
Handler

HIGH JUMP

Dog
X

Recall Path

X
Steward

X
Handler of
Honoring Dog

Start

Path of Working Dog

UNITED KENNEL CLUB, INC.

100 EAST KILGORE RD. • KALAMAZOO, MI 49001-5593 • 616-343-9020

1992 OBEDIENCE TRIAL SCORE BREAKDOWN
U.K.C. COMPANION DOG EXCELLENT (U-CDX)
Rules effective January, 1980
Revised January, 1991

Date _____ Dog No. _____ Open _____
(A or B)
Judge _____ Honor Dog No. _____ Height at Withers _____
Host Club _____ Breed _____ Jumps _____ High _____ Broad _____

EXERCISE	NON-QUALIFYING		QUALIFYING (OVER 50%)		Max. Pts	Pts. Lost	Net Score
	ZERO	LESS THAN 50%	Major (4 pts.)	Minor (½ - 2 pts.)			
HONORING DOG #____	Returns to Handler ....☐ Interferes with working dog or Handler ....☐ Dog leaves ring ....☐	Did not remain in place ....☐ Sits up ....☐ Barks or whines repeatedly ....☐	☐............Forced into position............☐ ☐............Whines ☐............Sits when Handler returns ....☐ ☐............Minor move when handler returns ....☐ ☐...Leaves ring between exercises		30		
HEEL OFF LEASH & Figure 8 (Place Steward To Walk) (Release Honor Dog)	Unqualified Heeling.................☐ Uncontrollable ....☐ Dog leaves ring ....☐	Handler continually adapts pace to dog ....☐ Leaves or breaks heel at stewards approach ....☐	Fig. 8 ☐..Extra commands or signals ☐ ☐ ☐..Improper heel position ☐ ☐ ☐..Lagging ☐ ☐ ☐..Forging ☐..Crowding handler ☐ ☐ ☐..No change of pace ☐fast ☐slow ☐..Heeling wide ☐..About Turn ☐..Lacks natural smoothness ☐ ☐ ☐..No Sit. ☐ Poor Sits ☐ ☐ ☐..Leaves ring between exercises		40		
DROP ON RECALL (Place Steward To Walk)	Does not drop on first command and/or signal ....☐ Does not come on first command and/or signal ....☐ Dog leaves ring ....☐	Anticipates Recall ....☐ Drop ....☐ Come ....☐ Sits out of reach ☐ Extra command and/or signal after handler leaves ....☐ Breaks Down position when Steward approaches ......☐	☐..Lies down or stands ....☐ ☐..Slow response....................☐ ☐..No sit in front ....☐ ☐..No finish ....☐ ☐..Touches Handler ....☐ ☐..Sits between feet ....☐ ☐..Lack of natural smoothness ....☐ ☐..Slow return....................☐ ☐..Poor Sit ....☐ ☐..Poor Finish ....☐ ☐..Leaves ring between exercises		30		
RETRIEVE ON FLAT	Fails to retrieve ....☐ Fails to go out on first command or signal ....☐ Sits out of reach ....☐ Dog leaves ring ....☐	Extra command and/or signal ....☐ Goes before command and/or signal ....☐	☐..Mouthing or playing ....☐ ☐..Slow ☐..Going ☐..Returning..☐ ☐..Poor delivery Touches handler..☐ ☐..Dropping dumbbell....................☐ ☐..Handler Error Poor finish..☐ ☐..No sit in front Sits between feet..☐ ☐..No Finish Poor Sit...☐ ☐..Leaves ring between exercises		20		
RETRIEVE OVER HIGH JUMP	Doesn't go out on first command and/or signal ....☐ Doesn't jump going or returning ....☐ Doesn't retrieve ....☐ Dog leaves ring ....☐	Leaves before command and/or signal ....☐ Jumps in only one direction ....☐ Sits out of reach ....☐ Extra command and/or signal to retrieve ....☐ Climbs Jump ....☐	☐..Mouthing or playing ....☐ ☐..Slow ☐..Going ☐..Returning..☐ ☐..Dropping dumbbell Touching Handler..☐ ☐..Touching Jump Sits between feet..☐ ☐..Poor delivery....................☐ ☐..Handler error....................☐ ☐..No sit in front Poor sit..☐ ☐..No finish Poor finish..☐ ☐..Leaves ring between exercises		30		
BROAD JUMP	Does not jump on first command and/or signal ....☐ Walks over any part ....☐ Dog leaves ring ....☐	Leaves before command and/or signal ....☐ Does not clear Jump .....☐ Sits out of reach ....☐	☐..Poor return....................☐ ☐..No sit in front....................☐ ☐..No finish....................☐ ☐..Minor jump touch....................☐ ☐..Touching Handler....................☐ ☐..Sits between feet....................☐ ☐..Poor finish Poor Sit..☐ ☐..Leaves ring between exercises		20		
SUB TOTAL					170		
LONG SIT (Group Exercise) (3 minutes)	Did not remain in place ....☐ Disturbed other dog................☐ Dog left ring ....☐	Repeatedly whines or barks ....☐ Stands or lies down before handler returns to heel position ....☐	Minor move before handler returns to heel position. ☐ ☐..Forcing into position ☐..Rough treatment ☐..Leaves ring between exercises	Minor move after handler returns to heel position. ☐ Minor whine or bark..☐ Handler error..☐	30		
				MAX. POINTS	200		

☐..H. Disciplining ☐..Shows Fear ☐..Fouling Ring ☐..Disqualified ☐..Expelled ☐..Excused — Less penalty for Unusual Behavior

Explanation of Penalty — **TOTAL NET SCORE**

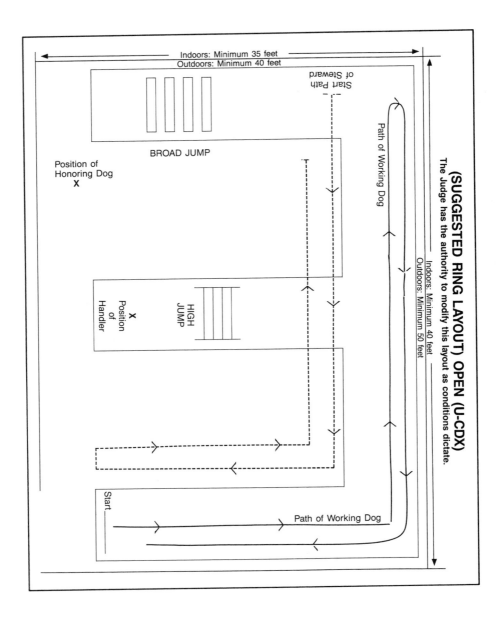

(SUGGESTED RING LAYOUT) OPEN (U-CDX)

The Judge has the authority to modify this layout as conditions dictate.

UNITED KENNEL CLUB, INC.

100 EAST KILGORE RD. • KALAMAZOO, MI 49001-5593 • 616-343-9020

1992 OBEDIENCE TRIAL SCORE BREAKDOWN
U.K.C. UTILITY DOG (U-UD)
Rules effective January 1, 1986
Revised January 1, 1992

Date _____ Dog No. _____

Judge _____ Non-Qual. Honor Dog No. _____

Host Club _____ Breed _____

Utility (A or B) _____

Article No. _____

Height at Withers _____

Jumps _____ High (24" max.)

EXERCISE	NON-QUALIFYING		QUALIFYING (OVER 50%)		Max. Pts.	Pts. Lost	Net Score
	ZERO	LESS THAN 50%	Major (4 pts.)	Minor (½ - 2 pts.)			
HONORING DOG #____	Interferes with working dog or handler ☐ Dog leaves the ring ☐	Honoring dog barks, whines or moves from a down ☐	☐ Sits as handler walks behind dog on return	Sits when handler is in heel position ☐	10		
SIGNAL EXERCISE (Release Honor Dog)	Handler adapting self to dog pace ☐ Unmanageable ☐ Unqualified heeling ☐ Any audible comm. ☐ Working dog goes to Honoring dog ☐ Dog leaves ring ☐ Failure on first signal to: Stand ☐ Stay ☐ Drop ☐ Sit ☐ Come ☐ Anticipated ☐	Sat out of reach ☐ Honoring dog barks or whines ☐	☐ Forging Crowding handler ☐ ☐ Lagging Sniffing ☐ ☐ No change of pace Fast ☐ Slow ☐ ☐ Heeling wide-on turns-abouts ☐ ☐ Extra signal to heel ☐ Sit ☐ ☐ Holding signals ☐ Slow response to signal to: ☐ Stand ☐ Down ☐ Sit ☐ Come ☐ ☐ No sit front finish Touching handler ☐ ☐ Lack of naturalness smoothness Sat between feet ☐ ☐ Poor sits☐ Poor Finish ☐		30		
SCENT DISCRIMINATION	No go out 1st command ☐ No retrieve ☐ Wrong article ☐ Dog leaves ring ☐	METAL Anticipated ☐ Extra command ☐ Sat out of reach ☐	☐ Handler roughness ☐ ☐ Does not sit after turn ☐ ☐ Doesn't work continuously ☐ ☐ Dropping article on return ☐ ☐ Slow response Picks up wrong article then dropped ☐ ☐ No sit in front Sat between feet ☐ ☐ No finish Poor sit ☐ ☐ Handler error Poor finish ☐ ☐ Leaves ring between exercises Touched handler ☐ Mouthing ☐		30		
DIRECTED (MARKED) RETRIEVE	Does Not: Go out on command ☐ Go directly to glove ☐ Retrieve right article ☐ Fails to retrieve ☐ Dog leaves ring ☐	Anticipated ☐ Extra signal ☐ Sat out of reach ☐	☐ Touching dog sending ☐ ☐ Excessive signals ☐ ☐ Slow response to command ☐ ☐ Mouthing Playing ☐ ☐ Dropping article Touching handler ☐ ☐ Poor delivery Sat between feet ☐ ☐ No sit in front Poor sit ☐ ☐ No finish Poor finish ☐ ☐ Lack of naturalness-smoothness ☐ ☐ Leaves ring between exercises		20		
DIRECTED (SIGNAL) RETRIEVE	Does Not: Go out on command ☐ Go directly to glove ☐ Retrieve right article ☐ Fails to retrieve ☐ Dog leaves ring ☐	Anticipated ☐ Extra signal ☐ Sat out of reach ☐ Does not stop ☐ Excessive signals ☐	☐ Does not sit on go out ☐ ☐ Touching dog sending ☐ ☐ Excessive signals ☐ ☐ Slow response to command ☐ ☐ Mouthing Playing ☐ ☐ Dropping article Touching handler ☐ ☐ Poor delivery Sat between feet ☐ ☐ No sit in front Poor sit ☐ ☐ No finish Poor finish ☐ ☐ Lack of naturalness-smoothness ☐ ☐ Leaves ring between exercises		30		
CONSECUTIVE RECALL	**ZERO** Recall - Drop Anticipated drop ☐ Sat out of reach ☐ Does Not: Come on 1st command ☐ Drop on 1st command ☐ Double command ☐ Sit or come ☐ Dog leaves ring ☐	Recall Anticipated drop ☐ Sat out of reach ☐ Does Not: Come on 1st command ☐ Double command ☐	☐ Slow response to command ☐ ☐ Does not stay sitting ☐ ☐ Touching handler ☐ ☐ No sit ☐ ☐ Poor sit ☐ ☐ No finish ☐ ☐ Poor finish ☐ ☐ Leaves ring between exercises		40		
DIRECTED JUMPING	HIGH BAR JUMP JUMP ☐ ☐ Does not leave on order ☐ ☐ Does not go substantially in right direction ☐ ☐ Does not stop on command ☐ ☐ Does not jump as directed ☐ ☐ Does not go at least 10' beyond jumps ☐ ☐ Climbing Jump ☐ ☐ Anticipated command ☐ ☐ Knocking bar off ☐ ☐ Dog leaves ring		☐ Holding signals ☐ ☐ Slow response to directions ☐ ☐ Slightly off direction ☐ ☐ Not back far enough ☐ ☐ Anticipated ☐ Turn ☐ Stop ☐ Sit ☐ ☐ Does not sit on command Poor sits ☐ ☐ Lack of naturalness- Touches handler ☐ smoothness ☐ No sit in front Sat between feet ☐ ☐ No finish Poor finishes ☐ ☐ Leaves ring between exercises		40		
			MAXIMUM POINTS		200		

☐ . .H. Disciplining   ☐ . .Shows Fear   ☐ . .Fouling Ring   ☐ . .Disqualified   ☐ . .Expelled   ☐ . .Excused

Less penalty for Unusual Behavior

Explanation of Penalty

TOTAL NET SCORE

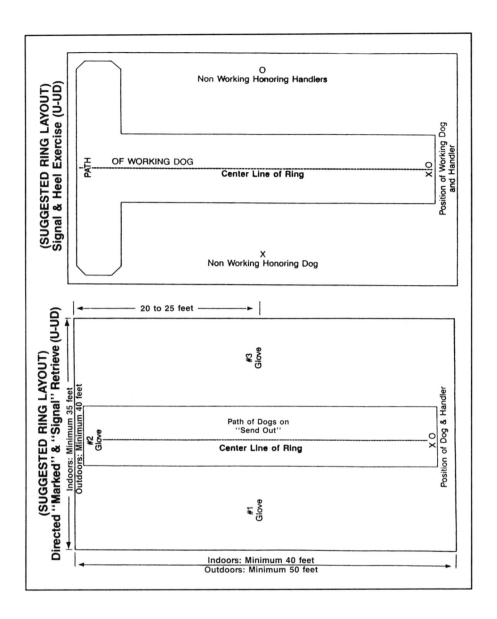

(SUGGESTED RING LAYOUT)
Signal & Heel Exercise (U-UD)

O
Non Working Honoring Handlers

PATH OF WORKING DOG

Center Line of Ring

X:O
Position of Working Dog and Handler

X
Non Working Honoring Dog

(SUGGESTED RING LAYOUT)
Directed "Marked" & "Signal" Retrieve (U-UD)

20 to 25 feet

#3
Glove

Indoors: Minimum 35 feet
Outdoors: Minimum 40 feet

#2
Glove

Path of Dogs on "Send Out"

Center Line of Ring

X O
Position of Dog & Handler

#1
Glove

Indoors: Minimum 40 feet
Outdoors: Minimum 50 feet

94

regulations. No correcting, praising or training are allowed in the ring during a trial.

Matches are much more informal and are held for practice. At many matches, the judge will allow you to do a certain amount of training in the ring. Your score will reflect any mistakes, of course, even if you are helping Fido, but that's what matches are for. Use them as a means to get ready for a trial.

Preparing for a Trial

The first step in preparing for a trial is to read and study the rules and regulations. If you have any questions, call the obedience department at each registry and ask. If a local trainer is a well-known competitor, ask for help.

Your next step is to go to a nearby trial and watch the competitors and the judges. Every judge will run his ring slightly different. The heel pattern might be different or the way he sets up the work in the ring. Some judges are more personable with the competitors, some sterner. Keep in mind, the judge is not there to win a personality contest but to give each exhibitor a fair evaluation of his performance.

Each competitor is going to be different, too. Watch for similarities, though. What do all the successful exhibitors have in common? Compare your style of training with what is being done? Are you making some mistakes? What are you doing right? Don't watch a successful competitor and then try to turn yourself into that person, though. Be yourself. Just watch the other competitors and see what you can learn from them.

When Fido is proficient in the basic exercises, go to a fun match and give it a try. Don't expect to go in the first time and bring home all the trophies offered. Instead, go in with the attitude that this is a learning experience to discover your strengths and weaknesses. Your performance can tell you what you need to practice before entering a trial.

Look at your training as objectively as possible. What mistakes did Fido make in the match competition? What mistakes did you make? Where do you need to make some changes in your training?

If there are any dog clubs nearby, join and work with one. Work with a friend who is also interested in competing. Meet at different places to train Fido and Rover. Train outside the pizza place or the ice cream store. Train at different parks. Make sure Fido sees people of various sizes, colors, shapes and sexes. Let him meet people wearing hats, raincoats, flowing dresses and beards. After all, you never know what your judge might look like!

Train Fido with distractions. Have someone eat a hot dog nearby while you do heelwork. Throw the ball while Fido does a sit/

The Subnovice or Beginners novice class is a nonregular class and is performed entirely on leash. Here a group of dogs do the one-minute sit/stay on leash.

stay. Make sure he understands that his training is applicable anywhere, under any conditions.

Finding Trials or Matches

Local pet professionals in your community should be able to point you toward any upcoming competitions; matches or trials. Local pet publications usually list upcoming dog events and local clubs. The AKC and UKC both publish magazines that list upcoming shows and trials. If you join a dog club, most publish monthly newsletters that also notify their members of upcoming dog events.

Sending in Your Entry

Most matches can be entered on the day of competition although many require that you enter prior to the start of judging. All AKC trials require that you pre-enter and the premium list, which gives you the information about the upcoming trial, will also list the pre-entry deadline, the cost of entry and where to send the entry blank. Most UKC and ASCA trials can be entered on the day of the event.

You will need your dog's registration to enter, and in most UKC events, you will also need proof of the dog's rabies vaccination. Many times bringing an up-to-date license or rabies tag is sufficient. However, if you are in doubt about what you need, call the match or show chairman before the show.

Most entry blanks are self explanatory but keep in mind a few things. First, list Fido's breed correctly. For example, it's a Labrador Retriever not a Lab. It's also a German Shepherd Dog, not just a German Shepherd. The dog-show-class blank is for conformation competition. Obedience classes are listed below that on the form. The blank for the full name of the dog is for exactly that, the full registered name, not what you call him at home.

As an example, see the entry blank that I have filled out for my Papillon, Chocho. Don't worry about any blanks that don't pertain to you. All the blanks do not have to be filled in. Do make sure that you sign the entry, though. It is not valid without a signature.

On the Day of the Trial

Make sure that Fido is clean, flea free, brushed and has had his nails trimmed or any other grooming that his breed requires. Bring his leash, collar, brush, fly spray if that is a problem in your area, a bowl and water, a crate and a few treats.

You should also look good. This is not the time to wear your grubbiest jeans. You don't need to dress for an evening on the town but you should be clean and neat. Don't forget to wear comfortable shoes.

Make sure Fido is used to training around ring ropes before you go to your first match or trial. (Australian Shepherd)

When you get to the show grounds, find your ring and check in with the steward. Pick up your armband and find out where you are in the judging line up. Are you the third dog in the ring or the twenty-first? Be ready. If it's your turn and you don't show up, you've lost. The judge does NOT have to take you later. Many will, but they don't have to do so.

Watch the competitors before you. What is the judge's ring pattern? Where does he do the slow heel, or the fast? Where does he do the recall?

When the competitor before you goes in the ring, give Fido a chance to go potty. Clean up after him, then do some quick heels and sits. Praise him and offer him a treat. Training is not allowed on show grounds but a quick warm up is allowed. Some competitors take advantage and push it as far as they can but that's poor sportsmanship. Abide by the rules and simply make sure that Fido is awake, alert and ready to listen to you.

When you go in the ring, take a deep breath and smile. It's good for you, good for the judge and good for Fido. Listen to the judge. Ask him questions if you don't understand what he said—then trust your training. You and Fido are ready for this. You're a team. Now is the time to show off!

If by chance, you have a bad performance in the ring, do NOT come out of the ring blaming the world. DON'T blame your trainer, the judge, the grass in the ring, the weather or your spouse. And, I had better not hear you blame Fido. Excuses are uncalled for and unnecessary. A good sport will look at that performance and try to use it constructively to improve the next one.

Keep in mind, dog obedience competition is a sport and is to be enjoyed. It doesn't matter whether you are aiming for High in Trial and 200 points out of the 200 available, or you are going for the fun of it. There is always another day, another trial and another opportunity. Enjoy it and be a good sport.

Chapter Seven

The Recall (Come) Exercises

Become the most positive and enthusiastic person you know.
"Life's Little Instruction Book," by H. Jackson Brown Jr.
Published by Rutledge Hill Press, Nashville, TN.

The Exercise

In the American Kennel Club obedience Novice class, the recall or come exercise demonstrates that Fido can be left in a sit, in one position and remain there until you call him. When called, Fido is to run directly to you, sit centered in front of you and wait until told to move to the heel position.

In the ring, the exercise will be performed as follows:

1. The judge positions Fido and Jack at one side of the ring, their backs toward the ring ropes. Fido is in a sit in the heel position.

2. The judge tells Jack: "This is the recall exercise. I will tell you to leave your dog. At that time, I want you to walk across the ring. I will give you a signal to call your dog and a signal to finish your dog. Do you have any questions?" At Jack's, "No," the judge tells him, "Leave your dog."

3. Jack tells Fido "Wait," giving a hand signal and/or a verbal command. Jack then walks quickly but naturally across the ring. Just before he reaches the ring ropes, making sure that he allows enough room for Fido to do a finish, he turns and faces Fido, his arms hanging naturally at his sides. Keeping an eye on the judge for his signal, he waits.

4. At the judge's signal, Jack smiles and calls, "Fido, Come!" in a pleasant, clear voice. He concentrates on standing still, not giving any unintentional body cues.

5. On Jack's command to come, Fido pushes himself off from the sit and runs quickly to Jack, centering himself in front of him so that Jack could easily reach out and touch him. Holding his sit, Fido waits for the next command.

6. After watching Fido run in and sit, Jack looks up at the judge, waiting for the signal to finish. The judge nods and signals. Jack says, "Fido, finish!"

7. Fido springs up to the left of Jack and swivels around, swinging his hips and coming to a sit by Jack's left side, in the heel position. He holds still, waiting for the release and Jack's praise.

8. Jack watches the judge. Nodding, the judge says, "Exercise finished! Good work!"

9. Jack steps forward as he tells Fido: "Fido, release! Good boy! All right," and he praises the dog.

Scoring

The American Kennel Club Novice class Recall Exercise:

EXERCISE	NON QUALIFYING ZERO	QUALIFYING SUBSTANTIAL / MINOR	Maxiumum Points	Points Lost	NET SCORE
RECALL	Didn't come on first command or signal ☐ Anticipated ☐ Extra command or signal to stay ☐ Moved from position ☐ Sat out of reach ☐ Leaving handler ☐	☐ Stood or lay down ☐ Slow response — Touched handler☐ ☐ No sit in front — Sat between feet☐ ☐ No finish — Poor sit☐ ☐ Failure to come directly to handler Poor finish☐ ☐ Failure to come at a brisk trot or gallop ☐ Handler arms not at side ☐ Handler error ☐	30		

A perfect AKC Novice recall exercise is worth 30 points and every dog that begins the recall exercise starts with those 30 available points. Each mistake lowers that total. Minor deductions (1/2 point to two points) might include crooked sits, crooked finishes, touching the handler on the sit or finish or sitting between the handler's feet.

Substantial deductions (three or more points) will be given for a slow response to the come command, standing or laying down during the sit/stay portion of the exercise, failure to sit in front, finish or sit after the finish. The dog will fail if he refuses to come on the first command, refuses to stay when left or sits out of reach when sitting in front.

The handler can lose points by not having his arms hang naturally by his sides when calling the dog, or by giving the dog extra signals or commands with his body language, or by moving his feet while the dog is coming to him.

In the AKC and UKC Open classes, the exercise and scoring are the same as the AKC Novice class except that Fido will be given a down signal or command while he is moving toward you on the come command and Fido must immediately lie down and remain there until you call him again. The emphasis is on the promptness of Fido's response to the drop command or signal. Fido will fail the exercise if

An illustraion of the AKC Open (CDX) Drop on Recall scoresheet and the UKC Open (CDX) class Drop on Recall exercise:

EXERCISE	NON QUALIFYING ZERO		QUALIFYING		Maxiumum Points	Points Lost	NET SCORE
			SUBSTANTIAL	MINOR			
DROP ON RECALL	Does not come on first command or signal.....☐ Does not drop on first command or signal.....☐ Extra com. or sig. to stay after handler leaves.....☐	Moved from place left.....☐ Anticipated: Recall.....☐ Drop.....☐ Come in.....☐ Sat out of reach.....☐	☐ Handler error.....☐ ☐ Stood or lay down.....☐ ☐ Finish.....☐ ☐ Slow response Touching handler.....☐ ☐ Failure to Come Briskly Sat between feet.....☐ ☐ Slow drop Poor Sit.....☐ ☐ No sit in front Poor finish.....☐ ☐ No finish ☐ Arms not at side		30		

EXERCISE	NON-QUALIFYING		QUALIFYING (OVER 50%)		Max. Pts.	Pts. Lost	Net Score
	ZERO	LESS THAN 50%	Major (4 pts.)	Minor (½ - 2 pts.)			
(Place Steward To Walk) DROP ON RECALL	Does not drop on first command and/or signal.....☐ Does not come on first command and/or signal.....☐ Dog leaves ring.....☐	Anticipates Recall.....☐ Drop.....☐ Come.....☐ Sits out of reach.....☐ Extra command and/or signal after handler leaves.....☐ Breaks Down position when Steward approaches.....☐	☐..Lies down or stands.....☐ ☐..Slow response.....☐ ☐..No sit in front.....☐ ☐..No finish.....☐ ☐..Touches Handler.....☐ ☐..Sits between feet.....☐ ☐..Lack of natural smoothness.....☐ ☐..Slow return.....☐ ☐..Poor Sit.....☐ ☐..Poor Finish.....☐ ☐..Leaves ring between exercises		30		

An illustration of the UKC Recall over the Jump scoresheet:

EXERCISE	NON-QUALIFYING		QUALIFYING (OVER 50%)		Max. Pts.	Pts. Lost	Net Score
	ZERO	LESS THAN 50%	Major (4 pts.)	Minor (½ - 2 pts.)			

RECALL OVER JUMP
(Place Stewards At Jump)
	Doesn't come on first command or signal.....☐
	Refused to jump.....☐
	Handler steps over jump.....☐
	Sits too far away.....☐
	Dog leaves ring.....☐
		Moved from position.....☐
		Extra command or signal to stay.....☐
		Anticipated recall.....☐
		Went around jump.....☐
		Climbs jump.....☐
			☐..Lay down or stood Poor sit..☐
			          Poor finish..☐
			☐..Slow response Touched handler..☐
			          Sat between feet..☐
			☐..Lack of natural smoothness.....☐
			☐..Touching jump
			☐..No sit in front
			☐..No finish
			☐..Leaves ring between exercises
					35		

he fails to go down within a couple of steps on the first command or if he doesn't remain in the down position until you call him to you.

In the UKC obedience program, in the Novice class (the equivalent to the AKC Novice class) Fido must do a recall over a jump. The exercise and scoring are very similar to the AKC's Novice exercise except that Fido can fail for refusing to jump or by going around the jump.

The UKC Utility class has a Consecutive Recall exercise. In the first recall, Fido will do the drop on recall just like the AKC Open class drop on recall. Immediately following that, he will do a straight recall with no drop, just like the AKC Novice recall. This is to make sure that Fido is listening to your commands and is not anticipating a drop halfway through the recall.

The United Kennel Club Utility class Consecutive Recall exercise:

EXERCISE	NON-QUALIFYING		QUALIFYING (OVER 50%)		Max. Pts.	Pts. Lost	Net Score
	ZERO	LESS THAN 50%	Major (4 pts.)	Minor (½ - 2 pts.)			
CONSECUTIVE RECALL	**ZERO** Recall - Drop Anticipated drop ....□ Sat out of reach ....□ Does Not: Come on 1st command ...□ Drop on 1st command ....□ Double command ....□ Sit or come ....□ Dog leaves ring ....□	Recall Anticipated drop ....□ Sat out of reach ....□ Does Not: Come on 1st command...............□ Double command ....□	□..........Slow response to command........□ □..............Does not stay sitting...........□ □................Touching handler............□ □....................No sit..................□ □.....................Poor sit................□ □.....................No finish...............□ □.....................Poor finish.............□ □..Leaves ring between exercises		40		

Practical Application

All dogs, no matter whether they are obedience competition dogs, tracking dogs, show dogs or pets, need to know, understand and respond quickly to a come command. An immediate response to a come command can save Fido from a speeding car or can bring him in from the backyard when it's time for dinner.

Other aspects of the recall exercise have practical uses, too. The sit in front is the most obvious and is one of the most useful because it can stop the dog from jumping on people. Most dogs jump on people to greet them and to get attention. Dogs greet each other face to face, puppies licking the dominant dog's face. Because people are so much taller, the dog jumps to reach the face or the hands.

Training Sequence (TS)
One repetition of a training step, followed by praise.
Second repetition of the same step, followed by praise.
Third repetition of the same step, followed by praise, a release ("Fido, Release! Good boy!") and a reward (His motivator, a toy or a treat).

Training Schedule
1. Do each step a minimum of three training sequences.
2. If the third TS has no mistakes and Fido is doing the step correctly, go on to the next step.
3. If Fido is having problems, go back one step and repeat the TS at that step.
4. If Fido is still confused, go back several steps to a place where Fido is sure of himself, and work back up.

Tigger, an Australian Shepherd, wanted badly to jump on her owners and would try it at any opportunity. Her owners tried many of the recommended corrections for jumping but Tigger would tolerate any correction and immediately go back to jumping. However, once she learned that the sit in front brought her the praise and attention that she craved, she stopped jumping. In fact, her sit in front became a slide into a sit, and then a sit and quiver as she waited for the attention that she knew would follow.

The sit in front can also solve a *keep-away* problem. Tasha, a Golden Retriever, liked to play keep away. She would run in towards her owner and then dash away, never going far but staying just out of reach. Tasha liked the game and enjoyed the attention that it brought, even the negative attention. Once she learned that the sit in front brought the positive attention that she wanted, she too, like Tigger, would slide into a sit and hold still, waiting for that praise.

The sit in front can also make the day-to-day aspect of living with a dog much easier. When Fido understands that sit in front means *sit in front and hold still,* the dog can have the collar and leash put on without playing catch me if you can. The dog can be touched, handled, examined and medicated without risk of being pawed or mauled.

The drop on recall is part of the open class recall exercise and is also a practical command. It can be used in emergency situations to stop the dog in his tracks or it can simply put the dog in one spot to keep him out from underfoot around the house.

The finish portion of the recall exercise is not as important as the come, the sit in front or the drop but it is a useful command because it puts the dog back in the heel position. After leashing the dog, or praising him, or if the dog is underfoot in front of you, you can tell him "Finish," and put him back where he belongs.

Teachng the Finish Exercise

In Chapter Four, Fido learned to sit, both in front of you

105

Your body language can help encourage Fido to come to you. Cameron kneels as he calls Desi, smiles and opens his arms to his dog. (Australian Shepherd)

Wilma dashes around Jane in a fast, right finish, positioning herself in a beautiful straight sit. (Weimaraner)

106

Sparky gets the height he needs for a snappy left finish, but is still clumsy. (Dalmatian)

while practicing the Watch me and by your left side in what is called the heel position. When teaching Fido to go to heel, or to finish, you will start with Fido in a sit in front and end up with Fido in a sit by your left side. To get Fido to the heel position, there are two directions the dog can go, to your left or to your right.

Right Finish. Fido can start by moving toward your right side and go around you, coming into the heel position from behind. This finish is particularly good for long-bodied dogs, slower moving dogs or dogs that have difficulty sitting straight.

Step 1. Sit Fido in front of you and do a *Watch me!* When Fido is watching, take the leash and motivator in your right hand and as you give Fido the finish command, sweep your right hand back behind you as you step back with the right foot. As soon as Fido starts to follow the hand and foot signal, praise him and encourage him to continue around. Bring the leash to your left hand behind your body and bring Fido up to a sit in the heel position. Praise him. Follow the training sequence and schedule.

Step 2. DECREASE THE MOVEMENT OF THE RIGHT FOOT until Fido is moving entirely for the verbal command and the right hand passing the leash behind the body. Follow the training sequence and schedule.

NOTE: This hand movement is in itself a signal to the dog and can be used as a command for the dog to finish. However, in competition, only one command can be given for the finish—either the verbal command or the hand signal—so you need to decide which one works better for the dog and then concentrate on that one command.

Step 3. PUT FIDO'S MOTIVATOR IN YOUR POCKET, OUT OF SIGHT and practice as in Step 2, using both your right hand with the leash and a verbal command. Follow the training sequence and schedule.

Step 4. Give the verbal command, "Fido, Finish," and if Fido doesn't start to move immediately, SNAP THE LEASH QUICKLY to start Fido moving around you. Follow the training sequence and schedule.

Left Finish. Fido can also finish by going directly to your left side, swinging around to position himself in the heel position. The swing finish is particularly flashy if the dog moves quickly and moves to the heel position with a leap as he's swinging.

You can teach Fido the swing finish just as you did the other, except that you will use the left hand and foot to help guide Fido. As you take the left hand (holding the leash and motivator) and left foot backwards, tell Fido: "Fido, Swing!" Fido should go back far enough to turn his body around so that he can stop in the heel position sitting straight. As Fido learns the exercise, encourage Fido to hop by popping the leash upwards with the motivator as you give Fido the command to swing. Use the same training steps above, except reverse the direction that Fido will go.

NOTE: Always train the finish exercise separately from the come. If you always call Fido to you and then always have him finish, pretty soon he will put two and two together. In competition, you will lose a lot of points when he anticipates the finish and goes directly to the heel position, forgetting about the sit in front.

Sit in Front. Although Fido was taught to sit in front in Chapter Four, little emphasis was placed on sitting straight, centered in front of you. However, in competition, Fido is required to sit straight, centered in front of you. This sit position can be of benefit to you in another way, too, besides competition. When Fido sits in front of you, it is much easier to get and keep his undivided attention. When he's paying attention to you, you know he's not distracted and that you can give him an additional command.

Step 1. With Fido sitting in front of you, take a couple of steps backward, as you hold the leash in one hand and motivator in another, both hands close together centered in front of your body at waist level. (See photo.) Encourage Fido to step forward and sit, praising him for a straight sit. Allow him to sniff toward the motivator and tease him with it. Allow him to nibble on it or play with it while you praise him after a good sit. Follow the training sequence and schedule.

Step 2. Repeat as in Step 1, except if Fido doesn't sit straight, LIGHTLY SNAP THE LEASH AS YOU STEP BACK AGAIN AND REPOSITION FIDO IN A STRAIGHT SIT. Help him by moving the motivator so that his eyes and head lead him to a straight sit. Praise him enthusiastically when he sits correctly. Follow the training sequence and schedule.

NOTE: Don't get frustrated and use your hands to position Fido. He may learn that *sit straight* means "Allow Mom to jerk me around" instead of what you really want it to mean. If Fido is having trouble understanding what you want, set up something to help him sit straight, such as a couple of lawn chairs or boards. Set them up so that they are just wide enough for Fido to walk between and then walk

Left: Sit in Front, Step 1. Jane has both hands centered at her waist to help guide Wilma into a straight sit in front. (Weimaraner) Right: Sit in Front, Step 5. Rachel has both hands by her sides, but Sparky is very slightly crooked. (Dalmation)

Fido between them a few times so he's not worried, then back up between the boards, encouraging Fido to follow you. Stop and have Fido sit. If he sits crooked the boards or chairs should stop him or make it uncomfortable. If he sits straight, praise him.

Step 3. With Fido in a sit in front, with the leash in the left hand and the motivator in the right hand, both hands centered at your belt buckle (or where a belt buckle would be if you were wearing one) back up a few steps but instead of backing straight, as you were, BACK UP IN A ZIG-ZAG PATTERN, challenging Fido to sit straight. Take two steps back and make a partial left turn. Then repeat with a right turn. And so on. Follow the training sequence and schedule.

110

Step 4. With Fido in a sit in front, have the leash and motivator BOTH IN THE LEFT HAND AND DROP THE RIGHT HAND TO A NORMAL POSITION BY YOUR SIDE. Practice as you did in Step 3. Follow the training sequence and schedule.

Step 5. With Fido in a sit in front, TUCK THE LEASH AND IF POSSIBLE, THE MOTIVATOR, IN THE TOP OF YOUR PANTS, CENTERED, AND DROP BOTH HANDS TO YOUR SIDE. Practice as in Step 3. Follow the training sequence and schedule.

NOTE: Train the sit in front all the time. Have Fido sit straight and centered when you give him dinner. Have him sit straight and centered when you ask him to sit to leash him. Have him sit straight and centered when you ask him to shake hands. You want this to become second nature.

The Drop in Motion. The drop in motion is the portion of the AKC and UKC Open class Drop on Recall exercise when the dog must respond to your command to down or drop, and do so instantly. Ideally, Fido should hear your *Down!* command and act as if he's hit a brick wall, dropping immediately to the ground. However, the general rule of thumb is that he should be totally down within one body length of receiving the command.

Step 1. Start teaching this command by reviewing the down that Fido learned in Chapter Two. Fido should be going down from a sit very quickly, with no hesitation. If he's slow, snap the leash sharply with your left hand as you give the down command. At the same time, hold the motivator in your right hand and give the down signal with your right hand and the motivator. When Fido is down, reward him with the motivator while he is still in the down position. Follow the training sequence and schedule.

Step 2. When he is going down quickly from a sit by your side, STEP OUT IN FRONT OF FIDO, AND GIVE HIM A DOWN COMMAND FROM A LEASH LENGTH AWAY, STILL HOLDING ONTO THE LEASH. If he hesitates, step back to him, lightly snap the leash and repeat your command. When he does it correctly, make sure you praise and reward him with the motivator. Follow the training sequence and schedule.

Step 3. Once he is going down quickly from a sit at a distance, START HEELING WITH FIDO AND AS YOU ARE WALKING, GIVE HIM THE

DOWN COMMAND. POINT TO THE GROUND IN FRONT OF HIM WITH YOUR RIGHT HAND AS THE LEFT HAND ON FIDO'S SHOULDER HELPS HIM GO DOWN QUICKLY. Once Fido is down, praise him. Heel him forward and try it again. Follow the training sequence and schedule.

Step 4. When Fido is going down easily, with no assistance needed, START WALKING FASTER WHEN YOU DROP HIM. Follow the training sequence and schedule.

Step 5. BACK AWAY FROM FIDO AND GIVE HIM THE DOWN COMMAND AS HE IS COMING TOWARDS YOU. Once he's down, back up to the end of the leash before you go back to him to praise him.

NOTE: If Fido will not go down without crawling to your feet, go back to practicing the drop from a sit/wait a leash length away. If he tries to crawl forward, step into him and give him a down signal directly in front of him and then step away again. Once he is doing this well, then leave him on a long line and drop him from gradually increasing distances. Then reintroduce the moving drop.

Drop in Motion, Step 2. Wilma goes down from a sit at the end of the leash. (Weimaraner)

112

Drop in Motion, Step 3. Joan praises DC for going down quickly from the heel. (Golden Retriever puppy)

The Come. Your goal is to teach Fido to come to you, at a run or gallop, ignore any distractions and come on the first command, every time you call him. To do this, you must keep the come positive. Never call him to come to do something nasty to him. Don't call him to come and flea spray him. Don't call him to come and give him a bath and never, ever call him to come and punish him for something. If you do, Fido will associate the last thing that happened—you calling him to come—with the punishment or the flea spray. And then the next time you call, he will hesitate, perhaps long enough to get hit by a car or to fail the obedience exercise.

If you have already ruined the word *come* by using it incorrectly, begin teaching this exercise using a different word. Use *Here* or *Front* or any other word that you will easily remember. Because the come is so important, we will be teaching it several different ways.

The "Cookie" Come. It's important to keep the come fun as well as positive. You can teach Fido that the come is a lot of fun by making a "cookie" container. Take a plastic container with a tight fitting lid, a small one is fine, and put some hard dog treats in it. This is your motivator for the come command.

Step 1. With Fido close to you, shake the container and in a high, happy tone of voice, ask Fido: "Do you want some cookies?" Promptly pop a "cookie" in his mouth. Follow the training sequence and schedule.

Step 2. WITH FIDO OUTSIDE, go to the back door, shake the container and repeat your question. Give him another treat. Follow the training sequence and schedule.

Step 3. When Fido is reacting when he hears the container, go outside and shake it, saying, "Fido, cookie? FIDO, COME! GOOD BOY!" Praise him as you pop a cookie in his mouth.

Step 4. Practice as in Step 4, except ELIMINATE THE WORD COOKIE FROM YOUR COMMAND, but continue shaking the container and popping the treat in his mouth.

Step 5. Fido is now associating the container shaking and the come command with both a cookie and your praise. Excellent! NOW PUT HIM ON A LEASH. With container in hand, back away from Fido as you very slightly rattle the motivator and call him: "Fido, come! Good boy!" Follow the training sequence and schedule.

Step 6. Repeat as in Step 5, except when he catches up to you, HAVE HIM SIT IN FRONT OF YOU, CENTERED AND STRAIGHT, BEFORE YOU GIVE HIM A COOKIE. Follow the training sequence and schedule.

Step 7. PUT YOUR TREAT CONTAINER AWAY. HAVE A TINY MOTIVATOR (a treat or toy) IN YOUR RIGHT HAND OR POCKET TO USE AS A REWARD. Back up and call Fido, as you did in Step 5. Reward with the motivator. Follow the training sequence and schedule.

NOTE: Keep the treat container around, don't get rid of it, you'll use it again. If Fido sneaks out the front door, use the treat container to bring him back to you. If he's chasing a cat in the back yard, use the treat container. If Fido backslides on the come command, bring back the treat container!

Long Line and Come. A long line is a 20- to 50-foot length of clothesline rope that acts as a long leash for Fido. When you take Fido out to run or to play Frisbee, he needs to understand that even in the heat of a chase, he must respond and come back to you as soon as you call him.

Joan backs up as she calls DC. The treat in hand is to encourage the puppy and to help shape the sit in front. (Golden Retriever puppy)

Step 1. Hook Fido up to the long line and let him drag it as you throw the ball or Frisbee. When you know Fido is distracted, grab the end of the line and back away from Fido as you call him to come: "Fido, Come! Good boy!" Use the long line to make sure that he comes directly to you with no detours. Praise him. Follow the training sequence and schedule.

Step 2. Practice as in Step 1 above except HAVE FIDO SIT IN FRONT WHEN HE CATCHES UP TO YOU. Praise him. Follow the training sequence and schedule.

Wait and Come. The *wait* command is very similar to the stay command that Fido learned in Chapter Four. You will give the same hand signal for the stay and the wait but with the stay, you always go back to Fido to release him and with the wait, you can call Fido to come to you.

Fido will learn, with practice, that he can go to sleep on the stay if he wants as long as he remembers what he's doing when he wakes up. But with the wait, you will call Fido to come, or release him to go through the door, or will allow him to jump in the car. We want Fido to understand that *stay* means statue: "Hold still until I come back and release you." But *wait* means: "Don't walk forward with me but pay attention, something else is going to happen."

Step 1. Have Fido sit by your left side and tell him "Fido, wait" as you give him the wait and stay hand signal. Take two steps away, holding on to the leash. If he moves from position, give him a verbal correction, "ACCKK!" and reposition him. Wait no longer than five seconds, then call him, "Fido, come!" Back away from Fido as you call him so that he can break into a trot to follow you. Stop and praise him. Follow the training sequence and schedule.

Step 2. Practice as in Step 1 except GO OUT TO THE END OF THE SIX-FOOT LEASH BEFORE YOU CALL HIM. Follow the training sequence and schedule.

NOTE: If at any time during the come exercises, Fido is not coming to you quickly, turn and run from him as fast as you can. Continue to hold on to the leash and if he doesn't go with you fast enough, snap the leash. The prey drive and chase instincts are very strong and chasing a moving target is much more exciting than a still one. If you need to spice up the come, run!

Bonnie backs up as she calls Jupiter, encouraging him to come quickly. (Golden Retriever)

Step 3. Practice as in Step 2 except HAVE FIDO SIT IN FRONT OF YOU, STRAIGHT AND CENTERED. Praise him. Follow the training sequence and schedule.

Step 4. Practice as in Step 3 except INCREASE THE WAIT TO 10 SECONDS BEFORE CALLING FIDO. Follow the training sequence and schedule.

Step 5. Practice as in Step 4 except ADD THE 20-FOOT LONG LINE. Hook the long line to Fido INSTEAD OF THE LEASH, leave Fido at a wait, GO OUT ABOUT 12 FEET. Then, after waiting about 10 seconds, call Fido to come, backing away from him slightly to encourage him to come faster. When he catches you, have him sit in front, straight and centered. Praise him. Follow the training sequence and schedule.

Step 6. Leave Fido in a sit/wait and GO ABOUT 20 FEET AWAY. Practice as in Step 5 above. Follow the training sequence and schedule.

Step 7. Practice as in Step 6, except DROP THE LONG LINE TO THE GROUND. Put your foot on the long line but keep your hands free. Call: "Fido, come! Good boy!" Praise him as he sits in front, straight and centered. Follow the training sequence and schedule.

> **NOTE:** Don't be in a hurry to get rid of the leash or long line.

The most common mistake that people make is taking the leash off too soon. If you take the leash off and the dog learns that you can't catch him or that you can't enforce the come command, you will have some major retraining to do—all on leash! Use the leash, long line and motivator—they are not crutches—they are training tools that you are using to build good habits, such as coming happily and quickly on the first command and coming straight to you without any detours.

Distractions. When Fido is working very reliably on the long line at a distance of about 30 feet, start supplying some distractions. Train with other dogs if you can, make funny noises, eat a sandwich, have a friend eat a hot dog, or borrow a neighbor's kid to ride a bicycle around the training area. Fido must learn to pay attention to you and concentrate on what he is doing regardless of what is going on around him. Use your long line and your voice to correct any mistakes. Most importantly, praise him enthusiastically when he has done the exercise correctly.

Are You Having Problems?

Is Fido reluctant to come to you? Have you punished him after calling him? Or have you flea sprayed him after calling him? If so, you may want to reteach the exercise using a different word. Use Front or Here or any other word that you will easily remember. When you're reteaching the exercise, remember to be enthusiastic and always positive.

Does Fido normally come to you but occasionally hesitates or comes slowly? You may be frowning instead of smiling, or your body language may look angry. In an obedience trial, years ago, I called my German Shepherd Michi to come and he refused. He looked at me and watched me, but didn't come. I called him again and he did come but very slowly. The judge came over to me and asked me: "What were you so angry about? His performance, up to now, was very good." I shook my head and said I wasn't angry. His reply: "I thought you looked angry. You were frowning and he obviously thought you were angry."

If Fido already had some bad habits concerning the come, your progress may be slower than a dog that did not have any bad habits. If Fido likes to play keep away or runs away from you when you call him, keep a long line on him when he's in the back yard and you can watch him to make sure he doesn't tangle it and choke himself. Then call him occasionally, using the long line to make sure he does come to you, and comes all the way in, not just outside of arm's reach. Make him sit in front and hold it until you release him. Don't take the long line off for training until you have gone a period of time without having to use it to correct Fido, and then put a shorter one on for a while before you eliminate it altogether.

When you practice the wait/come, use a long line as often as you need it and don't assume that you don't need it. Use it when you are practicing with distractions. Use it when you're training with new dogs, or in a new place. The long line allows you to keep control and to make sure that Fido does come and doesn't get away from you.

If Fido seems to run out of steam or get bored with the come, spice it up. When he's coming towards you and is kind of blah, then turn and run away from him, encouraging him to chase you. Praise him for chasing you. Bring back the treat container and use it once in a while. When he does a really good recall, nice and fast with a beautiful straight sit in front, give him a jackpot of praise! Love him up! Rewarding his efforts will make sure that he continues to try.

Jane calls Wilma, off lead, and has a treat in-hand to reinforce the straight sit in front. (Weimaraner)

A dependable down/stay can be used for something as simple as controlling the dog while you talk to friends. (Weimananer)

Chapter Eight
The Stay Exercises

A trained dog is a free dog.
Joachim Volhard

The Exercise

In the AKC obedience Novice class, the stay exercises demonstrate that Fido can be left in one position for a specified time, sometimes in close proximity to other dogs, without moving from that position. In Novice, there are three stays: the stand/stay (See Chapter Ten), the one-minute sit/stay and the three-minute down/stay.

In the ring, here's how the sit/stay will be performed:

1. After completion of the individual exercises, a ring steward will ask the competitors to line up outside the ring in the order of their armbands, or the order in which they performed the individual exercises, if that differs from armband order. At the judge's direction, the steward will bring the competitors back into the ring. All handlers should follow the steward in a single file, with dogs at a heel. The steward will direct the handlers to form a straight line along one side of the ring.

2. When lined up, Jane makes sure that Fido is in a good sit, in the heel position. She takes off Fido's leash and her armband and wraps the leash around the armband to weight it down. She then places the armband on the ground behind Fido.

3. The judge tells the handlers: "This is a one-minute sit/stay. I want you to walk across the ring and turn and face your dog. Are there any questions? Sit your dog."

4. Jane looks at Fido. He is sitting quietly.

5. The judge says, "Leave your dog."

6. Jane tells Fido, "Stay," and gives him a hand signal meaning stay. She then walks across the ring, turns around and faces Fido. With her arms by her sides, she stands quietly.

7. The judge times one minute and then says, "Return to your dog." As a group, the handlers go back to their dogs, walking around and behind the dogs to return to the heel position.

8. When all handlers are in the heel position next to their dogs, the judge says, "Exercise finished." Jane tells Fido: "Fido, release! Good boy! Fido sit."

9. After praising their dogs, the handlers will put their dogs back into the heel position in a sit. The judge will then introduce the down/stay exercise, which is handled in the same manner as the sit/stay except that it is for three minutes instead of one.

10. At the completion of both stays, the handlers must reattach the leashes to the dogs before leaving the ring and should not leave the ring until dismissed by the judge.

Scoring

The American Kennel Club Novice class Group stay exercises

EXERCISE	NON QUALIFYING ZERO	QUALIFYING		Maximum Points	Points Lost	NET SCORE
		SUBSTANTIAL	MINOR			
LONG SIT (1 Minute)	Did not remain in place ☐ Goes to another dog ☐ Repeated whines or barks ☐ Changes its position ☐	☐ . Stood or lay down after handler returns to heel position ☐ . Minor move before handler returns ☐ . Minor whine or bark ☐ . Forced into position ☐ . Handler error ☐		30		
LONG DOWN (3 Minutes)	Did not remain in place ☐ Goes to another dog ☐ Repeated whines or barks ☐ Changes its position ☐	☐ . Stood or Sat Down after handler returns to heel position ☐ . Minor move before handler returns ☐ . Minor whine or bark ☐ . Forced into position ☐ . Handler error ☐		30		

A total of 30 points is possible for each of the stay exercises in the AKC Novice class. Fido loses all 30 points if he gets up from the down, lies down on the sit, walks away, gets up to go to another dog, crawls to another dog, or repeatedly barks or whines.

Points can be deducted for one or two whines or barks, for minor movement, movement after the handler returns to the heel position or for handler errors. Substantial deductions will be made for the handler who must force the dog into either the sit or the down position before leaving the dog.

EXERCISE	NON QUALIFYING ZERO		QUALIFYING		Maximum Points	Points Lost	NET SCORE
			SUBSTANTIAL	MINOR			
LONG SIT (3 Minutes)	Did not remain in place _____ Goes to another dog _____	Stood or lay down before handler returns _____ ☐ Repeated whines ☐ or barks _____	☐ Forced into position ☐ Minor move before handler returns ☐ Minor whine or bark ☐ Handler error	Changes Position after handler returns to heel position _____ ☐ ☐	30		
LONG DOWN (5 Minutes)	Did not remain in place _____ Goes to another dog _____	Stood or sat before handler returns _____ ☐ Repeated whines ☐ or barks _____	☐ Forced into position ☐ Minor move before handler returns ☐ Minor whine or bark ☐ Handler error	Changes Position after handler returns to heel position _____ ☐ ☐	30		

The American Kennel Club Open class Group stay exercises

In the Open class, the stay exercises and the scoring are very similar. The differences are: the sit/stay is for three minutes, the down/stay is for five minutes, and when the handlers leave the dogs, they will leave the ring and go behind a partition or blind so that they are out of the dogs' line of vision.

The AKC Utility class does not have a group stay exercise, however there is a signal exercise in which the dog must respond to a stay signal. (See Chapter Twelve.)

In the UKC Novice, Open and Utility classes, each dog will do a down/stay while another dog is doing heelwork in the ring. This down/stay, called Honoring, is worth 35 points in Novice, 30 points in Open and 10 points in Utility. Deductions are very similar to the AKC Novice group exercises. Fido will fail if he breaks the stay, gets up, interferes with the working dog, or repeatedly barks or whines.

The UKC Novice class also has a one-minute sit/stay that is scored the same as the AKC Novice sit/stay and like the AKC exercise, is worth 30 points. The UKC Open class has another three-minute sit/stay with handlers out of sight, scored very much like the AKC sit/stay out of sight. Both the AKC and UKC three-minute sit/stays out of sight are worth 30 points.

Practical Application

The stay is obviously very important for all obedience competition dogs. It is equally important for home companion dogs, herding dogs, search and rescue dogs and workers in every other canine profession. The stay teaches Fido to hold still and to remain in the position in which he was left until released, no matter what the distractions.

The stays have innumerable uses at home. A down/stay by the foot of your chair keeps him in one spot while you visit with guests. A down/stay in the dining room doorway makes sure that Fido won't be begging under the table at mealtime. If Fido is doing a sit/stay while you're fixing his dinner, he can't knock his bowl out of your hand.

EXERCISE	NON-QUALIFYING		QUALIFYING (OVER 50%)		Max. Pts.	Pts. Lost	Net Score
	ZERO	LESS THAN 50%	Major (4 pts.)	Minor (½ - 2 pts.)			
HONORING	Return to Handler ....□ Interfered with working dog or Handler ....□ Dog leaves ring ....□	Did not remain in place ....□ Sat up ....□ Barked or whined repeatedly ....□	□................ Whined ....□ □...... Sits when Handler returns ....□ □..., Minor move when handler returns ....□ □.......... Forced into position ....□ □..............Leaves ring between exercises		35		

The United Kennel Club Companion Dog class Honoring exercise

EXERCISE	NON-QUALIFYING		QUALIFYING (OVER 50%)		Max. Pts.	Pts. Lost	Net Score
	ZERO	LESS THAN 50%	Major (4 pts.)	Minor (½ - 2 pts.)			
HONORING DOG #	Interferes with working dog or handler □ Dog leaves the ring ....□	Honoring dog barks, whines or moves from a down ......□	□ Sits as handler walks behind dog on return	Sits when handler is □ in heel position	10		

The United Kennel Club Utility class Honoring exercise

EXERCISE	NON-QUALIFYING		QUALIFYING (OVER 50%)		Max. Pts.	Pts. Lost	Net Score
	ZERO	LESS THAN 50%	Major (4 pts.)	Minor (½ - 2 pts.)			
HONORING DOG #	Returns to Handler ....□ Interferes with working dog or Handler ....□ Dog leaves ring ....□	Did not remain in place ....□ Sits up ....□ Barks or whines repeatedly ....□	□.................Forced into position.............□ □.....................................Whines ....□ □........ Sits when Handler returns ....□ □.... Minor move when handler returns ....□ □...Leaves ring between exercises		30		

The United Kennel Club Companion Dog Excellent class Honoring Dog exercise

EXERCISE	NON-QUALIFYING		QUALIFYING (OVER 50%)		Max. Pts.	Pts. Lost	Net Score
	ZERO	LESS THAN 50%	Major (4 pts.)	Minor (½ - 2 pts.)			
LONG SIT (Group Exercise) (1 minute)	Did not remain in place ....□ Disturbed other dog.................□ Dog leaves ring ....□	Repeatedly whined or barked ....□ Stood or lay down before handler returns to heel position ....□	Minor move before handler returns to heel position...□ □..Forcing into position □..Rough treatment □..Leaves ring between exercises	Minor move after handler returns to heel position...□ Minor whine or barks...□ Handler error...□	30		

The United Kennel Club Companion Dog class Long Sit exercise

EXERCISE	NON-QUALIFYING		QUALIFYING (OVER 50%)		Max. Pts.	Pts. Lost	Net Score
	ZERO	LESS THAN 50%	Major (4 pts.)	Minor (½ - 2 pts.)			
LONG SIT (Group Exercise) (3 minutes)	Did not remain in place ....□ Disturbed other dog ....□ Dog left ring ....□	Repeatedly whines or barks ....□ Stands or lies down before handler returns to heel position ....□	Minor move before handler returns to heel position...□ □..Forcing into position □...Rough treatment □..Leaves ring between exercises	Minor move after handler returns to heel position...□ Minor whine or bark...□ Handler error...□	30		

The United Kennel Club Companion Dog Excellent class, Long Sit exercise

Teaching the Exercise

Sit and Down Stay on Leash. Practice the stays with the leash on Fido so that you have some means of controlling him and preventing him from breaking the stays and getting away from you. To build a good dependable stay, make sure you follow the training steps carefully. This is not an exercise to take lightly. It's too important.

Keep in mind, that to Fido the stays are very boring. All he gets to do is sit or lie down in one spot. That can make all of his motivation disappear quickly. It's up to you to make sure that Fido is kept motivated. Follow the training steps carefully, and after each training sequence (See sidebar) release Fido so that he can play with his motivator, eat a treat and bounce around a little. Play with him, pet him and make a fuss over him. Make sure that his release is a minimum of one full minute. Then continue with his training.

To keep things upbeat and exciting for Fido, you can also do one training sequence of stays and then one training sequence of comes from Chapter Six. Mix in a few training sequences of foundation exercises from Chapter Four. Remember, it's your job to keep Fido motivated!

Step 1. Review the stay in Chapter Four, "Building a Sound Foundation." Make sure that Fido has completed Steps 1 through 8

Down/stay, Step 1. Cameron holds the end of the six-foot leash while Desi does a down/stay. (Australian Shepherd)

Stays with Distractions. A group of dogs learns to hold the sit/stay on leash while close to each other.

Stays with Distractions. Jupiter, Gracie, Desi and Cassie are doing a down/stay off leash in preparation for Novice competition.

from Chapter Four, and can do a one-minute sit/stay and down/stay with you 10 steps (about 20 feet) away. Do not go on to the next step until Fido can do both reliably. If he's having problems, go back to the steps that he can do and do well, and work back through the foundation exercises, following the training sequence and schedule.

Step 2. Hook Fido up to your 30- to 50-foot long line. A length of clothesline rope is fine. Stretch the line out so that it is flat on the ground away from Fido. With Fido in a sit, tell him, "Stay," and walk away from him, with hands free and line on the ground. GO ABOUT 15 STEPS AWAY, about five steps further than Step 1. Move your hands so that there is no doubt that Fido knows you are not holding the leash. If he moves, step on the long line, snap it, tell him, "ACCKK!" and put him back where he was. After about 40 seconds, go back to him and praise him. Follow the training sequence and training schedule.

Step 3. Repeat as in Step 2, staying at 15 steps, except INCREASE THE SIT/STAY TO ONE FULL MINUTE. Follow the training sequence and training schedule.

Step 4. Repeat as in Step 3, keeping the time one minute but IN-CREASE THE DISTANCE TO 20 STEPS OR ABOUT 40 FEET. Follow the training sequence and schedule.

Step 5. Repeat Steps 2 through 4 practicing the down/stay, except GRADUALLY INCREASE YOUR TIME TO A MINUTE AND A HALF. Follow the training sequence and schedule.

Step 6. Repeat Step 5, practicing the down/stay, INCREASING THE TIME TO TWO FULL MINUTES. Follow the training sequence and schedule.

Step 7. Repeat Step 6, INCREASING THE TIME TO THREE FULL MINUTES. If Fido is having a problem, break it into several smaller steps: two minutes, two and a quarter minutes, two and a half minutes and two minutes 45 seconds. Follow the training sequence and schedule.

NOTE: If Fido is breaking the stays, go back and review the foundation steps. Go through the steps methodically. Where does Fido start making mistakes? Is it distance? Or time? Is there a particular problem with the sit? Or the down? If you need to break these steps into even smaller steps, do so. You want Fido to be able to succeed, not fail. Set him up for success.

Training Sequence (TS)

One repetition of a training step, followed by praise.
Second repetition of the same step, followed by praise.
Third repetition of the same training step, followed by praise, a release ("Fido, Release! Good boy!") and a reward (His motivator, a toy or a treat).

Training Schedule

1. Do each step a minimum of three training sequences.
2. If the third TS has no mistakes and Fido is doing that step correctly, go on to the next step.
3. If Fido is having problems, go back one step and repeat the TS at that step.
4. If Fido is still confused, go back several steps to a place where Fido is confident, then work back up.

Stays with Distractions. Distractions are a part of life. The world will not stop, be quiet and stay still because Fido needs to concentrate on a sit/stay. So Fido needs to learn to concentrate when there are things happening around him. He needs to see traffic and hear motorcycles and trucks. He needs to hold a stay while a child throws a tennis ball or a Frisbee. He must learn that although his motivator might be food, food is not an excuse to break a stay.

With Fido on a long line, use the following steps to teach Fido to hold the stays around distractions.

Step 1. Sit/stay for 30 seconds at three steps away.

Step 2. Down/stay for 45 SECONDS at three steps away.

Step 3. Sit/stay for 30 seconds at FIVE STEPS AWAY.

Step 4. Down/stay for ONE FULL MINUTE at five steps away.

Left: Stays with Distractions. Ursa is concentrating on her stays even though there is a ring rope behind her and toys, balls and treats on the ground in front of her. Right: Out-of-sight Stays, Step 1. The long line allows you to increase your distance from the dogs on the stays. (Australian Shepherd)

NOTE: Follow the training sequence and schedule with each step even if Fido had worked far beyond this in the previous steps. Once we add distractions, it becomes a whole new ball game. It's just like it was a new exercise altogether.

While doing these stays, add ONE DISTRACTION AT A TIME. Dogs react differently to distractions, so find out what bothers (or interests) Fido the most. Some ideas: balls, Frisbees, bicycles, skateboards, kids, cats, birds, food, picnic baskets, lawn chairs upside down, umbrellas, other leashes, car keys, kites, other dogs, other dogs chasing balls and so on. You get the idea.

The hardest distraction for Care Bear, an Australian Shepherd, is food. A hot dog in a passing child's hand is torment. To Kody, a Newfoundland, a tennis ball is the ultimate distraction and yet Kato, a Bearded Collie, can ignore a tennis ball but goes crazy over a Frisbee. Wilma, a Weimeraner, can ignore just about everything but a bird flying overhead or worse yet, landing on the grass in front of her. Practice with a variety of distractions so that Fido learns that stay means exactly that.

You will need to practice in other places, too. Some good places include: schoolyards, parks, beaches, areas with high foot traffic, outside an ice cream store and outside a pizza delivery store. My husband and I used to train our German Shepherds outside a local ice cream store and then after our training sessions, we would reward the dogs and ourselves with a scoop of ice cream. Even though the distractions there were very difficult, the dogs learned that good behavior resulted in a jackpot reward, something very special. So we used that to help our training.

Out of Sight Stays. If Fido has been able to complete successfully all of the above training steps on the sit and the down stays, then you may start working on the out of sight stays. If he is having any difficulty at all, do not go on.

Step 1. Situate Fido so that you have a building corner or doorway to step around or into that is no more than 30 feet from Fido. Attach a long line to Fido and the other end to a fence or concrete block as an anchor. Have Fido's leash on him as well. With Fido in a sit or a down, tell him, "Stay," drop your end of the leash to the ground and walk away. Go around your corner, or in the doorway, count to five and return to Fido. Praise him. Follow the training sequence and schedule.

If he moves, the long line will prevent him from coming to find you, however you still need to let him know that you are unhappy with him breaking the stay. Use a verbal correction and replace him in the position and spot where you left him.

Step 2. Repeat as in Step 1, except COUNT TO 10 while out of sight. Alternate between sit and down/stay. Follow the training sequence and schedule.

Step 3. Repeat as in Step 2, except COUNT TO 20 while out of sight. Follow the training sequence and schedule.

NOTE: Out of sight stays can cause anxiety in many dogs. If Fido appears to be worried about you going out of sight, keep the time increments very short. Teach Fido that you are ALWAYS coming back. Increase the time very gradually.

Step 4. With Fido on the anchored long line and leash, have him sit or down by your left side. Unhook his leash and toss it to the ground in front of him. If he moves from the sit or down right away (as many dogs will!), step on the long line, correct him and reposition him. When he is sitting quietly by your side, tell him, "Stay," and step away. Go to your out-of-sight location, count to five and return to Fido. Praise him. Hook his leash back on his collar. Alternate between sit and down/stay. Follow the training sequence and schedule.

Step 5. Repeat Step 4 above, except INCREASE THE TIME TO A 10 COUNT. Follow the training sequence and schedule.

Step 6. Repeat Step 5 above, except INCREASE THE TIME TO A 20 COUNT. Remember to practice both the sit and the down/stays. Follow the training sequence and schedule.

Step 7. Remove Fido's long line but keep it close. With Fido sitting by your left side, unhook his leash and toss it to the ground in front of Fido. Tell him, "Stay," and step away from him. Walk 20 steps away and turn and face him. Count to 20 slowly (One Mississippi, two...) and return to Fido. Praise him. Do both sit and down stays. Follow the training sequence and schedule.

Step 8. Follow Step 7 above except INCREASE THE TIME TO A FULL MINUTE. Practice both the sit and down stays. Follow the training sequence and schedule.

NOTE: Remember to stop your training sessions on a high note. Not a made-up high note but a real one. Do something that Fido can do very well and give him a jackpot of praise! Good verbal praise, petting, his motivator and a chance to bounce around a little are perfect.

Step 9. Follow Step 8 above, remaining 20 steps away, in sight, IN-CREASING THE TIME TO TWO MINUTES on both the sit/stay and the down/stay. Practice each in its own training sequence.

Step 10. Follow Step 9, except INCREASE THE TIME TO THREE MINUTES on both the sit/stay and the down/stay.

Step 11. INCREASE THE DOWN/STAY ONLY TO FOUR MINUTES. Remain in sight, 20 steps away. RELEASE FIDO BETWEEN EACH REPETITION. Four minutes is a long time so make sure Fido gets a chance to bounce around between repetitions within the training sequence.

Step 12. INCREASE THE DOWN/STAY ONLY TO FIVE MINUTES. Again, release Fido between each repetition within the training sequence.

Step 13. With Fido in a sit or a down by your left side, unhook his leash and drop it to the ground BEHIND HIM. Tell him stay and walk away from him. Go out of sight. After TWO FULL MINUTES, go back to him and praise him. Follow the training sequence and schedule.

Step 14. Repeat Step 13 except INCREASE THE TIME OUT OF SIGHT TO THREE FULL MINUTES. Follow the training sequence and schedule, releasing Fido between each repetition in the sequence.

Step 15. With Fido in a DOWN ONLY, command Fido "Stay" and go out of sight for a FULL FIVE MINUTES. Release Fido between repetitions. Follow the training sequence and schedule.

Are You Having Problems?

Does Fido lay down on the sit/stay? Bring him back up to a sit each time he lays down and as you do, give him a verbal correction. Keep the sit/stays short for a while until he can do it without laying down. Then gradually extend the time.

Does Fido fight you going down? Or does he act like you're going to kill him, rolling over to bare his belly? Many dogs dislike the down/stay for a variety of reasons. Very dominant dogs consider the down a submissive position and dislike you or other dogs being near while they are doing a down. Submissive dogs may bare the belly, asking not to be hurt or corrected. Small dogs often feel very vulnerable in a down. Understanding why Fido might not like the down can help your training and your responses to Fido's actions, but Fido also needs to understand that if you tell him to lay down, he must do it. Keep the training consistent, don't make him go down in one situation and then back off in another.

Teach Fido not to crawl, or thrash around or sniff in the down/stay by using a verbal correction and a collar snap, or a squirt bottle

132

correction. Crawling and sniffing often cause a dog to forget what he's supposed to be doing. Let him know by your reactions that stay means exactly that, in one spot with only minor movement allowed.

If Fido is having problems holding the stay, repeat the training steps, keeping the time and distance both short. Don't move on until the problem has disappeared and then increase the time and distance very slowly. Break up your stay training sessions with other exercises so that you and Fido both don't get bored silly.

Use the long line as much and as long as you need it. Don't be in a hurry to take it off.

A good, reliable stay is one of your most useful commands. Ursa holds a stay with a ring gate behind her. (Australian Shepherd)

Practical Application. Anyone who has been pulled down the street by a dog and then has wlaked with a dog who understands the heel command, knows the benefits of "Fido, Heel!" (Great Dane)

Chapter Nine
The Heel Exercises

We can secure other people's approval if we do right and try hard; but our own approval is worth a hundred times more.

Mark Twain

The Exercise

A definition of the heel position is easy—teaching it is a little harder. Fido is to walk by your left side with his neck even with the side of your leg, about a hand's width away from your leg and is to maintain that position no matter what you do. If you speed up, slow down, make a right turn, left turn or about turn, he is to be in that same position. In both the AKC and UKC Heel exercises, Fido will have to demonstrate that he can do exactly that. Teamwork is the goal of this exercise.

The AKC Novice Heel on Leash and Figure Eight will be performed as follows:

> 1. The steward asks Jane and Fido to follow him into the ring. Before coming into the ring, Jane will make sure that Fido is in a sit in the heel position and is paying attention to her. Jane will also make sure that the leash is gathered up in her left hand and that the leash snap is hanging loose from Fido's collar (leash not tight). She will then tell her dog "Fido, Heel" as she follows the steward into the ring.

> 2. The judge walks up to Jane and says, "This is the Heel on Leash exercise. Are you ready?" Jane looks at Fido, who is sitting straight by her side, watching her. She smiles at Fido and answers the judge, "Yes. We're ready."

> 3. The judge says, "Forward." Jane says, "Fido, Heel!" and begins walking forward in a brisk pace. Her right arm is by her side, moving naturally and her left hand, holding the gathered-up leash, is at her waist. During the heelwork, she can give no corrections or cues to Fido but must rely on his previous training.

> 4. During the exercise, the judge will give various commands, including "Slow," "Fast," "About turn,"

"Left turn" and "Right turn." Jane should follow each command within two steps of hearing it. She cannot give Fido any additional commands for these actions. He must demonstrate his willingness to follow her lead. The only exception is that after a command to halt, Jane can give Fido another command to "Heel."

5. After the completion of the heel routine (which can vary in pattern, length and difficulty from judge to judge), the judge tells Jane, "Exercise finished." Jane praises Fido but makes sure that the praise is not so stimulating that he loses control.

6. Two stewards now come into the ring to stand as two posts for the Figure Eight exercise. Jane positions herself and Fido about two feet in front of the two stewards, centered, facing the judge. The judge asks, "Are you ready?" At Jane's yes, after checking Fido, the judge says, "Forward." Jane may start in either direction but opts to start to her left. "Fido, Heel."

7. Fido must yield to Jane and slow down on the inside circles of the Figure Eight and speed up on the outside portions. Jane can give no additional commands for Fido's change of pace. During the exercise, the judge says, "Halt" and Jane comes to a stop. The judge then says, "Forward," and Jane can give Fido a command to heel.

8. After the final halt, the judge says, "Exercise finished," and Jane praises Fido.

Scoring

Teamwork is the key to heelwork. The judges want to see Fido paying attention to Jane and expressing a willingness and desire to follow her lead.

The American Kennel Club Novice class Heel on Leash exercise

EXERCISE	NON QUALIFYING ZERO	QUALIFYING SUBSTANTIAL	MINOR		Maximum Points	Points Lost	NET SCORE
			Heeling	Fig. 8			
		□ ..No change of pace □ Fast □ Slow		□			
		□ ..Improper heel position............□		□			
HEEL	Unmanageable............□	□ ..Occasional tight leash..........□		□			
ON LEASH	Unqualified Heeling........□	□ ..Forging . . □ Crowding handler.......□		□	40		
AND	Handler continually	□ ..Logging . . . □ . . □ Sniffing............□		□			
FIGURE 8	adapts pace to dog ......□	□ ..Extra command to heel		□			
	Constant tugging on	□ ..Heeling wide □ Turns □ Abouts □		□			
	leash or guiding............□	□ ..No sits . . . . . □ Poor sits					
		□ ..Brisk pace.................................□		□			
		□ ..Handler error.............................□		□			

EXERCISE	NON-QUALIFYING		QUALIFYING (OVER 50%)		Max. Pts.	Pts. Lost	Net Score
	ZERO	LESS THAN 50%	Major (4 pts.)	Minor (½ - 2 pts.)			
HEEL ON LEASH & Figure 8 (On leash) (Release Honor Dog)	Unqualified Heeling ....☐ Uncontrollable ....☐ Dog leaves ring ....☐	Constant guiding or tight leash ....☐ Handler continually adapts pace to dog.................☐ Constant jerking on leash ....☐	☐..Extra command or signals ☐..Improper heel position ☐..Lagging ☐..Forging ☐..Crowding handler ☐..Sniffing ☐..No change of pace ☐ fast ☐ slow ☐..Occasional tight leash ☐..Heeling wide ☐..About Turn ☐..Lacks natural smoothness ☐..No Sit...☐ Poor sits ☐..Leaves ring between exercises	Fig. 8 ☐ ☐ ☐ ☐ ☐ ☐ ☐ ☐ ☐ ☐ ☐ ☐ ☐ ☐ ☐ ☐	35		

The United Kennel Club Companion Dog class Heel on Leash exercise

Jane will lose points or fail, depending upon the severity, by holding the leash too tight, jerking or correcting with the leash, giving additional commands or cues and by adapting her pace to Fido.

Fido will fail if he is unmanageable, leaves the ring or ignores Jane. He can lose points for following Jane but walking out of position, for failing to sit at each halt or for sitting crooked.

EXERCISE	NON QUALIFYING ZERO	QUALIFYING		Maximum Points	Points Lost	NET SCORE
		SUBSTANTIAL	MINOR			
HEEL FREE	Unmanageable...............☐ Unqualified heeling ....☐ Handler continually adapts pace to dog ......☐ Leaving handler...............☐	☐..No change of pace ☐ Fast ☐ Slow..........☐ ☐..Improper hand position.........☐ ☐..Forging .. ☐ Crowding handler................☐ ☐..Lagging .. ☐ Sniffing................☐ ☐..Extra command to heel................☐ ☐..Heeling wide ☐ Turns ☐ Abouts ☐ ☐..No sits ..... Poor sits...............☐ ☐..Brisk pace ....☐ ☐..Handler error................☐		40		

The American Kennel Club Novice class Heel Free exercise

EXERCISE	NON-QUALIFYING		QUALIFYING (OVER 50%)		Max. Pts.	Pts. Lost	Net Score
	ZERO	LESS THAN 50%	Major (4 pts.)	Minor (½ - 2 pts.)			
HEEL OFF LEASH	Unqualified Heeling ....☐ Uncontrollable ....☐ Dog leaves ring ....☐	Dog leaves handler..............☐ Handler continually adapts pace to dog.................☐	☐..Extra command or signal ....☐ ☐..Improper heel position ....☐ ☐..Forging................................☐ ☐..Lagging ....☐ ☐..Crowding handler.....................☐ ☐..Heeling wide ....☐ ☐..No change of pace .... ☐ fast ☐ slow ☐..Lack of natural smoothness............☐ ☐..Poor sits...☐..No Sit ☐..Leaves ring between exercises ....☐		35		

The United Kennel Club Companion Dog class Heel Off Leash exercise

The Novice Heel Off Leash exercises are judged and scored the same as the heel on leash, except that Fido is working without a leash and there is no figure eight exercise. Normally, the heel pattern is the same for heel off leash as it is for heel on leash, so there won't be any surprises.

Jane will walk in the same position as she did on leash, with left hand at her waist. Fido's working position is exactly the same, too, in a correct heel position.

EXERCISE	NON QUALIFYING ZERO		QUALIFYING SUBSTANTIAL MINOR		Maxiumum Points	Points Lost	NET SCORE
				Heeling	Fig. 8			
HEEL FREE AND FIGURE 8			□ ..Improper hand position................................□	□	40		
			□ Forging . . .□ Crowding handler...............□	□			
			□ Lagging . . . . . . □ Sniffing	□			
			□ .Extra command to heel..............................□	□			
	Unmanageable..................□ Handler continually		□ ..Heeling wide □ Turns □ Abouts □				
	Unqualified Heeling..........□ adapts pace to dog......□	□	□ No change of pace □ fast □ slow				
			□ :..No sits . . . . . . Poor sits...........................□	□			
			□ .Lacks naturalness smoothness....................□	□			
			□ Heel at brisk pace......................................□	□			
			□ Handler error...□	□			

The American Kennel Club Open class Heel Free exercise

EXERCISE	NON-QUALIFYING ZERO	LESS THAN 50%	QUALIFYING (OVER 50%) Major (4 pts.)	Minor (½ - 2 pts.)	Max. Pts.	Pts. Lost	Net Score
(Place Steward To Walk)				Fig. 8			
		Handler continually adapts pace to	□ . .Extra commands or signals	□ □			
	Unqualified	dog......................□	□ . .Improper heel position	□ □			
HEEL OFF LEASH	Heeling . . . . □		□ . .Lagging	□ □			
&			□ . .Forging	□ □			
Figure 8	Uncontrollable . . . . □	Leaves or breaks heel	□ . .Crowding handler	□ □	40		
		at stewards	□ . .Sniffing	□ □			
	Dog leaves ring . . . . □	approach . . . . □	□ . .No change of pace □fast □slow	□ □			
			□ . .Heeling wide	□ □			
			□ . .About Turn				
			□ . .Lacks natural smoothness	□ □			
			□ . .No Sit. . . .□ Poor Sits	□ □			
(Release Honor Dog)			□ . .Leaves ring between exercises				

The United Kennel Club Companion Dog Excellent class Heel Off Leash exercise

In the Open class for both the AKC and UKC, the heel free (or off leash) also includes a figure eight. The judging, commands and scoring are the same as for the Novice heel work.

Practical Application
Anyone who has owned a dog that pulls as an Iditarod sled dog knows the benefits of teaching a dog to heel. When Fido is paying attention to you, walking with you, changing pace, stopping and turning with you, taking Fido for a walk becomes a joy instead of a battle. Sore arms and shoulders and skinned knees become a thing of the past.

Teaching the Exercise
Watch Me. Go back to Chapter Two, section "Steps for Success" number 3 and Chapter Four, section "Teaching the Walk on

Lead," and review the Watch Me command. Practice the training steps 1 through 4 from Chapter Four, following the training sequence and schedule.

Give Fido as much enthusiasm as you want him to give you!

When Fido is watching you and paying attention to everything you do, he won't get into trouble. It's physically impossible for Fido to drag you down the street and do an attentive Watch Me at the same time. A good attentive Watch Me! eliminates the need for innumerable leash corrections for trouble that Fido got into when he wasn't paying attention.

Straight Sits. All the heelwork score sheets have a place for points lost due to poor sits. If every crooked sit is worth one point, that can add up very quickly.

A Straight Sit is defined as Fido being in proper heel position, with his backbone parallel to you as if there were a line drawn through you and Fido, front to back. If you have a hard time visualizing that, LIGHTLY (so that it won't pull out hairs) tape a string down Fido's backbone from his neck to his tail. Stand with your feet straight front to back (it will seem uncomfortable). Now look at your feet and look at Fido's backbone. Are they parallel?

You can use props to help position Fido if he's having a hard time finding the position. Have Fido sit between you and a wall, praising him when he sits straight. Make every sit a straight one to help build reliability and to make it a habit.

Don't try to rush things by positioning Fido with your hands. He will learn it better by doing it himself. You have to help him so that he CAN do it himself.

Leash Awareness. Go back to Chapter Four to reread the section on leash awareness and practice training steps 1 through 3, following the training sequence and schedule, EVEN IF YOU HAVE DONE THIS EARLIER. A good refresher never hurts.

Beginning the Heel. Again, review Chapter Four "Beginning the Heel" and practice the training steps 1 through 3, following the training sequence and schedule.

Heel Position. When you are standing still, Fido should be sitting by your left side, his neck by your left leg. Obviously the position of a St. Bernard is going to be different from that of a Papillon but the same directions apply. Fido should be one hand's width from your leg so that he isn't interfering with your walking. When he's walking forward, he should maintain the position he was

Wilma heels nicely by Jane's side. She is paying attention to Jane and maintaining a nice heel position. (Weimaraner)

in when he was sitting. He should not be walking sideways down the street but rather his body should be parallel with yours, front to back.

In the heel position, you can turn the upper part of your body SLIGHTLY to look at Fido, but as soon as you do look forward again. If you constantly look back, the power of your face, your eyes and your posture will cause Fido to lag, to hang back. Your left hand should hold the leash at your waist. The left hand, during training, can also hold the motivator.

NOTE: The motivator is for training only and is not allowed in the ring for competition.

Quick Right and About Turns. Turns cause problems for many dogs—dogs may tend to lag on the outside of a right or about turn and the outside of a figure eight. Fido needs to learn how to compensate and to increase or decrease his pace to match yours.

Step 1. With Fido on leash, sitting by your left side, put motivator in your left hand. Gather up the excess leash (also in your left hand) so that it is taut but not tight. Tell Fido, "Fido, Watch me. Heel" and step

140

Watch Me in the Heel Position. Topo pays close attention to Ken, who is using a treat to motivate Topo's "Watch me." (Toy Poodle)

Quick Right Turns and About Turns.Left: Sparky starts to turn with Rachel as soon as her left foot moves toward the right. Right: Sparky has almost completed his about turn before Rachel has. Look as the arch of his body around hers. Very nice! (Dalmation)

forward briskly. After a couple of steps, turn to the right and at the same time, put Fido's motivator in front of his nose and tell him, in a high-pitched tone of voice, "Watch me. Quick, quick, quick!" Praise him when he catches up to you, stop and sit him, then praise him again. Follow the training sequence and schedule.

NOTE: Your footwork can either help Fido corner quickly or make it more difficult for him. When you make an about turn or a right turn, take several small steps around the corner rather than a single large step with a pivot. If you pivot step, Fido will have to jump your extended leg or rush to catch up.

Step 2. Repeat Step 1 above, except offer the motivator as Fido is COMING OUT OF THE TURN, about half way through. Follow the training sequence and schedule.

Step 3. Repeat as in Step 2 above except that if Fido lags behind, snap his leash quickly an instant before offering his motivator. Follow the training sequence and schedule.

NOTE: Don't go overboard with snapping Fido's leash. Many dogs, expecting a correction on the turns, will start to lag going into each turn.

Training Sequence (TS)

One repetition of a training step, followed by praise.
Second repetition of the same step, followed by praise.
Third repetition of the same step, followed by praise, a release ("Fido, Release! Good boy!") and a reward (His motivator, a toy or a treat).

Training Schedule

Do each step a minimum of three training sequences (TS).
1. If the third TS has no mistakes and Fido is doing the step correctly, go on to the next step.
2. If Fido is having problems, go back one step and repeat the TS at that step.
3. If Fido is still confused, go back several steps to a place where Fido is confident and then work back up.

Slow Left Turns. Fido needs to learn to slow down on the inside of left turns and the inside of a figure eight.

Step 1. With Fido in a sit in the heel position and the leash gathered up in the left hand held at the waist, tell Fido, "Fido, Watch me. Heel" and step off briskly. After a few steps, turn into Fido, making a left turn. If he backs off a little as you turn, praise him. Stop, sit him and praise him. Follow the training sequence and schedule.

Step 2. Repeat as in Step 1 above, except that if Fido doesn't back off on his own as you make the left turn, SNAP THE LEASH QUICKLY BACK TOWARD HIS TAIL WITH YOUR LEFT HAND. Continue as above. Follow the training sequence and schedule.

Changes of Pace. The slow and fast are really quite easy. When you are training the heel, practice walking at different speeds. Slow, extra slow, normal, brisk and jog. Don't give Fido any additional commands, simply change your pace.

When you do speed up or slow down, do it gradually. Take about two steps to change into the new pace so that Fido can see you changing and has a chance to do it with you.

Figure Eight. Set up two trash cans, or two kitchen chairs about eight feet apart. Stand with Fido about two feet in front of the chairs, centered.

Step 1. Tell Fido, "Fido, Watch me. Heel. Good boy," and step toward the chair on your left so that the first turn has Fido on the inside. Use your back snap to encourage Fido to slow down. As you come toward the center, encourage Fido to speed up. As you curve around the other chair, Fido will be on the outside and will need to speed up. Use his motivator in front of his nose and LIGHT snaps to help him catch up. After one time around, stop and sit Fido and praise him. Follow the training sequence and schedule.

Spicing up the Heel. Heel work looks awful if Fido is moving with you but has his ears plastered back and his tail tucked between his legs. The judges are looking for obvious willingness and a desire

Figure Eight. Left: Pam uses Gracie's motivator to speed her up on the outside of the figure eight. Right: Gracie shows excellent form on the inside of the figure eight. She is slowing down and giving way to Pam and is curving her body around the post; (Basset Hound)

144

Spicing up the Heel, Step 1. Rachel uses Sparky's motivator to speed him up when he lags. Look at the happy tail and the prancing front feet— Sparky's happy! (Dalmation)

to please. You will feel a lot better if Fido is happy about what he's doing.

Step 1. Use Fido's motivator to make the heelwork happier. If his motivator isn't doing the job, find something that will: a new squeaky toy, a foxtail (a ball with a tail on it), a new tennis ball, a bit of hot dog. With Fido sitting by your left side, gather up the leash so that the leash is taut but not tight and hold it in your left hand. With the motivator in your left hand, also, do a watch me with Fido and begin heeling. Use your voice to praise him and when he loses interest, looks away or falters, lightly snap the lead and put his motivator in front of his nose for a second and then take it back to your waist. Stop after about 20 feet, sit Fido, praise him and reward him with his motivator for a few seconds. Then follow the training sequence and schedule.

Step 2. Repeat as above, except ADD SOME TURNS TO THE HEEL WORK. Follow the training schedule.

Step 3. Repeat as above, except SHOW FIDO HIS MOTIVATOR AS YOU GIVE HIM THE WATCH ME AND HEEL COMMANDS, but do not give it to him or show it to him again until he sits and is praised.

NOTE: This is an important step. Don't hurry. If Fido is losing interest or starts to sniff or look around, go back to Step 2. Remember, it's YOUR job to keep Fido motivated.

Heel Off Leash. There are several different methods to get Fido heeling dependably off leash. The key to all of them is don't rush it. If you take the leash off too soon and Fido learns that he can get away from you and that you can't catch him, you've got troubles. Go through all the steps and make sure that Fido is good at each step before moving on to the next one.

Step 1. Hook Fido up to two leashes. Take one leash and invert it through the hand loop, making a large circle out of the leash. Step through it and draw it up around your waist. Pull it tight so that it doesn't fall down and trip you. You should now have a leash circled around your waist and hooked to Fido's collar. This is your umbilical cord. It connects Fido to you throughout the off-lead training so that Fido learns that you will continue to have control, even when you take off his leash.

Hold on to the other leash as you do normally for heeling. Do some heelwork practice. Then sit Fido and after you praise him, take the leash and put it up over your shoulders. Keep your left hand at your waist. You have two leashes on Fido but your hands are not holding either of them.

Use your voice to control Fido. If he makes a mistake or does something very good, talk to him. If you need to use the leash, correct him with the one over your shoulder (not the umbilical) and then drop the leash again. Follow your training sequence and schedule.

Step 2. Follow the same exercise as above, except that after doing some heelwork, REACH DOWN AND UNHOOK THE TRAINING LEASH THAT IS HANGING OVER YOUR SHOULDERS. Let it hang freely and continue to work Fido. The umbilical will prevent Fido from taking off if he chooses to, but do NOT use the umbilical for corrections. Go back and forth, hooking and unhooking the leash a minimum of six times during this training step. Follow the training sequence and schedule.

Step 3. Follow the same exercise as above, except when YOU UN-HOOK THE LEASH, DROP IT TO THE GROUND IN FRONT OF FIDO. Then continue with your heelwork. Again, go back and forth, hooking and unhooking the lead a minimum of six times during this training step, each time you unhook it, toss it to the ground. Follow the training sequence and schedule.

Step 4. Unhook the umbilical from Fido's collar but keep the training leash attached as you start the heelwork. After Fido is watching you and paying attention, toss the leash over your shoulder, as you did in Step 1. Follow the training sequence and schedule.

Step 5. Follow Step 4 above, except that as you do your heelwork, reach down and unhook the leash from Fido's collar. Use the watch me and your voice to make sure that Fido is paying attention to you. Stop and praise him and re-attach the leash. Go back and forth, rapidly, a minimum of six times during one training step. Follow your training sequence and schedule.

Step 6. Follow Step 5 above, except that as you unhook the leash, toss it to the ground in front of Fido. Continue with your heelwork training. Go back and forth between leash and no leash a minimum of six times this training step. Follow the training sequence and schedule.

NOTE: Do not be in a hurry to go completely off leash for your heelwork training. Make sure Fido is able to heel without a leash but do most of your training on leash.

Are You Having Problems?

Be aware of your feet. If you stumble and stagger as you walk, Fido will heel wide so that he doesn't get stepped on or kicked. If you can't walk a straight line, Fido will look bad simply because he's following you. On a fast change of pace, don't stomp when you run or you'll scare Fido away, especially if Fido is a small or toy breed dog. On your right or about turns, don't pivot and stick out your feet or you will cause Fido to lag behind or force him to jump over your leg or foot, both of which will look clumsy and will cost you points.

If Fido is not responding the way you would like, consider changing motivators or training collars. Both are simply training tools and a variety are available for your use.

Don't forget to practice ON LEASH around a variety of distractions and in different places. Take Fido to the local street fair or farmer's market. Take him to the lumber yard. Let him look around at first and satisfy some of his curiosity. (Make him behave, too, though!) Then teach him to pay attention and heel properly in all these different situations.

Straight Sit in the Heel Position. Wilma is in beautiful position and looks ready for anything Jane would want her to do. (Weimaraner)

Chapter Ten
The Stand Exercises

Personally, I'm always ready to learn although I do not always like to be
taught.
Winston Churchill

The Exercise

The Novice Stand for Exam exercise demonstrates that Fido will stand and not resist any positioning that might be needed to stand him comfortably. Fido is also required to remain in the standing position when left and must allow the judge to touch him, displaying no shyness or resentment, and should remain in the standing position until you return to him and release him at the completion of the exercise.

In the ring, the exercise will be performed like this:

1. After the completion of the Heel on Lead and Figure Eight, the judge will ask for Fido's leash. After Jack removes the leash and hands it to the judge or the steward, the judge will tell him, "This is the Stand for Exam. Stand your dog and leave when ready."

2. Jack turns to Fido and says, "Fido, stand." He can use both a hand signal and a verbal command but should not repeat the commands. Jack looks at Fido's legs and slightly moves one foot to make sure that Fido is standing square and comfortable. After deciding that Fido is stable and steady, Jack stands up, back in the heel position, both hands at his sides, not touching Fido.

3. Leaning over slightly, Jack gives Fido the stay hand signal as he says, "Fido, stay," and he then steps away. Walking six feet away and no further, he turns and faces Fido, hands hanging naturally by his sides.

4. The judge then steps in to the dog and touches Fido's head, shoulders and hips—putting slight pressure at each point. Walking around the dog, the judge then steps away. Watching to make sure the dog doesn't move, he then tells Jack, "Back to your dog."

5. Jack walks around Fido, back to the heel position and stops.

6. The judge checks Jack's positioning and then says, "Exercise finished."

Scoring

EXERCISE	NON QUALIFYING ZERO	QUALIFYING SUBSTANTIAL MINOR	Maximum Points	Points Lost	NET SCORE
STAND FOR EXAMINATION	Sits or lies down before or during examination..☐ Growl or snaps ....☐ Moves away before or during examination..☐ Shows shyness or resentment.............☐	☐ ..Moving Slightly Before or During ☐ ..Moves Feet............................☐ ☐ ..Moving after examination................☐ ☐ ..Sits after exam.......................☐ ☐ ..Heel Position........................☐ ☐ ..Extra Signal or Command................☐ ☐ ..Handler error.......................☐	30		

The American Kennel Club Novice class Stand for Examination exercise

EXERCISE	NON-QUALIFYING ZERO LESS THAN 50%	QUALIFYING (OVER 50%) Major (4 pts.) Minor (½ - 2 pts.)	Max. Pts.	Pts. Lost	Net Score
STANDING FOR EXAMINATION (Off Leash)	Growls or snaps ......☐ Sits before or during examination ....☐ Dog leaves ring ......☐	Moves away before or during exam...........☐ Shows shyness or resentment...........☐ Extra command after leaving ....☐	☐ ..Resistance to handler posing ....☐ ☐ ..Moving feet........................☐ ☐ ..Moves after examination completed......☐ ☐ ..Sits as handler returns................☐ ☐ ..Handler error ....☐ ☐ ..Lack of natural smoothness ....☐ ☐ ..Leaves ring during exercises...........☐	30		

The United Kennel Club Companion Dog class Standing for Examination exercise

A flawless AKC or UKC Novice Stand for Exam is worth 30 points. Fido can lose points for shuffling his feet or moving slightly when you return to the heel position. You can lose points by having a hand on Fido when you tell him "stay" or by not returning to the proper heel position when sent back to Fido. You can also lose many points by backing away from Fido when you leave him after giving the stay command.

Fido will fail if he shows any shyness or resentment during the exercise or if he growls or threatens the judge. He will also fail if he sits, lies down or moves away during the exercise.

In the Utility Moving Stand and Examination, you will tell Fido to stand while you are heeling and without stopping or hesitating, you will continue walking away from Fido for 10 to 12 feet. The judge will then examine Fido, quite thoroughly, and when he is finished with his exam, he will tell you to "Call your dog to heel." Fido should, on your command, return to the heel position without sitting in front of you.

EXERCISE	NON QUALIFYING ZERO		QUALIFYING SUBSTANTIAL MINOR	Maxiumum Points	Points Lost	NET SCORE
MOVING STAND AND EXAMIN-ATION	☐ Sat out of reach ☐ Displays Fear or Resentment ☐ Sitting ☐ Lying down ☐ Growling or snapping ☐ Repeated whining or barking	Failure to: Heel ☐ Stand and stay ☐ Accept examination ☐ Return to handler ☐	☐ . Forging . . ☐ Lagging ☐ Wide ☐ . .Moves Slightly on stand............☐ ☐ . .Handler Hesitates or Pauses............☐ ☐ . .Fails to return briskly ....☐ ☐ . .Poor sit ....☐ ☐ . .Return to Heel position............☐ ☐ . .Slow response ....☐ ☐ . .Handler error............☐ ☐ . .Poor finish ....☐	30		

The American Kennel Club Utility class Moving Stand and Examination exercise

This exercise is worth 30 points. Fido can start losing points in the very beginning for improper heel position during the initial heelwork prior to the stand command or signal. All appropriate penalties from the Novice Heel Free, Stand for Exam and Recall exercises shall apply in the same circumstances. Fido can also lose points for moving slightly on the stand, returning slowly when moving toward the heel position or for sitting crooked, and you can lose points by hesitating while giving the stand command or signal.

Fido will fail if he moves from the stand, as with the Novice Stand for Exam, if he shows any resistance to being examined, or if he fails to heel, stand and stay, or return to you on command.

Practical Application

The stand for exam is not as important as the come or stay commands but it still has some very practical uses. Obviously, the most important use for the stand for exam would be during a visit to the veterinarian. When Fido is comfortable standing and staying while being touched and handled, the visit to the animal clinic is much less traumatic for the dog and much easier for your vet.

Your dog's groomer is another professional who will appreciate the stand for exam. Many groomers will teach a dog to stand on the table if the dog doesn't seem to know, so make sure you tell the groomer what commands Fido knows and understands and how to enforce them so that Fido isn't confused by different words or signals.

You can use the stand for exam at home when you brush the dog, when you want to towel off his paws before he comes in the house or when you want him to hold still but not sit—perhaps when the ground is wet or muddy.

Teaching the Exercise

Stand. You want Fido to understand that stand means "stand up, all feet comfortable, and stand still while someone touches you."

Stand, Step 5. Pam told Gracie to stay and then stepped out to the end of the leash. (Basset Hound)

Step 1. With Fido in a sit by your left side, reach over with your right hand and take hold of the front of Fido's collar. If Fido is on a slip collar, take hold of the collar not by the choke but by the links. Pull Fido forward so that he stands up on his own as you tell him, "Fido, stand." Use your left leg to brace against his body to help anchor him and use your left hand to tickle his left flank gently so that he doesn't want to sit back down. Reassure him: "Good boy to stand." After a few seconds, when he has stopped trying to sit, pat his ribcage with your left hand and tell him, "OK! Good Boy!" Return him to the sitting position. Follow the training sequence and schedule.

NOTE: If Fido tries to sit, use your right hand on his collar to step him forward slightly as you tell him, "Acck! Fido, stand," and keep the left hand under the flank. If Fido is determined to sit and refuses to stand, hold his motivator in your right hand as you encourage him up to position.

Step 2. With Fido in a sit by your left side, hold his collar with LEFT HAND and urge him forward as you tell him, "Fido, stand." At the same time, YOUR RIGHT HAND MAKES A SWEEPING UPWARD MOVEMENT in front of him that ends in a stay signal. This will be your stand hand signal. Repeat as in Step 1 above. Follow training sequence and schedule.

NOTE: If Fido is not watching your hand, hold his motivator in your right hand as you make the signal.

Step 3. With Fido in a sit by your left side, give him the stand signal and command, and then PICK UP AND MOVE SLIGHTLY ONE LEG, REPOSITIONING IT, so that you can place him in a square, steady comfortable position. If Fido is a small- or medium-sized dog, lift his chest and let the front legs set on the ground straight down from the shoulder. Only lift two legs at a time; do NOT lift the entire dog off the ground because that is an automatic failure. Repeat as in Step 1 above. Follow the training sequence and schedule.

Training Sequence (TS)
One repetition of a training step, followed by praise.
Second repetition of the same training step, followed by praise.
Third repetition of the same training step, followed by praise, a release (Fido, Release! Good Boy!) and a reward (his motivator; a treat or a toy).

Training Schedule
Do each step a minimum of three training sequences.
If the third TS has no mistakes, Fido is doing that step correctly and is not fighting the training, go on to the next step.
If Fido is having problems, go back one step and repeat the TS at that step.
If Fido is still confused, go back several steps to a place where Fido is confident, then work back up.

Step 4. With Fido in a sit by your left side, give him the stand signal and verbal command and reposition his feet, making sure that he is standing square and comfortable. Once he's set, TELL HIM, "FIDO, STAY" using the same hand signal and the verbal command that you used in both the sit/stay and the down/stay. Step one step away. Count to three (One Mississippi, two...) and go back to Fido and praise him. Follow the training sequence and schedule.

Step 5. Repeat as in Step 4 above, except STEP OUT TO THE END OF THE LEASH once you tell Fido stay. Follow the training sequence and schedule.

Step 6. Repeat as in Step 5 above, except INCREASE THE TIME TO 10 SECONDS. Follow the training sequence and schedule.

Step 7. Repeat as in Step 6 above, except INCREASE THE TIME TO 20 SECONDS. Follow the training sequence and schedule.

Step 8. With Fido in a sit by your left side, give him a stand command and signal, position his feet, tell him, "Fido, Stay." Step out to the end of the leash, about three steps. Turn and face Fido. Wait about 20 seconds and then return to Fido, APPROACHING HIM FROM THE RIGHT AS YOU LOOK AT HIM, WALKING AROUND BEHIND HIM AND UP TO THE HEEL POSITION. Praise him and release him. Follow the training sequence and schedule.

 NOTE: If Fido won't or can't hold still as you walk around him, create a smaller step prior to Step 8. Leave Fido in a stand, tell him stay and then step away from him one step, walk a circle around him and return to the heel position. Follow the training sequence and schedule.

Stand, Step 8. Tony has come back to Jazzy, walking around him and putting himself back in the heel position. (Weimaraner)

154

The Examination. Being touched by someone while having to hold a stay is very difficult for Fido. His first reactions might range from wanting to greet a familiar person to moving away from a stranger rather than holding still. Make sure you keep your patience when teaching this exercise.

Step 1. Stand Fido and give him the stay command but remain close to him. Have an assistant walk up to Fido, offer her hand for a quick sniff and then gently touch Fido's head and walk away. Return to Fido, praise him and resit him. Follow the training sequence and schedule.

NOTE: If Fido is worried, have the examiner offer him a tiny piece of a treat as he steps up to him. Or have the helper praise Fido after you do an exam. Remember, don't correct fear—build confidence.

Step 2. Stand Fido and leave him with a stay but remain within a step of Fido. Have your helper walk up to Fido, let Fido sniff, and then TOUCH FIDO'S HEAD, SHOULDERS AND HIPS before walking away. Return to Fido quickly, praise him and return him to a sit. Follow the training sequence and schedule.

Step 3. Repeat as above, except have THE HELPER DO A MORE THOROUGH EXAM. Have her touch Fido's head, neck, shoulders, rib cage, back and hips. Follow the training sequence and schedule.

Step 4. Repeat as above, except STEP OUT TO THE END OF THE LEASH prior to the helper doing an exam. Follow the training sequence and schedule.

Step 5. Stand Fido with signal and verbal command, tell him, "Fido, Stay," and as you step away from him, DROP THE LEASH TO THE GROUND. Go only six feet away, have the helper step up to Fido and examine him, then go back to Fido, going around him to the heel position. Praise him! Follow the training sequence and schedule.

Return to Heel. Fido learned the finish exercise in Chapter Seven. The return to heel is just like a finish except that Fido will be starting the finish from a distance away and won't be sitting in front of you.

Step 1. Brush up on the finish by having Fido sit in front and do a few of them. Use your hand signal with his motivator in hand or a small leash snap to make sure he's moving quickly. Follow the training sequence and schedule, even if Fido normally finishes very well.

Step 2. HAVE FIDO SIT ABOUT FOUR FEET AWAY in front of you and give him the finish command. Make sure you give the finish command and not the come command. If he hesitates, encourage him and use the leash to help (but not correct!) him. Praise him enthusiastically once he's returned to the heel position. Follow the training sequence and schedule.

Step 3. Have Fido sit ABOUT 10 FEET AWAY in front of you, WITH A LONG LEASH ATTACHED IN PLACE OF HIS REGULAR LEASH. Repeat as in Step 2 above. Follow the training sequence and schedule.

Step 4. Have Fido sit about 10 feet away but VARY THE DIRECTION. Have Fido sit at an angle to you, off to the left and over to the right. You want to teach Fido that the finish command means to go back to the heel position regardless of where he was when you gave the command. Repeat as in Step 3. Follow the training sequence and schedule.

Step 5. STAND FIDO AND LEAVE HIM WITH A "WAIT." (Review the wait in Chapter 7.) Tell Fido, "Fido, Finish." If he's confused and refuses to move, take one step toward him and encourage him back to

The Examination, Step 5. Tony gives Wilma a thorough exam as Jane stands still and Wilma concentrates on holding her stay. (Weimaraner)

you. Don't allow him to sit in front, help him back to the finish position. Praise him. Follow the training sequence and schedule.

NOTE: Don't go on until you are sure that Fido understands.

Stand Signal While Heeling. Fido learned the stand signal at the beginning of this chapter but only from a sit. Now you will teach him that the signal is the same from a sit or from a moving heel.

Step 1. With Fido walking by your left side, tell him, "Fido, Stand" as you give him the stand hand signal with your right hand. With your left hand, be ready to touch his flank to stop any attempts to sit or to walk forward. As soon as Fido is standing still and comfortable, praise him and resit him. Follow the training sequence and schedule.

Step 2. Repeat as in Step 1 above, except AFTER FIDO IS GIVEN THE COMMAND TO STAND, WALK ABOUT TWO STEPS AWAY FROM HIM. If he walks forward, tell him, "ACCK!" and stop him. Then step away from him again. Go back to him and praise him. Follow the training steps and sequence.

Step 3. Repeat as in Step 2 above, except AFTER FIDO IS GIVEN THE COMMAND TO STAND, WALK FOUR STEPS AWAY. Follow the training sequence and schedule.

Step 4. Repeat as in Step 3 above, except that once you have walked away from Fido, HAVE YOUR HELPER EXAMINE FIDO. Go back to him and praise him. Follow the training sequence and schedule.

Step 5. Repeat as in Step 4 above, except once the helper has examined Fido, TELL FIDO TO FINISH. Encourage him to the heel position. Follow the training sequence and schedule.

NOTE: Vary your training, occasionally doing a stand, examine, return to your dog and sometimes a stand, call to finish. Don't let Fido get pattern trained (anticipating the order the exercises are always in). It's more important that he watch and listen to you and respond to your commands.

Are You Having Problems?

If Fido is refusing to stand, he may be confused. In the beginning of his training, you put a lot of emphasis on the sit and he may have learned that standing was unwanted. Don't try to force Fido into position or to pull him up. Instead, take a step forward, as if you were walking away, and as Fido moves forward, catch him in the flank with the left hand and put his motivator in his mouth with the right hand. Praise him. Follow the training sequence and schedule.

Stand Signal while heeling, Step 1. Tony praises Jazzy for standing for the stand signal. (Weimaraner)

If Fido is moving his feet, reposition each one individually so that Fido understands that you are concerned about his feet. Don't pick up the entire dog to reposition him.

Chapter Eleven
The Retrieving Exercises

Be quick to praise, slower to criticize.
Unknown

The Exercise

The AKC Open class Retrieve on the Flat exercise demonstrates that Fido will wait while a dumbbell is being thrown and when sent after the dumbbell, will run directly to it, picking it up. After picking up the dumbbell, he must bring it back to his handler, sitting in front and holding the dumbbell until told to release it. He will then finish as in the Novice Recall.

In the ring the exercise looks like this:

1. Fido will be in the heel position, off leash. Jack will hold the dumbbell.

2. The judge says, "This is the Retrieve on the Flat. Are you ready?" Jack looks at Fido, who is sitting straight by his side and is watching him, and says, "Yes, we're ready."

3. The judge says, "Throw it." Jack tells Fido, "Wait," and throws the dumbbell at least 20 feet. It lands on an end and rolls a little, then comes to a stop.

4. The judge says, "Send your dog." Jack tells Fido, "Take it," and Fido runs straight out to the dumbbell. Picking it up, he turns toward Jack and returns, sitting in front, holding the dumbbell.

5. The judge says, "Take it." Jack reaches down and takes the dumbbell from Fido.

6. The judge says, "Finish." Jack tells Fido, "Fido, heel," and Fido returns to the heel position.

7. The judge says, "Exercise finished."

Scoring

Fido will fail the exercise if he fails to go out on the first command or anticipates the command to get the dumbbell. He will also fail if he refuses to bring the dumbbell back. He can lose substantial points for mouthing or playing with the dumbbell, drop-

EXERCISE	NON QUALIFYING ZERO		QUALIFYING SUBSTANTIAL MINOR	Maximum Points	Points Lost	NET SCORE
RETRIEVE ON FLAT	Fails to go out on first command or signal................☐ Fails to retrieve...............☐ Goes before command or signal..................☐	☐ Extra command or signal Sat out of reach.......☐	☐ .Slow .....☐ Going ....☐ Returning ☐ Mouthing ....☐ Dropping ☐ Directly to dumbbell ..☐ Poor Delivery ☐ No sit .....Poor sit......................☐ ☐ Anticipate finish.........................☐ ☐ Arms not at side ☐ No finish ....☐ Poor finish.............☐ ☐ .Handler error.............................☐ ☐ .Touched Handler........................☐	20		

The American Kennel Club Open class Retrieve on the Flat exercise

EXERCISE	NON-QUALIFYING ZERO	LESS THAN 50%	QUALIFYING (OVER 50%) Major (4 pts.) Minor (½ - 2 pts.)	Max. Pts.	Pts. Lost	Net Score
RETRIEVE ON FLAT	Fails to retrieve ....☐ Fails to go out on first command or signal ....☐ Sits out of reach..........☐ Dog leaves ring ....☐	Extra command and/or signal ....☐ Goes before command and/or signal ....☐	☐ .. Mouthing or playing........................☐ ☐ .. Slow ☐ .Going ☐ ..Returning.........☐ ☐ .. Poor delivery Touches handler.. ☐ ☐ .. Dropping dumbbell.........................☐ ☐ .. Handler Error Poor finish... ☐ ☐ .. No sit in front Sits between feet.. ☐ ☐ .. No Finish Poor Sit.. ☐ ☐ .. Leaves ring between exercises	20		

The United Kennel Club Companion Dog Excellent class Retrieve on the Flat exercise

EXERCISE	NON QUALIFYING ZERO			QUALIFYING SUBSTANTIAL MINOR	Maximum Points	Points Lost	NET SCORE

SCENT DISCRIMI-NATION	No go out 1st comm.
	
	☐L
	
	☐M
		No retrieve
		
		☐L
		
		☐M
			Wrong article
			
			☐L
			
			☐M
				LEATHER
				Anticipated......................☐
				Extra command..............☐
				Sat out of reach ....☐
				METAL
				Anticipated......................☐
				Extra command..............☐
				Sat out of reach ....☐
					L M
					☐ ☐ . Handler Turn in place
					☐ ☐ . Directly to articles..........................☐ ☐
					☐ ☐ . Slow Going & Returning...............☐ ☐
					☐ ☐ . Doesn't work continuously.............☐ ☐
					☐ ☐ . Dropping article on return..............☐ ☐
					               Mouthing L M
					☐ ☐ Dropping Article Touched handler..☐ ☐
					☐ ☐ Slow response Sat between feet..☐ ☐
					☐ ☐ No sit in front Poor sit...........☐ ☐
					               Poor finish.............☐ ☐
					☐ ☐ Handler error........☐ ☐ No finish........☐ ☐
						LEATHER
						30
						
						METAL
						30		

The American Kennel Club Utility class Scent Discrimination exercise

EXERCISE	NON-QUALIFYING ZERO	LESS THAN 50%	QUALIFYING (OVER 50%) Major (4 pts.) Minor (½ - 2 pts.)	Max. Pts.	Pts. Lost	Net Score
SCENT DISCRIMINATION	No go out 1st command...............☐ No retrieve ....☐ Wrong article ....☐ Dog leaves ring ....☐	METAL Anticipated ....☐ Extra command ....☐ Sat out of reach ....☐	☐ ....Handler roughness...............☐ ☐ ....Does not sit after turn...........☐ ☐ ....Doesn't work continuously...........☐ ☐ ....Dropping article on return...........☐ ☐ ....Picks up wrong article then dropped...☐ ☐ Slow response Sat between feet...☐ ☐ No sit in front Poor sit........☐ ☐ No finish Poor finish........☐ ☐ Handler error Touched handler....☐ ☐ .. Leaves ring between exercises Mouthing....☐	30		

The United Kennel Club Utility class Scent Discrimination exercise

160

EXERCISE	NON QUALIFYING ZERO	QUALIFYING SUBSTANTIAL MINOR	Maximum Points	Points Lost	NET SCORE
DIRECTED RETRIEVE	Does Not: Go out on command ☐ Go directly to glove ☐ Anticipated ☐ Extra signal ☐ Retrieve right article ☐ Sat out of reach ☐ Fails to retrieve ☐	☐ Facing Glove ☐ . .Touching dog sending ....☐ ☐ . .Excessive Motions.............☐ ☐ . .Slow response to command........☐ ☐ . .Mouthing . ☐ Playing ☐ ....☐ ☐ . .Slow Going & Returning...........☐ ☐ Dropping article Touching handler......☐ ☐ Poor delivery Sat between feet........☐ ☐ No sit in front Poor sit.........☐ ☐ No finish Poor finish..........☐ ☐ Turn in place.................☐ ☐ Handler error................☐	30		

The American Kennel Club Utility class Directed retrieve exercise

EXERCISE	NON-QUALIFYING ZERO	LESS THAN 50%	QUALIFYING (OVER 50%) Major (4 pts.)	Minor (½ - 2 pts.)	Max. Pts.	Pts. Lost	Net Score
DIRECTED (MARKED) RETRIEVE	Does Not: Go out on command ☐ Go directly to glove ☐ Retrieve right article ☐ Fails to retrieve ☐ Dog leaves ring ☐	Anticipated ☐ Extra signal ☐ Sat out of reach ☐	☐ ....Touching dog sending ....☐ ☐ ....Excessive signals ....☐ ☐ ....Slow response to command ....☐ ☐ Mouthing Playing .....☐ ☐ Dropping article Touching handler......☐ ☐ Poor delivery Sat between feet ......☐ ☐ No sit in front Poor sit......☐ ☐ No finish Poor finish....☐ ☐ ......Lack of naturalness-smoothness .....☐ ☐ ..Leaves ring between exercises		20		

The United Kennel Club Utility class Directed (Marked) Retrieve exercise

EXERCISE	NON-QUALIFYING ZERO	LESS THAN 50%	QUALIFYING (OVER 50%) Major (4 pts.)	Minor (½ - 2 pts.)	Max. Pts.	Pts. Lost	Net Score
DIRECTED (SIGNAL) RETRIEVE	Does Not: Go out on command ☐ Go directly to glove ☐ Retrieve right article ☐ Fails to retrieve ☐ Dog leaves ring ☐	Anticipated ☐ Extra signal ☐ Sat out of reach ☐ Does not stop ☐ Excessive signals ☐	☐ ....Does not sit on go out ....☐ ☐ ....Touching dog sending ....☐ ☐ ....Excessive signals ....☐ ☐ ....Slow response to command ....☐ ☐ Mouthing Playing .....☐ ☐ Dropping article Touching handler.....☐ ☐ Poor delivery Sat between feet ......☐ ☐ No sit in front Poor sit......☐ ☐ No finish Poor finish.....☐ ☐ ....Lack of naturalness-smoothness .....☐ ☐ Leaves ring between exercises		30		

The United Kennel Club Utility class Directed (Signal) Retrieve exercise

ping the dumbbell and for refusing to sit when bringing the dumbbell back. Jack can lose points for body language when giving commands or when Fido is bringing the dumbbell back. Fido can lose minor points for crooked sits or poor finishes.

The scent discrimination exercise demonstrates that Fido can find and retrieve an article that is scented by his owner from among a number of identical articles that are scented by the judge or steward.

The scoring is similar to the Novice Recall exercise and the Retrieve on the Flat for those portions of the exercise. Fido must go directly to the articles and when he has selected the correct article must bring it back quickly, sitting in front until released, then must finish. When searching for the scented article, Fido must work continuously.

In the AKC competition, Fido will do the exercise twice, once for a metal article and once for a leather. Each exercise is worth 30 points. In UKC competition, Fido will do it once for a metal article, again, worth 30 points.

Fido will fail if he does not go to the articles on the first command. He will fail if he chooses the wrong article, if he does not bring the article back or if he needs a second command to find the article. Substantial points are deducted if he picks up a wrong article, even if he drops it to pick up the correct one. Substantial points can also be lost for stopping his search, for working slowly and for handler errors. Minor points are lost for crooked sits in front and crooked finishes.

These exercises demonstrate that Fido will stay until told to retrieve and will retrieve a single article by directional command. In addition, the UKC Directed Signal exercise requires the dog to do a go out, turn and sit as is required in the AKC Directed Jumping exercise. (See Chapter 13 for the Go Out exercise.)

Fido will fail if he refuses to stay until sent after the article or fails to retrieve it. He will also fail if he retrieves the wrong article. Other scoring is similar to the Retrieve on the Flat.

Practical Application

These exercises are a complicated combination of many things, all of which have practical uses. The retrieve itself is very important. A good retrieve is an excellent way to exercise Fido for both play and to use up excess energy. Make Fido feel useful and give him a job to do while you're working around the house. Have him retrieve the dirty clothes for you or the newspaper, or the weekly TV schedule.

A good retrieving dog can play Frisbee and compete in Frisbee competitions. A field dog or gun dog obviously needs a solid retrieve. Search and rescue dogs and working dogs need to retrieve. Many training schools for guide dogs, hearing service dogs or dogs for the disabled require that a puppy accepted for their program must have a strong retrieving instinct.

A directed retrieve allows you to send Fido to something without throwing it first. A scented retrieve teaches Fido to search for the object to be retrieved. He can find your keys, or your lost wallet, or the baby's shoe. The uses are unlimited.

162

One repetition of a training step, followed by praise.
Second repetition of the same step, followed by praise.
Third repetition of the same step, followed by praise, a release and a reward.

Training Schedule

1. Do each step a minimum of three training sequences.
2. If the third TS has no mistakes, go on to the next step.
3. If Fido is having a problem, go back one step and repeat the TS at that level.
4. If Fido is still confused, go back several steps and work your way back up.

Teaching the Exercise

Review the Retrieve. Review the retrieve in Chapter Four. Repeat the guidelines in Chapter Four for several different items that you want Fido to retrieve, using the same commands. "Take it," "Hold," "Bring it back" and "Give" all apply to the ball, the dumbbell, the Frisbee and anything else that you might want Fido to get for you.

Guidelines for a Good Retrieve. When you have Fido retrieving, never chase him, even in play, to get the ball or Frisbee back. The game then becomes a keep away or chase game and Fido will try even harder to keep it away from you. After all, the one with the toy wins. If Fido likes to play keep away, let him play with the long line on and teach him to come to you with the toy using the long line. (See Chapter Six for a review on using the long line.)

The other thing you can do to teach Fido that keep away stops the game is to do exactly that, stop the game. If he doesn't bring the ball back, stop playing. Just sit down on the grass or in the lawn chair, look at the sky or read the evening paper. Ignore Fido, no matter how cute he is trying to get your attention. When he drops the ball at your feet or in your lap, then come to life and resume the game.

Keep your retrieving sessions short, both your games and your training sessions. Always stop leaving Fido wanting more. During the training period, never run Fido until he's exhausted unless he's a retrieving maniac that nothing could discourage.

Retrieving Games for Natural Retrievers. If Fido is a natural

Wilma is a tennis ball fool, so Jane uses the tennis ball as a motivator and to make retrieving fun.

retriever, a dog that loves to chase things, get them and bring them back, you can use that instinct to teach him the retrieving commands. Use several different toys when you play games with him so that he understands that the commands apply to what he is doing and not specifically to one toy.

When you throw the toy and Fido is already running after it, tell him, "Fido, Take it! Good boy!" It may seem ridiculous, after all you know that Fido is going after it already, but giving him the commands now will help teach him what to do when you put it under more formal control. As he is bringing the toy back to you, tell him, "Bring it here. Good boy," and when you take it from him, tell him, "Give," and don't let him wrestle with you.

If you have more than one dog available, either yours or some training friends' dogs, and you know the dogs all get along, use them to help make the retrieve better. Have each dog do a down stay while one or more of the other dogs get to play retrieving games. Rotate it so that each dog gets a chance. This anticipation and jealousy can work to your advantage, making the retrieving something special instead of work.

Retrieving Games for Not-so-Natural Retrievers. If Fido is not a natural retriever, if he watches you throw the ball and waits for you to go get it, sometimes the retrieving games will teach him that this can be fun. Review the retrieve in Chapter Four so that Fido is acquainted with the ball, has licked peanut butter off it and, you hope, will pick it up.

If a training friend has a friendly dog that likes to retrieve, let Fido run with this dog a while, watching Rover retrieve and get praised for it. While Fido is running with Rover, ignore him. Don't tell him, "Take it! Take it!" while Rover is retrieving. Instead, praise Rover for the wonderful job he's doing. Work on Fido's jealousy, if he has any.

Then have Fido do a down/stay while Rover retrieves, again praising Rover for his wonderful work. Then put a long line on Fido and let him have a chance. Throw the ball just a few feet. If Fido runs after it, praise him but don't distract him. If you praise too much, he might forget the ball and come back to you for more praise. Tell him, "Take it" as he puts his jaws on the ball and then encourage him to bring it back to you. Kneel down, open your arms and invite him to bring it back. Then praise him as much as you want. Make him squirm with happiness.

Sometimes playing tug of war with Fido can stimulate the prey drive and as a result, the retrieving instincts. A rolled-up towel with a couple knots in it makes a good soft tug-of-war toy. Encourage Fido to grab it and gently encourage him to tug and pull on it. Get him

Care Bear returns a foxtail (a toy that is a ball with a tail). This is one of Bear's favorite toys and is a great motivator for his retrieving training. (Australian Shepherd)

excited about the game and praise him when he pulls.

On and off throughout the game, tell him, "Enough" and have him sit. Tell him, "Give," and take the tug toy away from him. If he resists or if he doesn't know the word *give* reach over the top of his muzzle, pressing the skin against his top teeth on both sides of his mouth and at the same time, tell him, "Fido, give." Praise him when he opens his mouth.

Once he's excited, have him release the tug toy to you and throw it several feet away. Encourage Fido to chase it, telling him to "Take it!" and praise him when he does. Repeat the tug game and chase game, using the verbal commands.

A word of caution, though. Tug-of-war games are not normally recommended for dogs with aggressive tendencies as the game can teach Fido to use his strength against you. If you do play the tug-of-war game, make sure that Fido understands that the game stops on your command and that you can always take the tug toy away from him. When played under these guidelines, a tug-of-war game can be a very constructive training tool.

With not-so-natural retrievers, make sure you always keep the retrieving sessions very short. Always stop before he's had enough, is tired or gets bored. Stop leaving him wanting more.

Teaching the Take It. When you send Fido after the dumbbell or toy, you want him to grab it quickly and hold it securely.

Step 1. With Fido on a leash, show him a treat (a very special treat that

There are a variety of dumbbells on the market, including handmade ones. A properly fitting dumbbell should allow one finger width between the dog's muzzle and the end pieces. It should not poke the dog's eyes or obstruct the dog's vision. (Australian Shepherd)

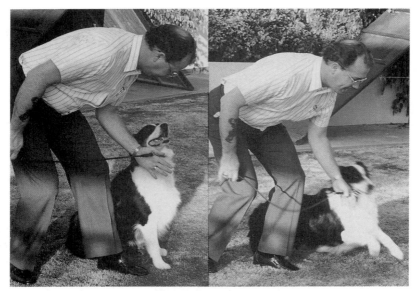

Paul has his hand through Ursa's leash near her collar (left) and as he gives her the retrieve command, his hand will urge her forward as he signals (right).

you know he loves), and as you hand it to him, tell him, "Take it." Do it six times. Follow the training sequence and schedule.

Step 2. Smear the dumbbell with the treat. OFFER FIDO THE DUMBBELL, placing it immediately in front of his muzzle, telling him, "Take it." As soon as he acknowledges the dumbbell in any form: smelling, licking, touching or if you're lucky, grabbing it, reward him with enthusiastic verbal praise and a treat. Repeat six times. Follow the training sequence and schedule.

Step 3. Repeat Step 2 above, except now YOU WILL REWARD ONLY A TOUCH ON THE DUMBBELL. Smelling the dumbbell is not good enough now. Repeat six times. Follow the training sequence and schedule.

Step 4. Repeat Step 3 above, except now YOU WILL REWARD ONLY OPENING HIS MOUTH. He doesn't need to grab the dumbbell yet, but he does need to show that he's willing to open his mouth to it, even touching it just a little. Repeat six times. Follow the training sequence and schedule.

Step 5. Repeat Step 4 above, except NOW YOU WILL REWARD ONLY GRABBING THE DUMBBELL. It must be in his mouth, even for an instant, to be rewarded. Tell him, "Give" when he spits it out. Repeat six times. Follow the training sequence and schedule.

NOTE: This is a very important step. Don't be in a hurry and try to bypass this step. If Fido does this by himself, you can be assured that he understands. If Fido keeps pushing the dumbbell in your hand, licks it and tries everything else that has worked before but he still doesn't grab the dumbbell, you may need to make another step in between Steps 3, 4 and 5.

Alternative Step. Offer Fido the dumbbell, and if he doesn't grab it, open his mouth gently and place the dumbbell in his mouth. Gently cup his mouth closed for a second, praise him, tell him, "Give" and then remove the dumbbell and give him his treat. Repeat six times. Follow the training sequence and schedule.

Do not go on to any additional steps until Fido is grabbing the dumbbell when it is placed directly in front of his muzzle.

Step 6. Offer Fido the dumbbell directly in front of his muzzle, tell him, "Take it," and when he grabs it, IMMEDIATELY BACK UP A STEP OR TWO and tell Fido, "Bring it here! Good boy!" When he steps toward you with the dumbbell, tell him, "Give," take it from him and give him his praise and treat. Repeat three times. Follow the training sequence and schedule.

Step 7. Repeat Step 6 above, except ONCE YOU GIVE FIDO THE DUMBBELL, TELL HIM, "HOLD IT," AND CUP YOUR HAND AROUND HIS MUZZLE. Then back up a couple of steps, tell him, "Give," take it from him, reward him and praise him. Do three times. Follow the training sequence and schedule.

Step 8. Repeat Step 7 above, except BACK UP SEVERAL STEPS. Do three times. Follow the training sequence and schedule.

Step 9. HOLD THE DUMBBELL ABOUT THREE INCHES IN FRONT OF FIDO'S NOSE, tell him, "Take it," and encourage him to reach forward. When he grabs it, tell him, "Hold it," and back up several steps, tell him, "Give," take the dumbbell and praise and reward him. Do three times. Follow the training sequence and schedule.

Step 10. Repeat Step 9 above, except HOLD THE DUMBBELL ABOUT SIX INCHES IN FRONT OF HIS MUZZLE.

Step 11. Repeat Step 10 above, except HOLD THE DUMBBELL ABOUT 10 INCHES AWAY.

Left: When teaching the retrieve, make sure Fido is returning the dumbbell to you without any detours. Center: There is a right way to carry the dumbbell and a wrong way. Care Bear is carrying it incorrectly. Right: Here he is bringing it back the way he should. (Australian Shepherd)

Step 12. Repeat Step 11 above, except LOWER THE DUMBBELL TO THE GROUND. Keep your hand on it, and be ready to help Fido pick it up if he hesitates. Continue to back up and praise him as in Step 8 above.

Reviewing the Sit in Front. When Fido has completed the steps above, you can show him that he can still do the sit in front, just as he has done before, but with a dumbbell or a toy in his mouth.

Step 1. With Fido on a leash, practice the sit in front without any retrieving. Back up and when Fido follows you, stop and have him sit in front. Praise him. Repeat three times. Follow the training sequence and schedule, even if he does it well.

Step 2. HOLD THE DUMBBELL SIX INCHES IN FRONT OF FIDO and tell him, "Take it." When he takes it, tell him, "Hold," back up several steps, encouraging him to follow you. Stop and have him sit in front of you. If he doesn't do it on his own, cup one hand under his muzzle to prevent him from spitting out the dumbbell, and with the other hand, help him to sit. Do this all as gently as you can. As soon as he sits, tell him, "Give" and take the dumbbell from him. Immediately praise and reward him. Repeat six times. Follow the training sequence and schedule.

Teaching the Retrieve and the Retrieve Signal. During a retrieve, you want Fido to run, on command or signal, after the dumbbell quickly, with tail wagging.

Step 1. With Fido sitting in the heel position, gather up the excess leash in your left hand so that the leash is taut but not tight. Hold the dumbbell in your right hand. Toss the dumbbell about three feet in front of you and at the same time, tell Fido, "Take it," and move your left hand and the leash forward in a sweeping movement pointing toward the dumbbell. At the same time, start moving quickly toward the dumbbell. When Fido picks it up, tell him, "Hold," and take a couple of steps backwards, have him follow you then sit in front. Tell him, "Give," take the dumbbell from him, praise and reward him. Talk to him, praise and encourage him throughout the exercise but not to the extent that he forgets what he's doing. Repeat three times. Follow the training sequence and schedule.

Step 2. Repeat Step 1 above, except TOSS THE DUMBBELL ABOUT

When teaching Fido to retrieve, teach him to retrieve a variety of things, including squeaky toys, rings, flying discs, balls, dumbbells, scent articles and gloves. (Australian Shepherd)

171

SIX FEET AWAY. Follow the training sequence and schedule.

Step 3. Repeat as above, except TOSS THE DUMBBELL 12 FEET AWAY. Follow the training sequence and schedule.

Step 4. At this point, if Fido is running toward the dumbbell on command and signal, start running with him but ALLOW HIM TO PULL AHEAD OF YOU. Extend the leash, or drop it so that you don't give him any inadvertent corrections. When he picks up the dumbbell, don't catch up with him but instead simply start backing up from where you are. Watch him carefully, though, and if he doesn't immediately pick up the dumbbell, catch up with him and have him pick it up. Then back away again and have him sit in front. Repeat three times. Follow the training sequence and schedule.

Step 5. Repeat as above, except TOSS THE DUMBBELL 20 FEET AWAY. Follow the training sequence and schedule.

Step 6. Repeat as above, except TOSS THE DUMBBELL 12 FEET AWAY TO THE SIDE. Vary the direction. One time throw it to the right, another time to the left, another time off center. Give the signal with the left hand and leash toward the dumbbell. Follow the training sequence and schedule.

Step 7. With Fido in a sit by your left side, DROP YOUR LEASH OR LONG LINE TO THE GROUND BEHIND FIDO. Tell him, "Wait," and hold his collar with your left hand. Toss the dumbbell out about 12 feet. Give the sweeping forward signal with the left hand as you tell him, "Fido, take it!" If he begins moving on his own, stay where you are. When he picks up the dumbbell, call him back and use your hands in front to encourage him to sit straight in front. (Review sit in front in Chapter Seven.) Tell him, "Give," and take the dumbbell from him. Immediately praise and reward him. Follow the training sequence and schedule.

Step 8. Repeat as in Step 7 above, except VARY THE COMMAND USED TO SEND THE DOG. One time give hand signal only, the next time use verbal command only and the third time use both verbal and hand signal. Fido needs to understand both commands: hand signal and verbal command. If at any time, Fido fails to respond to either command, use your left hand on his collar to urge him forward. Follow through as in Step 7 above. Follow the training sequence and schedule.

Care Bear is holding a metal scent article. Some dogs dislike having metal in their mouths. If so, they can get over it by licking peanut butter off a metal spoon. (Australian Shepherd)

Cup your hand over Fido's nose to give him your scent, but don't force him. He KNOWS what you smell like! (Australian Shepherd)

Ursa has found the article with Paul's scent from among a number of other objects (ALL toys) scented with the author's scent. (Australian Shepherd)

The gloves used for the directed retrieve should be plain, cotton work gloves that are predominately white. (Australian Shepherd)

NOTE: Do not go on to the following steps until Fido will go after the dumbbell for both commands or either command.

Teaching the Retrieve Over the High Jump. Read Chapter Thirteen for a definition of a high jump and more detailed instructions on teaching Fido to jump.

Step 1. Set up the high jump with one board or the equivalent of half the height to Fido's elbow, or as close as possible. For example, if Fido's elbow is 12 inches off the ground, put a six-inch board in the jump. However, if you just have boards in eight-inch or two-inch increments, an eight-inch board is fine. If Fido's elbow is eight inches high, put a four- or a six-inch board in the jump, preferably the four. Stand about three feet in front of the jump and as you tell Fido "Heel," walk forward, step over the jump as you tell him, "Jump" or "Over," and praise him. Repeat six times. Follow the training sequence and schedule.

Step 2. Repeat as in Step 1 above, except STAND ON THE OTHER SIDE OF THE JUMP AND CALL FIDO OVER TO YOU. Have him sit in front, then praise him. Repeat six times. Follow the training sequence and schedule.

Step 3. With Fido in a sit in the heel position, place yourselves about three feet in front of the jump. Throw the dumbbell so that it lands about four feet on the other side of the jump. Immediately, as it lands,

Paul has sent Ursa after the center glove. (Australian Shepherd)

tell Fido, "Take it," and chase the dumbbell with him, jumping the jump and making sure he goes directly to the dumbbell. As soon as he picks it up, back up a few steps and have him sit in front. Tell him, "Give," and take the dumbbell. Praise and reward him. Follow the training sequence and schedule.

Step 4. Repeat Step 3 above, except when Fido chases the dumbbell, extend the leash and walk forward a step or two but DON'T JUMP WITH HIM THIS TIME. When he picks up the dumbbell, back up a few steps, URGING HIM TO COME OVER THE JUMP BACK TO YOU and complete the exercise as in Step 3 above. Follow the training sequence and schedule.

Step 5. With Fido sitting by your left side, tell him, "Wait" before you toss the dumbbell. Hold his collar lightly and make him hold it about three seconds (One Mississippi, two...) before sending him. Complete the exercise as in Step 3 above, calling him back over the jump and having him sit in front. Follow the training sequence and schedule.

Step 6. Repeat as in Step 5 above, except have Fido HOLD THE WAIT ABOUT FIVE SECONDS before sending him. Complete as before. Follow the training sequence and schedule.

Step 7. SET YOURSELF AND FIDO UP ABOUT EIGHT FEET IN FRONT OF THE JUMP. Tell Fido, "Wait" WITHOUT HOLDING HIS COLLAR, let him wait about five seconds, send him after the dumbbell but DON'T STEP TOWARD THE JUMP. When he picks up the dumbbell, call him back over the jump and take a couple of steps backwards to encourage him to come sit straight in front. Tell him, "Give," and take the dumbbell. Praise and reward him. Follow the training sequence and schedule.

Step 8. Repeat Step 7 above, except DON'T CALL HIM BACK OVER THE JUMP, let him come back on his own. As soon as you can see that he is going over the jump without your direction, verbally praise him. Don't give him so much praise that he forgets what he's doing, though. Complete as in Step 7 above.

NOTE: Don't forget some of the important rules of the retrieve. When you are training a retrieve exercise, it's still important to maintain a sense of fun. Keep the praise upbeat and the rewards important. Use a motivator that Fido likes. Vary the article to be retrieved, sometimes use the wooden dumbbell, sometimes use a ball and occasionally use another toy.

Ursa has brought the glove back to Paul and holds it until he tells her to release it. (Australian Shepherd)

Step 9. With Fido in a sit in the heel position about eight feet in front of the jump, tell Fido, "Wait," and toss the dumbbell so that it lands about 10 or 12 feet past the jump. Wait about three seconds and send Fido, "Fido, Take it!" He should run directly to the dumbbell and immediately turn, facing you and the jump, and bring it back to you over the jump. If you stand still, he should sit in front, holding on to the dumbbell until you tell him, "Give." TELL HIM, "FINISH." Follow the training sequence and schedule.

Step 10. Repeat Step 9 above except toss the dumbbell off to one side when you throw it. Be ready to stop Fido should he go around the jump either going or coming back. Don't correct him severely, instead interrupt his run, bring him back and send him over the jump. Then praise him. Vary the directions that you throw the dumbbell so that Fido understands completely that he has to go over the jump even when the dumbbell is not in line with the jump. Repeat six times. Follow the training sequence and schedule.

179

Teaching Scent Discrimination. "Find it!" games can be very exciting to Fido and teach him to use his nose. Start with a treat. Have Fido sit and stay, show him a treat and walk away with it. Place it out of sight but close, like behind a chair or under the picnic table. Tell Fido to find it and make a big deal out of his efforts. "Find it! Where is it? Go look for it! Good boy!" When he finds it, he is rewarding himself by eating the treat and your verbal praise compound it. Repeat the game with toys.

When teaching scent discrimination you will need a set of six leather and six metal scent articles, a bag to carry them in, a pair of tongs and several wire coat hangers cut and bent into anchors. (Take a six-inch piece of coat hanger wire and bend it into a U shape. Make a half dozen anchors.)

The scent articles can be a pre-made set of dumbbells (See photo) or they can be identical articles of everyday use. Some handlers use soda cans for the metal articles and pieces of leather belt for the leather.

Make sure each article is numbered. Number the leather articles one through six and the metal, one through six. Touch only one metal and one leather article with your hands. (For example, number six metal and number six leather.) Touch the others only with the tongs. If you do touch the other articles, they can be de-scented by airing them out in the fresh air for a day or two.

The goal of this exercise is to teach Fido to search for an item that has your scent on it. The item or article may be hidden or mixed in with identical items that have not been scented by you.

Step 1. Take one metal article and one leather article and set the rest of the articles away. Practice the retrieve as in "Teaching the Retrieve and Retrieve Signal," Steps 1 through 8, above. Make sure that Fido will bring back either article willingly. Follow the training steps and sequences.

NOTE: If Fido is hesitant about picking up a metal article, and some dogs are, give him a big spoon smeared with peanut butter and let him lick it. Put the spoon on the kitchen floor and let it clang as he licks it. Let him pick it up and carry it if he wants and even encourage him to hold it in his mouth. Then smear some peanut butter on his metal scent article and let him lick it until he's lost his hesitation over the metal.

Step 2. With Fido in a sit in the heel position, toss the leather article in medium- length grass (about six inches high). Cup your hand over Fido's nose so that he inhales your scent, then send Fido after the article. "Fido, find mine!" Run after him. If he hesitates, encourage him to search. When he finds the article, back up a few steps so that he brings it to you, take it from him and praise and reward him. If he does not find it quickly or acts as if he doesn't understand, call him to the article and without touching it, point it out to him. Praise him when he gets it even if you had to point it out. Repeat 6 times. Follow the training sequence and schedule.

NOTE: You can scent your article by rubbing it between your hands for 20 seconds or so. You don't have to go overboard. Don't rub it under your arm. Fido's nose is very good, he doesn't need that kind of help!

Step 3. Repeat Step 2 above, except toss the dumbbell TOWARD THE BASE OF BUSHES, INTO TALLER GRASS OR INTO OTHER LAND-SCAPING. Don't make the search too difficult. We still want Fido to succeed but we also want him to use his nose. Repeat 6 times. Follow the training sequence and schedule.

Step 4. TURN FIDO SO THAT HIS BACK IS TO THE TRAINING AREA. Tell him to stay and then walk out and place the article in the open, not hidden by anything. Cup your hand around his nose and then TELL HIM, "FIDO, HEEL." TURN AND FACE THE TRAINING AREA AND HAVE FIDO SIT. Wait only a second or two, then send him after the article. "Fido, find mine!" Follow through as with a regular retrieve. Repeat 6 times. Follow the training sequence and schedule.

Step 5. REPEAT STEPS 2 THROUGH 4 WITH A METAL ARTICLE.

Step 6. With Fido on a stay placed so that he cannot see what you are doing, take one leather article that has not been scented and with the tongs, carry it to the grass in your training area. Take one of the coat hanger anchors and push the anchor into the dirt so that the article is held firmly down.

Bring Fido back and place him so that his back is to the train-ing area. Leave him on a stay and take your scented leather article out and place it about 18 inches from the anchored, unscented one. Cup your hand around his nose, tell him to heel and turn so that you are facing the articles. Send him with his find it command and run after him. If he runs to the unscented one, let him sniff. If he then runs over to the scented one, praise him and after he picks it up, call him back to you a couple of steps.

If he tries to pick up the unscented one, don't correct him or try to make him feel bad. He's just learning. If you correct Fido for going to the wrong article, you may be giving Fido the wrong idea. Does he think he's being corrected for sniffing? For investigating? For retrieving? Or for going out to the articles? Instead, let him work. If he seems confused and looks like he going to stop sniffing, then encourage him over to the correct article. Repeat six times. Follow the training sequence and schedule.

NOTE: If you train inside, you can use a piece of peg board and use ties or string to anchor the articles.

Step 7. Repeat as above, except ADD ANOTHER UNSCENTED ARTICLE, placed about eight inches from the other unscented article. Follow the training sequence and schedule.

Step 8. Repeat as above, except ADD A THIRD UNSCENTED ARTICLE. Follow the training sequence and schedule.

Step 9. Repeat as above, except ADD A FOURTH AND FIFTH UNSCENTED ARTICLE. Repeat the training sequence and schedule.

Step 10. PUT THE LEATHER ARTICLES AWAY AND REPEAT STEPS 6 THROUGH 9 WITH THE METAL ARTICLES.

Step 11. Have Fido in a sit, facing the training area. Set your scented articles aside. With your tongs, place two metal and two leather unscented articles out in the training area, about six inches apart, about 10 feet from Fido. Anchor them down. Place the scented article in the group, about six inches from the other articles. Go back to Fido and WITHOUT turning him away, GIVE HIM YOUR SCENT WITH YOUR HAND AND SEND HIM AFTER THE ARTICLE. When he picks up the right article, let him retrieve it to you and follow through as with a regular retrieve. Have him sit in front and hold the article until you tell him to "Give." Praise and reward him. Follow the training sequence and schedule.

Step 12. Repeat as in Step 11 above, except ADD MORE UNSCENTED ARTICLES, LEATHER OR METAL, per training sequence until there are four leather and four metal unscented articles out. Continue to anchor them.

Step 13. Repeat the training exercise as in Step 11 with all eight articles out as in Step 12, except AFTER THE ARTICLES ARE SPREAD OUT AND ANCHORED DOWN, TURN FIDO AWAY FROM THE

ARTICLES before PLACING THE SCENTED ONE. Give Fido your hand to sniff before turning him. Tell him, "Heel," and have him sit straight in the heel position facing the articles. Then send him. Follow the training sequence and schedule.

Teaching the Directed Retrieve. The goal of this exercise is to demonstrate that Fido can retrieve an object with a directional signal.

Step 1. Review "Teaching the Retrieve and Retrieve Signal" in this chapter.

Step 2. Introduce Fido to the cotton work gloves he will need to retrieve. Do some play retrieves with the gloves and some straight retrieves, letting Fido chase the glove as you throw it and then do a wait while you throw them. Follow the training sequence and schedule for each aspect of the retrieve.

Step 3. Review the sit straight in the heel position from Chapter Nine. Tell Fido, "Fido, heel," and pivot one step to the left. He will need to move backwards a bit to allow you room to turn. Help Fido sit straight next to you. Using his motivator or your hands, show him where you want him to be. Follow the training sequence and schedule.

NOTE: Steps 3, 4 and 5 are very important to the directed retrieve. If Fido is not sitting straight when you give the signal, he could end up going to the wrong place or retrieving the wrong article.

Step 4. Do the same thing as Step 3, except TO THE RIGHT. Fido will need to come forward into the heel position as you turn away from him. Again, encourage the straight sit. Follow the training sequence and schedule.

Step 5. Repeat Steps 3 and 4, except MAKE AN ABOUT TURN, turning around in place. Fido will have to move with you, again coming up to a straight sit. Follow the training sequence and schedule.

Step 6. With Fido in a sit in the heel position, leave him with a stay and walk about 20 feet away. Place a glove on the ground directly in front of Fido. Go back to him and send him with the retrieve command and signal, giving the signal with your left hand, right next to his head. Follow through as with a regular retrieve (as in Step 7 of "Teaching the Retrieve and Retrieve Signal" above). Follow the training sequence and schedule.

The herding instinct and prey drive are very close in relationship. The dogs with these strong drives usually also have good retrieving onctincts, which can make training much easier. (Australian Shepherd)

Step 7. Repeat Step 6 above, except PLACE THE GLOVE OFF TO THE RIGHT SIDE. Have Fido heel with you as you turn to face the glove, then send him with a signal and command. Do the same thing with the glove to your left side. Practice both directions. Follow the training sequence and schedule.

Step 8. TURN FIDO AWAY FROM THE TRAINING AREA. PLACE ONE GLOVE TO THE LEFT AND ONE GLOVE TO THE RIGHT, EACH ABOUT 20 TO 30 FEET FROM THE CENTER LINE THAT IS EVEN WITH FIDO. Decide which glove you will send Fido after and turn in place to face that glove. Send Fido with signal and command. Praise him for getting it, and when he comes back to you, have him sit in front and take the glove from him. Praise and reward him. Practice both directions. Follow the training sequence and schedule.

Step 9. PUT ALL THREE GLOVES OUT: ONE IN THE CENTER DIRECTLY ACROSS FROM FIDO, AND ONE TO EACH SIDE, about 20 to 30 feet away. Practice turning to face all three, and sending Fido to them. Do three or four each training sequence. Follow the training sequence and schedule.

   NOTE: Vary the retrieves. Do not always send him to left, center, right. Sometimes make it right, left center or center, right, left. Or center, right, right, left.

Reviewing the Go Out. The Go Out will be taught in Chapter Thirteen. Look at the section, "Teaching the Go Out." In the UKC Utility class, the go out is combined with a directed retrieve to make the Directed Signal Retrieve. If Fido understands both exercises, he will not have a problem with this exercise. Teach both the Directed Retrieve and the Go Out separately and make sure Fido understands and is doing both with no problem before trying to combine them.

Are You Having Problems?

Try to keep the retrieve fun and make sure you always stop both the training sessions and the play sessions prior to Fido losing interest. Use the tug-of-war game occasionally if that helps make it fun for Fido.

If Fido is having problems at any point during these exercises, go back to the basics. Go back to the beginning steps and work your way back up to the area where Fido had problems. During this review, watch Fido carefully and make sure he is doing each step well. Don't assume that he understands.

If you need to break a step into smaller steps, do so if that will increase Fido's understanding.

Signals can also be used for other than obedience training. Pam is using a hand signal meaning "Speak" for Gracie during a trick training routine. (Basset Hound)

Chapter Twelve
The Signal Exercises

Every good thought you think is contributing its share to the ultimate result
of your life.
Greenville Kleiser

The Exercise

The goal of the AKC Utility class Signal Exercise is to demonstrate the dog and owner's teamwork, their ability to work together and the dog's ability to follow a series of hand signals.

The exercise will be performed as follows:

1. The judge asks Jack, "Are you ready?" Jack looks at Fido, and replies, "Yes, we're ready." The judge says, "Forward." Jack signals Fido to heel, giving no verbal commands.

2. The exercise progresses like a Novice or Open Heel free exercise, with the judge giving commands for slow, fast, left turn, right turn and about turn. The commands may be given in any order and may be repeated although the judge will use the same pattern for every dog.

3. During the heel, while the team is walking a normal pace, the judge will say, "Stand your dog." Jack signals Fido to stand and remains standing by Fido's side.

4. The judge then says, "Leave your dog." Jack signals Fido to stay and walks across the ring and turns to face Fido. The judge signals Jack to drop his dog, then to sit his dog and to call his dog. Jack can only give a signal, no verbal commands allowed. After the come, with Fido sitting in front, the judge will signal Jack to finish his dog.

5. After Fido's finish, the judge will say, "Exercise finished."

Scoring

The AKC Utility class Signal exercise is worth 40 points if performed flawlessly. The UKC Utility class Signal exercise is worth 30

EXERCISE	NON QUALIFYING ZERO		QUALIFYING SUBSTANTIAL MINOR	Maximum Points	Points Lost	NET SCORE
SIGNAL EXERCISE	Handler adapting self to dog pace ☐ Unmanageable ☐ Unqualified Heeling ☐	Audible command or Failure on first signal to: Stand ☐ Stay ☐ Drop ☐ Sit ☐ Come ☐ Anticipated ☐ Sat out of reach ☐	☐ . Forging . . ☐ Crowding handler ☐ ☐ . Lagging . . ☐ Sniffing ☐ ☐ No change of pace ☐ Fast ☐ Slow ☐ ☐ .Heeling wide - on turns - abouts ☐ ☐ .Extra command to heel ☐ ☐ . . . . Holding signals ☐ Slow response to signal to ☐ Stand . Down . Sit . Come . Touching handler ☐ ☐ Walk Forward Sat between feet ☐ ☐ No sit front-finish Poor sits ☐ ☐ Anticipate finish Poor finish ☐ ☐ Handler error ☐	40		

The American Kennel Club Utility class Signal exercise

EXERCISE	NON-QUALIFYING ZERO	LESS THAN 50%	QUALIFYING (OVER 50%) Major (4 pts.) Minor (½ - 2 pts.)	Max. Pts.	Pts. Lost	Net Score
SIGNAL EXERCISE (Release Honor Dog)	Handler adapting self to dog pace ☐ Unmanageable ☐ Unqualified heeling ☐ Any audible comm. ☐ Working dog goes to Honoring dog ☐ Dog leaves ring ☐ Failure on first signal to: Stand ☐ Stay ☐ Drop ☐ Sit ☐ Come ☐ Anticipated ☐	Sat out of reach ☐ Honoring dog barks or whines ☐	☐ . Forging .... Crowding handler ☐ ☐ . Lagging .... Sniffing ☐ ☐ No change of pace .... Fast ☐ .... Slow ☐ ☐ .... Heeling wide-on turns-abouts ☐ ☐ .... Extra signal to heel .... ☐ Sit .... ☐ ☐ .... Holding signals .... ☐ Slow response to signal to: ☐ ...... Stand .... Down .... Sit .... Come ...... ☐ ☐ No sit front finish .... Touching handler .... ☐ ☐ Lack of naturalness smoothness .... Sat between feet ☐ ☐ Poor sits ☐ .... Poor Finish ☐ ☐ . . Leaves ring between exercises	30		

The United Kennel Club Utility class Signal exercise

points. In both classes, Fido and Jack can lose minor points for crooked sits, poor finishes or poor heeling. Substantial points can be lost for poor heeling, no change of pace, extra signal to heel or holding the signals. The exercise is failed if Fido leaves the ring, fouls the ring, fails to respond to a signal or if Jack gives Fido a verbal command.

Practical Application

Many of the exercises that you are already using have signals associated with them. Fido already knows signals that mean sit, down, stand and stay. The signals for these commonly used commands simply ensure that Fido hears and/or sees the command. When used in this manner, the signal is double insurance. However, there are many instances (when Fido is out in public or in a noisy environment, for example) in which the ability to get and keep Fido's attention without having to give a verbal command is very handy.

Teaching the Exercise

Signals. You will be teaching Fido to respond to hand signals instead of the combination of verbal commands and signals that you are now using. Fido's attention to you is very important now. If he doesn't pay attention, he will not see a hand signal. Work on your

Anything you do with your hands or body can be considered a signal. Here Miles uses his hands and body language to encourage a puppy to follow him. (Australian Shepherd)

watch me command, even going back to Chapter Four and reviewing the basics.

If, at any time during the teaching of the signals, you lose Fido's attention, immediately do a training sequence of the watch me. Because the signal exercises require so much concentration, you may find that Fido will get tired or lose his concentration more quickly than he normally does. Keep the training sessions short and sweet, with lots of praise and rewards. Make sure the release at the completion of each training sequence is for one full minute—don't skimp. And last, mix up Fido's training to keep it exciting. For example, do a training sequence of watch me, then a training sequence of signals, followed up by a some retrieves and some heel work.

When you start giving Fido signal commands, you can exaggerate your signal and your movements, using body language or leaning or stretching to show Fido what you want. However, eventually and especially before competition, Fido will need to respond to a smooth, simple signal with no extra body language. Go ahead and exaggerate now because it helps Fido understand, but keep in mind the body language is for teaching only and will have to disappear.

The actual signals can be anything you wish them to be. Descriptions of signals are given in this chapter as guidelines. The signals used here are fairly common and you can see them used all over the country with minor variations. However, you don't have to use these particular motions.

Watch Me. The watch me signal is a quick upward movement from Fido's nose to your eyes. It is for attention purposes only, not for competition. As Fido gets better, the signal can decrease in size until it is just a slight movement between you and Fido.

The hand signal for the sit is an diagonal movement upwards finishing across the chest. (Basset Hound)

Bonnie uses her right hand to make a "Watch Me" signal. (Golden Retriever)

Step 1. With Fido in a sit in the heel position, have Fido's motivator in your right hand. Let Fido see or sniff his motivator with your hand close to his nose; tell him, "Fido, Watch me!" as you take the motivator toward your eyes. Praise him. Follow the training sequence and schedule.

Step 2. Practice Step 1 above, except DO NOT GIVE FIDO A VERBAL COMMAND. Use the motion of your right hand and the motivator to make Fido look at your face. Follow the training sequence and schedule.

Step 3. DURING YOUR HEEL WORK, GIVE FIDO THE WATCH ME SIGNAL. If Fido doesn't pay attention, snap the leash to get his attention and repeat the signal with a verbal command. If he does pay attention to the signal, verbally praise him. Follow the training sequence and schedule.

Sit Signal. Fido learned the sit signal used with a verbal command in Chapter Four. The signal is an upward movement of the arm, starting by your side and ending in a diagonal across your chest.

191

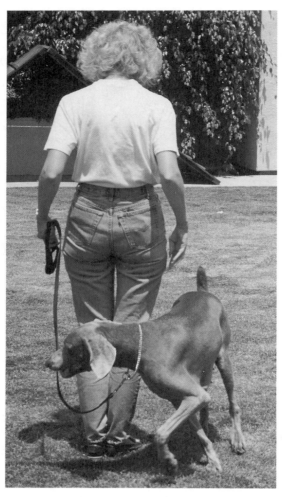

Since Wilma finishes to the right, Jane gives the finish signal with her right hand. (Weimaraner)

Paul gives Ursa a finish signal with her motivator (a treat) in the hand giving the signal. (Australian Shepherd)

Step 1. Let Fido have the freedom of his leash. Slowly step backwards a couple of steps so that Fido looks at you. Give him a verbal command, "Fido, sit," and at the same time give him the sit signal with his motivator in the hand that is giving the signal. Follow the training sequence and schedule.

Step 2. Practice Step 1 above, except DO NOT GIVE HIM A VERBAL COMMAND AS YOU SIGNAL. Continue to have his motivator in your hand as you signal, though. Follow the training sequence and schedule.

Step 3. Practice Step 2 above, except HAVE HIS MOTIVATOR IN YOUR POCKET INSTEAD OF IN YOUR HAND. Follow the training sequence and schedule.

Step 4. TELL FIDO TO STAND AND THEN STEP IN FRONT OF HIM. GIVE HIM A VERBAL COMMAND TO SIT AND AT THE SAME TIME, GIVE HIM A SIT SIGNAL WITH MOTIVATOR IN HAND. If he responds right away, praise him verbally. If he does not respond right away, repeat the signal, showing him his motivator, and if he needs help, use the leash in the other hand to shape him into a sit in front of you. Follow the training sequence and schedule.

Step 5. Practice Step 4 above USING A VERBAL COMMAND AND A SIGNAL, except PUT HIS MOTIVATOR IN YOUR POCKET AND GIVE THE SIGNAL WITH AN EMPTY HAND. Follow the training sequence and schedule.

Step 6. Practice Step 5 above, except HAVE HIS MOTIVATOR IN HAND AGAIN, AND USE ONLY A SIGNAL, NO VERBAL COMMAND. If he responds right away, praise him. If he does not react right away, repeat the signal with the motivator and at the same time, use the leash in your other hand to shape him into a sit. Follow the training sequence and schedule.

Step 7. Practice Step 6 above, except PUT HIS MOTIVATOR IN YOUR POCKET. Follow the training sequence and schedule.

Step 8. HAVE FIDO LIE DOWN, THEN STEP IN FRONT OF HIM. GIVE HIM A VERBAL COMMAND TO SIT AND AT THE SAME TIME GIVE HIM A SIT SIGNAL, WITH HIS MOTIVATOR IN YOUR HAND. If he sits up right away, praise him. If he doesn't, help him up with the leash. Follow the training sequence and schedule.

When Ken taught Chica to lay down by holding a food treat to the ground, that taught Chica to watch and follow his hand, and that movement became a hand signal meaning "Lay Down." (Poodle)

Step 9. Practice Step 8 above, except DO NOT GIVE A VERBAL COMMAND. Continue to use his motivator in the hand giving the signal. Follow the training sequence and schedule.

Step 10. Practice Step 9 above, except put his motivator in your pocket. Follow the training sequence and schedule.

Step 11. VARY THE POSITIONS. Have Fido do a down to a sit, a stand to a sit and a walk to a sit, all with signals with motivator in hand. Vary the order. Do six sits per step of the training sequence.

Stand Signal. In Chapter Ten, you taught Fido the stand command and the stand hand signal. The signal, a sweeping upward movement that ended in a stay hand signal in front of Fido's nose, was used with a verbal command.

Step 1. With Fido in a sit in the heel position, gather up the excess lead in your left hand. Have Fido's motivator, something you know he likes, in your right hand. Take one step forward, telling Fido, "Fido, heel," following that command with "Fido, stand" as you signal him to stand. The signal is with your right hand, moving across your body towards Fido in an arc coming up in front of Fido's nose, stopping as a stay signal. Watch Fido carefully and if he starts to sit, use your left hand to gently touch his flank, directly in front of the rear leg, to prevent him from sitting. Make him hold it for a count of five (One

Mississippi, two...) and then heel him forward again with praise. Give him his motivator. Follow the training sequence and schedule.

Training Sequence
One repetition of a training step, followed by praise.
Second repetition of the step, followed by praise.
Third repetition of the same step, folloowed by praise, a release and a reward.

Training Schedule.
1. Do each step a minimum of three training sequences.
2. If the third TS has no mistakes, go on to the next step.
3. If Fido is having problems, go back one step and repeat the TS at that level.
4. If Fido is still confused, go back several steps and work your way back up.

Step 2. Practice Step 1 above, except DELAY YOUR VERBAL COMMAND, giving it a second after the signal. Use the left hand in the flank as needed. Follow the training sequence and schedule.

Step 3. Practice as in Step 2 above, except ELIMINATE YOUR VERBAL COMMAND. If Fido starts to sit, use the left hand in the flank.

Step 4. PUT FIDO'S MOTIVATOR IN YOUR POCKET. Practice as in Step 3 above, except give the signal with an empty right hand. Follow the training sequence and schedule.

Step 5. With Fido in a sit in the heel position and his motivator in your pocket, DO SOME HEEL WORK WITH FIDO, INCORPORATING THE STAND SIGNAL. Heel and sit, right turn and sit, heel and stand with signal. Heel and about turn, heel and stand with signal. Vary your training so that Fido is paying attention and responding to your commands. Follow the training sequence and schedule.

Step 6. If Fido is reliably heeling off leash, PRACTICE STEP 5 ABOVE, OFF LEASH. Follow the training sequence and schedule.

Heel Signal. The heel signal is a forward sweeping motion of the left hand. Starting with the left hand at your waist in the normal position for heeling, take the hand down to your side and sweep forward from behind Fido's head, forward past the end of his nose. Then return the hand to your waist. It should be one smooth, continuous motion.

Step 1. With Fido in a sit in the heel position, on leash, gather up the excess leash so that there is very little slack in the leash. Tell Fido, "Fido, Watch me! Heel" as you give a signal with the left hand and leash and immediately begin walking forward. If Fido is lagging and not moving forward with you, gently snap the leash with your left hand as you return that hand to your waist. After a few steps, stop and sit Fido, praising him. If Fido is moving with you immediately as you give the command and signal, praise him verbally. Follow the training sequence and schedule.

Step 2. With Fido in a sit in the heel position, on leash, GIVE HIM THE WATCH ME SIGNAL AND THEN THE HEEL SIGNAL. If he doesn't respond immediately, give him a gentle snap of the leash and repeat the commands verbally. If he does respond right away, praise him verbally. Vary your heel work, keeping the heel portion short and sweet so that you and Fido don't get bored silly. Follow the training sequence and schedule.

Rachel uses an exaggerated signal combined with body language so that Sparky has a better understanding of what she wants him to do. (Dalmation)

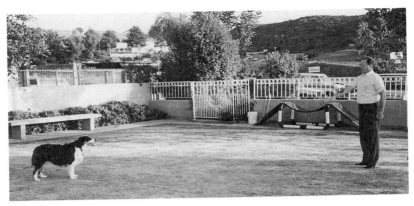

Paul signals Ursa to drop from a stand (top), to come up to sit from the down (center and bottom). (Australian Shepherd)

Step 3. With Fido in a sit in the heel position, OFF LEASH, repeat step 2 above, GIVING HIM A VERBAL CORRECTION INSTEAD OF A LEASH CORRECTION if he doesn't react right away to the signals. Follow the training sequence and schedule.

Finish. The finish command will be a sweeping movement from Fido's position in the sit in front, toward the direction that Fido finishes. If Fido does a right finish, going around you to come up in the heel position, your hand signal will be with the right hand, starting in front of you and moving toward your right side. If Fido finishes to your left, the signal will be with your left hand, moving toward your left. The signal should be one smooth, continuous motion.

Step 1. Review Fido's finish, using a verbal command only, making sure that he is moving quickly to the heel position. Follow the training sequence and schedule.

NOTE: Do Step 1 even if Fido already knows the finish. Use it as a review.

Step 2. With Fido in a sit in front, on leash, the leash held in the hand that will be giving the finish signal, give Fido a verbal command to finish and at the same time a signal with the hand holding the leash. If he moves toward the heel position, praise him verbally. If he doesn't, gently snap the leash as you move your hand. Follow the training sequence and schedule.

NOTE: If Fido is hesitant, hold his motivator in your hand with the leash and let him see it before giving him the signal.

Step 3. Practice as in Step 2 above, except DON'T GIVE FIDO A VERBAL COMMAND. Use the signal, with leash in hand, or leash and motivator in hand, only. Follow the training sequence and schedule.

Step 4. With Fido in a sit in front, OFF LEASH, practice as in Step 3 above. Follow the training sequence and schedule.

Step 5. With Fido ON LEASH, SIT HIM IN DIFFERENT PLACES IN FRONT OF YOU AND THEN SIGNAL HIM TO FINISH. Have him off to one side, then another. Sit him three feet away, then six inches. Follow the training sequence and schedule.

Come. The come signal is a very obvious signal. The right arm goes straight out to your side then moves forward in a wide sweeping movement, coming back to your chest and finishes in a sit signal.

Step 1. With Fido in a sit on leash, tell him, "Wait," and step out to the end of your six-foot leash. Tell him, "Fido, come! Good Boy!" as you back up and signal Fido to come. Let him catch up to you and sit him in front as you. Verbally praise him. Follow the training sequence and schedule.

Step 2. Practice Step 1 above, EXCEPT ELIMINATE THE VERBAL COMMAND. Continue to praise verbally if Fido responds right away to your backing away and the hand signal. Follow the training sequence and schedule.

Step 3. PUT FIDO ON A 20-FOOT LINE OR LONG LEASH. Have Fido sit, tell him, "Wait," and step about 10 feet away. Signal Fido to come as YOU VERBALLY CALL HIM, TOO. Do NOT back away from him. Follow the training sequence and schedule.

NOTE: The backing away from Fido is also a signal telling him to come or to follow you.

Step 4. Practice Step 3 above, except DO NOT USE A VERBAL COMMAND OR BACK AWAY. If Fido does not immediately move toward you, gently snap the leash, repeat the signal and use a verbal command. If he does move toward you on the first signal, praise him verbally. Follow the training sequence and schedule.

Step 5. Practice Step 4 above, EXCEPT USE THE ENTIRE LENGTH OF THE 20-FOOT LINE. Again, do not use a verbal command or back away when you give the come signal. However, if Fido does not immediately start towards you when you signal, signal again and back away quickly, snapping the long line as you do. DO NOT GIVE A VERBAL COMMAND.

Down Signal. The down signal is the same as the one you used in Chapter Four when you taught Fido to lay down using his motivator. Go back to Chapter Four and review that section.

Drop in Motion or Drop at a Distance Signal. The drop in motion or drop from a distance signal is a quick motion of the right arm. The arm should leave the side and go directly straight up in the air, then dropping back to the side. It is a very visible arm motion. The drop in motion or drop from a distance is different from a down in the heel position.

Step 1. Review the Drop in Motion in Chapter Seven. Make sure Fido is going down quickly when you give him the drop command.

Step 2. With Fido on leash, sitting in front of you, have his motivator in your right hand as you tell him, "Fido, drop," and give the drop signal. If he hesitates, step in to him and with your left hand, holding the leash, gently guide him to the ground. As soon as he lays down, praise him while he's still down, and then bring him back up to a sit and you give him his motivator. Repeat six times. Follow the training sequence and schedule.

Step 3. Repeat Step 2 above, except HAVE FIDO ABOUT SIX FEET AWAY when you give him the verbal command and signal. Don't allow him to crawl forward when you signal. If he crawls, step into him, put him back where he was when you signaled, and step away again. Repeat six times. Follow the training sequence and schedule.

Step 4. Repeat Step 3 above, except HAVE FIDO ON A LONG LINE AND STAND ABOUT 12 FEET AWAY when you give him a verbal command and signal. Follow the training sequence and schedule.

Step 5. With Fido on a long line, have him sit and tell him, "Fido, wait," and step about six feet away. DO NOT GIVE HIM A VERBAL COMMAND as you signal him to drop. If he does not immediately drop, step in to him and snap the leash lightly as you position him in the down. Do not give the verbal command now, either. Praise him verbally after he has dropped. Alternate between leaving him in a sit or in a stand. Follow the training sequence and schedule.

Step 6. With Fido in a sit in the heel position, tell him to wait and step in front of him. CALL HIM TO COME, verbally, and back up. After he's up and moving, signal him to drop and step in toward him, just a step or two, so that he goes directly down and doesn't try to crawl. Go back to him and praise him while he's down. Follow the training sequence and schedule.

Step 7. Repeat as in Step 6 above, except HAVE FIDO ON THE 20-FOOT LINE and go out to the end of the line before you call Fido. Follow the training sequence and schedule.

NOTE: Mix up some straight recalls with your drop on recall so that Fido doesn't assume that every come command or signal is going to result in a drop. If he becomes hesitant about the drop, go back to the very basic recalls, backing up and calling him with extra praise and rewards.

Step 8. Repeat as in Step 6 and 7 above, except VARY THE PLACE WHERE YOU DROP FIDO. Sometimes have him drop right after you call him, or half way across the yard or almost at your feet. Follow the training sequence and schedule.

Step 9. With Fido on a six-foot leash, stand him with a signal and step away from him. Signal him to drop and step back to him to praise him. Don't let him get up and then step away from him again. Signal him to sit. Verbally praise him. Then signal him to come. Back up if he comes in slowly. When he sits in front, signal him to finish. Give him a jackpot of praise! Super! Follow the training sequence and schedule.

Step 10. Repeat Step 9 above, except USE A 20-FOOT LINE and vary the order of exercises. Do a stand, sit, down, sit, come. Or do a stand, down, sit, down, come. Don't let Fido assume that A follows B follows C. You want him to think and to react to your commands. Follow the training sequence and schedule.

Are You Having Any Problems?

Fido should be comfortable with reacting to hand signals. You have been using them since the beginning of training. However, if he is having a hard time, hold his motivator in your hand as you signal. You might even want to use a motivator that makes noise, like a squeaky toy.

If he still doesn't seem to see the signals, or if he reacts to the signals on the six-foot leash but not the 20-foot line, Fido might have some vision problems. Talk to your veterinarian about Fido's vision.

Chapter Thirteen

The Jumping Exercises

It was the saying of Bion that though the boys throw stones at frogs in
sport, the frogs do not die in sport but in earnest.
Plutarch

The Exercise

The AKC Utility class Directed Jumping exercise demonstrates that Fido will run away from his owner, in the direction his owner sends him, will stop and turn when told, and will then jump as directed. This is a complicated exercise with many parts.

In the ring, it will be performed like this:

1. The judge will position Jane and Fido at one side of the ring, facing across the ring. The bar jump and solid high jump are both set up so that Jane is looking across the ring in between both jumps.

2. The judge explains, "This is the Directed Jumping exercise. Are you ready?" Jane looks at Fido and says, "Yes, we're ready."

3. The judge says, "Send your dog." Jane tells Fido, "Go away," and Fido runs away from Jane, across the ring, running between the jumps. When he reaches the other side of the ring, Jane calls out, "Fido, sit." Fido stops and turns toward Jane, sitting facing her, so that he has turned around from his direction of travel.

4. The judge says, "Bar jump." Jane gives Fido a hand signal, pointing her arm to the side in the direction of the bar jump as she tells Fido, "Fido, over!" Fido gets up from the sit and moves quickly to the bar jump, jumping it cleanly. He then comes to Jane who has pivoted in place toward the jump as Fido jumped. Fido sits in front. The judge says, "Finish," and Jane tells Fido to finish, as in the Novice recall exercises.

5. The judge then repeats the exercise, exactly as before, except that Fido is sent over the high jump instead of the bar.

EXERCISE	NON QUALIFYING ZERO		QUALIFYING SUBSTANTIAL MINOR	Maxiumum Points	Points Lost	NET SCORE
DIRECTED JUMPING	HIGH JUMP Does Not: Leave on order . . . . ☐ Stop on command . . . ☐ Jump as directed . . . ☐ Climbing jump . . . . . ☐ ☐ . Anticipated command ☐ . .Does not go at least 10' beyond jumps	BAR JUMP Does Not: Leave on order............☐ Stop on command ....☐ Jump as directed ....☐ Knocking bar off............☐ ....☐ ....☐	☐ . .Holding signals..................☐ ☐ . . .Slow response to directions.........☐ ☐ . .Slightly off direction...............☐ ☐ . . . .Not back far enough............☐ ☐ . . .Anticipated ☐ Turn ☐ Stop ☐ Sit ☐ . . .Does not sit on command ☐ . Hesitation or reluctance to jump.......☐ ☐ No sit in front Touched handler.....☐ ☐ Anticipate Finish Sat between feet.....☐ ☐ No finish Poor sits ....☐ Poor finishes.........☐ ☐ . . Handler error................☐	40		

The American Kennel Club Utility class Directed Jumping exercise

EXERCISE	NON-QUALIFYING		QUALIFYING (OVER 50%) Major (4 pts.) Minor (½ - 2 pts.)	Max. Pts.	Pts. Lost	Net Score
DIRECTED JUMPING	HIGH BAR JUMP JUMP ☐......☐....Does not leave on order ☐......☐....Does not go substantially in right direction ☐......☐....Does not stop on command ☐......☐....Does not jump as directed ☐......☐....Does not go at least 10' beyond jumps ☐......☐....Climbing Jump ☐......☐....Anticipated command ☐......☐....Knocking bar off ☐......☐....Dog leaves ring		☐..............Holding signals.............☐ ☐..............Slow response to directions.......☐ ☐..............Slightly off direction...........☐ ☐..............Not back far enough...........☐ ☐ . Anticipated ☐ Turn.....☐ Stop....☐ Sit ☐ Does not sit on command Poor sits... ☐ Lack of naturalness- Touches handler.... smoothness ☐ No sit in front Sat between feet.....☐ ☐ No finish Poor finishes.....☐ ☐..Leaves ring between exercises	40		

The United Kennel Club Utility class Directed Jumping exercise

A flawless AKC or UKC Utility Directed Jumping exercise is worth 40 points. Minor points can be lost for crooked sits in front after the jump or crooked sits on the finish. Points can be lost for a slow go away, for hesitation in jumping or for a minor touch of the jump during a jump.

Substantial points can be lost for a poor go away, for antici-pating the turn and sit or for a failure to sit on the go away. Fido will fail the exercise if he climbs over the jump, hits the jump or knocks the bar off. He will also fail if he anticipates the go out command, doesn't go out where directed, doesn't stop on command or anticipates the jump command.

In this exercise, Fido must wait until sent over the jump, must jump cleanly and return to the handler in a straight sit in front. He must then finish as in the Novice Recall exercise. Both the AKC and UKC Open class Broad Jump exercises are worth 20 points if performed perfectly. Minor points can be lost for a crooked sit in front after the jump, a poor finish or hesitation to jump. Substantial points can be lost for anticipating the finish, touching the jump, handler errors, no sit in front or no finish. Fido will fail the exercise if he re-

EXERCISE	NON-QUALIFYING		QUALIFYING (OVER 50%)		Max. Pts.	Pts. Lost	Net Score
	ZERO	LESS THAN 50%	Major (4 pts.)	Minor (½ - 2 pts.)			
BROAD JUMP	Does not jump on first command and/or signal .... ☐ Walks over any part .... ☐ Dog leaves ring .... ☐	Leaves before command and/or signal .... ☐ Does not clear Jump ...... ☐ Sits out of reach .... ☐	☐ . Poor return............................ ☐ ☐ ..No sit in front .... ☐ ☐ . No finish .... ☐ ☐ . Minor jump touch .... ☐ ☐ . Touching Handler .... ☐ ☐ . Sits between feet .... ☐ ☐ . Poor finish Poor Sit...☐ ☐ . Leaves ring between exercises		20		

The United Kennel Club Companion Dog Excellent class Broad Jump exercise

EXERCISE	NON QUALIFYING		QUALIFYING		Maximum Points	Points Lost	NET SCORE
	ZERO		SUBSTANTIAL	MINOR			
RETRIEVE OVER HIGH JUMP	Fails to go out on first command or signal................. ☐ Fails to jump going or returning .... ☐ Fails to retrieve .... ☐ Goes before command or signal .... ☐	Jumps only one direction............☐ Sat out of reach ....☐ Extra command Climbing jump............☐	☐ .Slow ..... ☐ Going.... ☐ Returning ☐ .Mouthing ... ☐ Dropping ☐ .Directly to dumbbell .. ☐ Poor Delivery ☐ .No sit .... Poor sit .... ☐ ☐ .Anticipate finish .... ☐ ☐ .Touches jump .... ☐ ☐ .Arms not at side .... ☐ ☐ .Pause, Hesitation or reluctance at jump .... ☐ ☐ .No finish ... ☐ Poor finish............. ☐ ☐ .Handler error........................... ☐ ☐ .Touched Handler .... ☐		30		

The American Kennel Club Open class Retrieve over the High Jump

EXERCISE	NON-QUALIFYING		QUALIFYING (OVER 50%)		Max. Pts.	Pts. Lost	Net Score
	ZERO	LESS THAN 50%	Major (4 pts.)	Minor (½ - 2 pts.)			
RETRIEVE OVER HIGH JUMP	Doesn't go out on first command and/or signal .... ☐ Doesn't jump going or returning .... ☐ Doesn't retrieve .... ☐ Dog leaves ring .... ☐	Leaves before command and/or signal .... ☐ Jumps in only one direction................ ☐ Sits out of reach .... ☐ Extra command and/or signal to retrieve .... ☐ Climbs Jump .... ☐	☐ . Mouthing or playing..................... ☐ ☐ . Slow . ☐ Going ☐ . Returning........... ☐ ☐ . Dropping dumbbell Touching Handler.. ☐ ☐ . Touching Jump Sits between feet.. ☐ ☐ . Poor delivery .... ☐ ☐ . Handler error .... ☐ ☐ . No sit in front Poor sit... ☐ ☐ . No finish Poor finish... ☐ ☐ . Leaves ring between exercises		30		

The United Kennel Club Companion Dog Excellent class Retrieve Over the High Jump

EXERCISE	NON QUALIFYING		QUALIFYING		Maximum Points	Points Lost	NET SCORE
	ZERO		SUBSTANTIAL	MINOR			
BROAD JUMP	Refuses to jump on first command or signal................. ☐	Goes before command or signal........... ☐ Does not clear jump........ ☐ Sat out of reach .... ☐	☐ Poor return Touching handler............... ☐ ☐ No sit in front Sat between feet............... ☐ ☐ Anticipate finish Poor sit .... ☐ ☐ No finish Poor finish............... ☐ ☐ Hesitation, Pause or Reluctance to jump............ ☐ ☐ Touches jump ☐ Arms not at side ☐ Handler error................ ☐		20		

The American Kennel Club Open class Broad Jump exercise

205

fuses to jump on the first command, anticipates the jump command or doesn't clear the jump.

This exercise is worth 30 points when performed flawlessly. Fido must wait while the dumbbell is being thrown, jump over the jump going to the dumbbell, pick up the dumbbell without playing with it and return over the jump while bringing the dumbbell back to the handler. The sit in front and finish are the same as in the Novice Recall.

Minor points are deducted for poor sits, crooked finishes or minor handler errors. Substantial points are lost for running slowly after the dumbbell instead of quickly. Substantial points can also be lost for touching the jump, for mouthing or dropping the dumbbell, and for anticipating the finish. Fido can fail the exercise if he climbs the jump, refuses to jump, refuses to retrieve, goes around the jump, anticipated the retrieve command or required a second command.

Practical Application

Teaching Fido to jump is a practical skill. When Fido understands a command that means "jump over" or "jump on" you can then have him jump in the car, out of the car, onto the groomer's table or the veterinarian's table. When you go for a walk, Fido can get some extra exercise and have fun by jumping benches or walls. When you go hiking or camping, you can help direct Fido with verbal commands.

Working dogs, search and rescue dogs, law enforcement dogs and customs dogs must all know how to jump and be able to do so on command and all must be able to combine it with a retrieve.

Teaching the Exercise

Retrieve. Review the retrieve in Chapter Eleven. Make sure Fido is comfortable and happy retrieving anything you send him after.

Identifying the Jumps. There are three different jumps that Fido will face in AKC and UKC competition. The high jump is a solid jump, made of wood with boards that can be added or removed to make different heights at variables of two inches. The jump is five feet wide and needs to make a maximum height of 36 inches and is painted flat white.

Each dog must jump one and a quarter his height at the shoulder, with a few exceptions. For example, if Fido is 20 inches tall at the shoulder, one and a quarter times his height is 25 inches. However, the jumps are set to the nearest increment of two inches, so Fido would jump 26 inches.

Several breeds have exceptions to the height ruling. The following breeds are to jump their height at the withers or 36 inches, whichever is less: Bloodhounds, Bernese Mountain Dogs, Bullmastiffs,

This is a solid, high jump, set at 24 inches tall.

Great Danes, Great Pyrenees, Greater Swiss Mountain Dogs, Mastiffs, Newfoundlands and St. Bernards. The following breeds will jump their height at the shoulder or eight inches, whichever is greater: Clumber Spaniels, Sussex Spaniels, Basset Hounds, Dachshunds, Cardigan and Pembroke Corgis, Australian Terriers, Cairn Terriers, Dandie Dinmont Terriers, Norfolk and Norwich Terriers, Scottish and Sealyham Terriers, Skye Terriers, West Highland White Terriers, Maltese, Pekingese, Bulldogs and French Bulldogs.

The bar jump consists of two upright poles that are self supporting and marked in increments of two inches, from eight inches off the ground to 36 inches. A five-foot-long pole, width two inches square, painted alternately black and white in three inch increments must be able to be set on the uprights at various heights. Holes drilled in the uprights to fit small dowels to use as supports are acceptable.

The height of the bar jump is the same as the high jump. If Fido jumps 20 inches over the high jump, he will have to jump 20 inches over the bar jump, too.

The Broad Jump is made of four hurdles, each of boards eight inches wide, painted white. The hurdles are made to telescope together for ease of handling and storage. The smallest board is about four feet six inches long and the largest board is five feet long. Each board is set at an angle so that the low end is toward the dog as he jumps. The smallest board is set at one inch on the low end to three inches on the high end. The largest board is four inches tall at the lowest end and six inches tall at the high end.

The number of boards used for each dog depends upon the distance the dog must jump. Each dog must jump a distance equal to twice the height of the high jump. If Fido must jump 20 inches on the high jump, then he will need to jump 40 inches over the broad jump. Four boards are used for distances of 48 inches to 72 inches. Three boards for 28 inches to 44 inches and two boards for 16 inches to 24 inches. The highest or largest hurdle is always removed first when adjusting the width of the jump.

Training Sequence

One repetition of a training step, followed by praise.
Second repetition of the step, followed by praise.
Third repetition of the same step, folloowed by praise, a release and a reward.

Training Schedule.

1. Do each step a minimum of three training sequences.
2. If the third TS has no mistakes, go on to the next step.
3. If Fido is having problems, go back one step and repeat the TS at that level.
4. If Fido is still confused, go back several steps and work your way back up.

Introducing Jumping. Contrary to public perception, many dogs do not know how to jump. Fido can jump enough to get through day-to-day routines, but unless he is faced with a situation that requires him to jump and to jump precisely, he never learns how to really jump. Jumping accurately and safely requires Fido to see an obstacle and judge what he is going to have to do to clear that obstacle. He needs to learn what to do with his body: his head, neck and shoulders, his front legs, back legs, his back and even his tail. And he needs to develop some muscles that he hasn't used before.

Step 1. Set up the high jump first. If Fido is normally active, set the height at his elbow level. If he is sedentary, set it at about half that height. Decide upon your jumping command and then with Fido on leash, start about 10 feet back from the jump and run toward it, telling Fido, "Fido, over!" Head Fido toward the center of the jump. If you are athletic, you can jump the jump with him or if you wish, go around the upright. After he jumps the jump, run Fido away from the jump in a straight line for a few feet, praising him verbally. If Fido is hesitant, as you run toward the jump, show him his motivator and toss it across

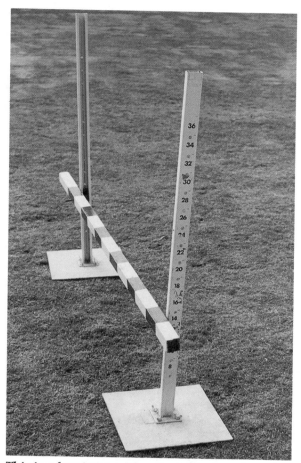

This is a bar jump with adjustable dowels so that the height can be set at two-inch increments.

This is the broad jump spaced here at 40 inches, which is the proper width for a dog that jumps a 20-inch-high jump.

When Fido is comfortable jumping the bar jump with the high jump, set up the bar jump alone but lower the height so Fido will jump it easily and not try to duck under it. (Australian Shepherd)

the jump ahead of him, encouraging him to jump and chase it. Follow the training sequence and schedule.

NOTE: Never yank the dog over the jump or swing him over by the leash and collar. Never give the leash a jerk or pull once the dog has started moving. A correction or yank given as the dog is moving will spoil his concentration, can cause him to hit the jump or land improperly and can cause him to hurt himself.

Step 2. Practice just as you did in Step 1, except LEAVE FIDO IN A SIT/WAIT ABOUT 10 FEET IN FRONT OF THE JUMP. Stand at the end of the leash, toward the jump, but to the side, out of Fido's path. When you give Fido the command to jump, run towards the jump but let Fido pass you. Follow up as in Step 1. ALWAYS praise Fido for his jump. Follow the training sequence and schedule.

Step 3. Practice as you did in Step 2, except TAKE OFF FIDO'S LEASH. If he hesitates or even looks as if he wants to go around the jump, toss his motivator over the jump ahead of him. Follow the training sequence and schedule.

Step 4. SET THE BAR JUMP IN FRONT OF THE HIGH JUMP, about

The bar jump is set at Ursa's elbow height and the high jump at half that. This teaches her to jump the bar without allowing her to crawl under it. (Australian Shepherd)

211

six inches in front, with the bar set about two inches lower than the high jump. Practice ON LEASH as you did in Step 2. Follow the training sequence and schedule.

NOTE: If Fido tries to go around a jump, don't yell "No!" at him. That will only serve to teach him to be wary of the jumps and jumping and could cause to stop all voluntary jumping. Instead, stop all positive reinforcement (including praise) and take him back to the jump and have him jump it. Put him on the leash if you need to but don't overload him with corrections. Show him what you want him to do.

Step 5. REVERSE THE JUMPS, setting the bar jump behind the high jump, adjusting the height so that the bar jump is about two inches higher than the high jump. Practice on leash as you did in Step 2. Follow the training sequence and schedule.

Step 6. ADJUST THE TWO JUMPS SO THAT THE HIGH JUMP IS ONLY HALF THE HEIGHT OF THE BAR JUMP. For example, the high jump is eight inches tall and the bar jump is 16 inches tall. The highest of the jumps should still be no higher than the dog's elbow. Practice as in Step 2. Follow the training sequence and schedule.

Step 7. MOVE THE TWO JUMPS APART so that there is a minimum of three of the dog's body lengths between the high jump and the bar jump. Make sure the jumps are in a straight line so that the dog can run them one after the other. Practice on leash. Follow the training sequence and schedule.

NOTE: If you have any additional jumps, or anything that can be used as a jump, add them now. Make a line of a high jump, bar jump, propped up board, picnic bench on its side or an agility jump. Just make sure that the jump is secure, that Fido can't hurt himself on it and that you introduce him to it as a jump.

Step 8. REMOVE FIDO'S LEASH and practice running the line of jumps. Vary the distance between jumps so that Fido learns to judge his landings and take-offs. Follow the training sequence and schedule.

Step 9. REMOVE THE EXTRA JUMPS, KEEPING OUT ONLY THE HIGH JUMP. Set up two boards of the broad jump, one in front of the high jump, one after. Practice on leash, as in Step 2, doing a sit/wait/over. Follow the training sequence and schedule.

A series of jumps that Fido can jump freely will help teach him how to judge his take-offs and landings and how to pace himsself between jumps. (Australian Shepherd)

Teach Fido to jump anything you direct him towards, such as these two homemade jumps. (Australian Shepherd)

Directed Jumping, Step 1. Position Fido behind the high jump and centered. (Australian Shepherd)

Directed Jumping, Step 8. Position Fido slightly toward the center of the training area so he isn't centered on the jump. (Australian Shepherd)

Step 10. LOWER THE HIGH JUMP TO TWO-THIRDS THE HEIGHT AT FIDO'S ELBOW. Add one more broad jump board, placing it to the front of the high jump. Practice on leash, as in Step 9. Follow the training sequence and schedule.

Step 11. REMOVE FIDO'S LEASH and practice as in Step 10 above. Follow the training sequence and schedule.

NOTE: Very gradually increase the height of the high jump and bar jumps and the width of the broad jump. Fido's physical fitness and normal activity level can help you decide how slow or fast to increase the height and width. If Fido is normally very active and jumps to catch Frisbees, chases rabbits and swims daily, you will be able to work up to full height fairly quickly. However, if Fido is not as active, take your time to build up those muscles. No athlete, canine or human, enjoys sore muscles.

Teaching the Individual Jumps

High Jump and Bar Jump. Fido will need to be able to jump the high jumps in both the AKC open and utility classes and the UKC novice, open and utility classes. Fido will need to be able to jump it coming to you on a recall, going away from you after a dumbbell,

215

Paul is still using exaggerated body language to direct Ursa to the jumps. (Australian Shepherd)

Directed Jumping, Step 15. Fido is positioned as he would be in competition. (Australian Shepherd)

A PVC jump set at Fido's elbow height, situated between two boards of the high jump will help teach Fido to jump high and not walk across the jump. Another PVC jump set at right angles will help Fido make a U-turn to sit straight in front of you and not take a short cut across the jump. (Australian Shepherd)

bringing the dumbbell back and coming to you after a directional command to jump.

Step 1. After completing the 11 jumping training steps above, set up a high jump at elbow height. Refresh Fido's skills by running him over the jump a few times on leash and a few times off leash, with you running toward the jump with him. When he's jumping eagerly, have him sit/wait about 10 feet in front of the jump, off leash. Walk around the jump and standing in the center behind the jump, touch the center of the jump with your hand, say, "Fido, Come! Over!" Praise him as he jumps and then back up about eight to ten feet. When Fido catches up with you, stop and have him sit in front of you. Follow the training sequence and schedule.

Step 2. Repeat step 1 above, except STAND ABOUT FOUR FEET BEHIND THE JUMP WHEN YOU CALL FIDO. Follow the training sequence and schedule.

Step 3. Repeat Step 2 above, except STAND 10 FEET BEHIND THE JUMP, still centered. Follow the training sequence and schedule.

Step 4. STAND ABOUT TWO FEET BEHIND THE JUMP, SLIGHTLY OFF CENTERED TO THE LEFT. Tell Fido, "Fido, Over," and at the same time, stick your right arm straight out, pointing to the right. If Fido doesn't immediately move, swing your right arm toward the center of the jump but bring it back out in the directional signal right away. Praise Fido. Follow the training sequence and schedule.

Step 5. SET UP THE BAR JUMP ABOUT 10 FEET AWAY FROM THE HIGH JUMP, side by side about 10 feet away, evenly spaced in your training area. Continue Step 4 above, working from both the left side and the right side, using the opposite hand to signal. Ignore the bar jump. Follow the training sequence and schedule.

NOTE: Don't forget your verbal praise!

Step 6. Stand about 10 feet back from the high jump, and off to the left side far enough that Fido can see you without looking over the jump. He sees you to the side of the jump. As you give the jump command and the directional signal with your right arm, lean to the right, exaggerating the direction. If Fido starts to go around, run up to the jump and encourage him over. Follow the training sequence and schedule.

Step 7. Practice Step 6 above, except ALTERNATE BETWEEN STANDING TO THE LEFT AND RIGHT SIDES OF THE JUMP and giving signals to the left or right. Follow the training sequence and schedule.

Step 8. When you position Fido on the sit/wait, instead of placing him in the center of the jump, position him to one side, the side that you will be moving toward. If he tries to come straight to you instead of over the jump, intercept him and guide him back to the jump. Follow the training sequence and schedule.

Step 9. Practice Steps 1 through 8 above, except over the BAR JUMP. Follow the training sequences and schedules for each step.

Step 10. Set up the bar jump and high jump, end to end, about 10 feet apart. Have both jumps set at elbow height. Position Fido slightly

The broad jump with PVC aids from Fido's perspective. (Australian Shepherd)

Go Out, Turn and Sit. Set up ring ropes or ring gates so that Fido learns that he can run toward them. Have him turn and sit after he reaches the barrier. (All American)

off center, closer to the jump that you will be sending him over, about 10 feet back from the jump. Position yourself about 10 feet back on the opposite side of the jumps, again slightly off center toward the jump that you will be sending Fido over. Send Fido over the jump, giving a verbal command, "Fido, over," and an arm signal straight out from your side, with your arm horizontal and pointing toward the jump. At the same time, use lots of body language (leaning and stepping toward the jump) so that you are giving Fido plenty of help understanding what you where you want him to go. If Fido moves to the jump, stand back upright and turn to face Fido as he jumps. Call him into sit in front. Praise him. Follow the training sequence and schedule. If Fido doesn't start moving toward the jump right away, move toward the jump, going as far as to touch the top board, then again, back up as he moves. If Fido tries to come directly to you, interrupt his forward motion, verbally, and try to direct him toward the jump.

Step 11. Practice Step 10 above, except PRACTICE IT FROM BOTH SIDES OF THE JUMPS. Have the high jump on the right and then on the left. Follow the training sequence and schedule.

Step 12. Practice Step 11 above, except DECREASE THE BODY LANGUAGE AND STEP TOWARD THE JUMP. Follow the training sequence and schedule.

Step 13. POSITION FIDO ABOUT 10 FEET BACK FROM THE JUMPS BUT CENTERED, an equal distance from both jumps. Keep your position slightly off center, toward the jump to be jumped. Follow the training sequence and schedule.

Step 14. POSITION YOURSELF ABOUT 10 FEET BACK FROM THE JUMPS, CENTERED BETWEEN THEM, OPPOSITE FIDO. Lean into your signal. Follow the training sequence and schedule.

Step 15. DECREASE YOUR BODY LANGUAGE, ELIMINATE THE LEAN AS YOU SIGNAL. Practice sending Fido both directions with the jumps on either side. Follow the training sequence and schedule.

Broad Jump

Step 1. Set up the bar jump, at elbow height, and put one broad jump board in front of it and one behind. (If you have a very small dog, set up one board in front of the bar.) Leave Fido at a sit/wait about 10 feet in front of the jump and then run him toward and over the jump. Let him pass you as he jumps and call him to you, shaping him into a sit in front. Follow the training sequence and schedule.

Step 2. Leave Fido in a sit/wait and then STAND JUST IN FRONT AND TO THE RIGHT SIDE OF THE JUMP. Send Fido over the jump as you take a couple of steps toward the right side. Again, let Fido pass you as he goes over the jump. Encourage him back to a sit in front. Follow the training sequence and schedule.

Step 3. Determine what distance Fido is going to need to jump and if necessary, ADD ANOTHER BOARD. Repeat Step 2 above. Follow the training sequence and schedule.

Step 4. With the jump set up as above, with bar jump and two or three broad jump boards, leave Fido at a sit/wait 10 feet in front of the jump. STAND TWO FEET TO THE RIGHT of the jump, facing the jump with your left side toward Fido. Send him over the jump, stepping to your right as you do to encourage his movement. As he just, step back into position, pivoting so that you are facing the back of the jump, your left side toward the jump. Smile at Fido as he lands and looks at you. En-

221

221

courage him into a sit in front. Follow the training sequence and schedule.

Step 5. Practice as in Step 4 above, except ADD ANOTHER BOARD IF NEEDED. Follow the training sequence and schedule.

Step 6. REMOVE THE BAR AND LEFT UPRIGHT. Keep the upright closest to you. Practice as in Step 4 above. Follow the training sequence and schedule.

Step 7. POSITION THE RIGHT UPRIGHT BEHIND THE LAST BOARD. Practice as in Step 6 above. Follow the training sequence and schedule.

Teaching the Go Out

In the Go Out portion of the Directed Jumping exercise and the UKC Directed Signal retrieve exercise, Fido must run directly away from the owner, in a straight line, until told to stop and sit. When he is called, he must turn around and face the handler and sit waiting for direction to either jump or retrieve.

Train the turn and sit and the go out as two different exercises. Combine them only when Fido knows them both and is not making any mistakes.

Turn and Sit

Step 1. With Fido on a loose leash, allow him to get up and move around. Back up a step or two and tell him, "Fido, sit." When you say his name, jiggle the leash so that he looks at you. If he sits immediately, praise him. If he does not sit immediately, step in and help him sit. Follow the training sequence and schedule.

NOTE: If Fido's favorite motivator is a squeaky toy, use that to get him to look at you.

Step 2. Repeat Step 1 above, except HAVE FIDO ON A 20-FOOT LINE. Don't allow him to move forward when you tell him to sit. He should turn towards you but sit immediately. Tell him, "OK," and let him get up again. Follow the training sequence and schedule.

Step 3. With Fido moving freely on a long line, toss a toy ahead of him (without any commands) and let him run towards it. Before he gets to the toy, tell him, "Fido, sit." If he continues toward the toy, use the long line as a brake. Praise him when he sits. Tell him, "OK," and let him get up. Follow the training sequence and schedule.

Teaching the Go Out

Step 1. With Fido in a sit-in-the-heel position, let Fido smell a treat (his motivator or another treat) and then walk away from him, to a spot about 30 feet away. Put the treat on the ground in a very obvious manner, calling Fido's attention to it. Go back to Fido and send him to the treat, telling him, "Fido, go out!" Run with him to the treat, pointing it out to him if you need to do so. Praise him. Follow the training sequence and schedule.

Step 2. Repeat Step 1 above, except LET FIDO RUN AHEAD OF YOU. Run with him but let him pull ahead. Don't point out the treat unless you have to, if he can't find it. Follow the training sequence and schedule.

Step 3. Repeat Step 2, except SET UP A RING ROPE, RING GATE OR STANCHION THAT FIDO CAN USE AS A VISUAL GUIDE. Put the treat JUST BEYOND the visual guide. Fido should still be on the long line. Send Fido with the go out command, and follow behind him. Praise him for going to or under the ring ropes. Follow the training sequence and schedule.

Step 4. Repeat Step 3, except DO NOT FOLLOW FIDO. Follow the training sequence and schedule.

Step 5. Repeat Step 4 above, except do it in different locations with different backgrounds. Keep the long line on him and run with him only if you need to. Teach Fido that go out means run directly away from you regardless of the location.

Retrieving over the Jumps

Review the retrieve in Chapter Eleven. When Fido is jumping happily and eagerly, add a play retrieve to the jumps, tossing a ball, dummy or squeaky toy over the jumps and sending Fido after them. Keep it upbeat and fun.

When Fido is comfortable with both the jumping and retrieving, and the combination of both, then review the instructions in Chapter Eleven for retrieving over the jumps.

Are You Having Any Problems?

If Fido is reluctant to jump, get him to your veterinarian for a thorough physical. Many physical problems can cause discomfort jumping, including hip or elbow dysplasia, vision problems, back or joint injuries, foot problems, long toe nails or a variety of other things. Don't assume that it's something to do with training until you have ruled out a physical problem.

If Fido is sound physically and is still reluctant to jump, get down on your knees and look at the jump from Fido's perspective. Is the grass too tall? Can he see to take off? Can he see where he's landing? Is there a gully or dip where he has to take off? Is the grass wet? Is he sliding? You want to build Fido's confidence in you and in himself, so help him, don't hurt him.

Some dogs have fun jumping from the first day they are introduced to it. Other dogs are worried or afraid or look upon jumping as work. After all, why should Fido have to put forth the effort to jump when it's so easy to go around? It's up to you to show Fido that jumping can be fun and results in lots of praise and a chance to play. Teach him also, though, that he does have to jump when you ask him to do so.

Don't be afraid to review training steps. If Fido is having a problem taking directions, take it slow and go over the steps again. Make sure he understands before you go on.

Ursa is almost up to her full jumping height of 26 inches, but she still needs work on carrying the dumbbell properly. (Australian Shepherd)

PART III. MORE INFORMATION

Most dog obedience instructors teach classes because they love dogs and want to make a difference in dogs' lives.

Chapter Fourteen

For Instructors: Teaching an Effective Class

I may disapprove of what you have to say but I will defend to the death
your right to say it.
S. G. Talentyre

Why do People go to an Obedience Class?

The majority of people who attend obedience classes do so because they are having a problem (or two) with their dogs. The dogs are jumping on people, digging up backyards, chewing on sprinkler systems or furniture or barking too much. The dogs probably drag them down the street when they go out for a walk and may not even be housetrained.

The class that teaches only the basic commands, heel, sit, down, stay and come, without addressing the problem behavior is failing the student. The student leaves class unhappy, the trainer will not get any word-of-mouth referrals and the dog may end up at a Humane Society facility because of the unresolved problem behavior.

Every student in class needs to know how these basic commands can help him, individually. How does the sit in front help a jumping-on-people problem? When the student learns how the commands can be used in his day-to-day routine and how they can affect Fido's behavior at home, he will have more motivation to use them and as a result, your class will be a success.

The common behavior problems need to be discussed during class, too. It only takes 15 to 20 minutes during one training class to talk about why dogs get into trouble, how problems can be prevented and how the dog can be taught not to get into any more trouble. The time spent will be well worth it.

Teacher or Trainer?

In many dog training clubs and schools, it has been the tendency to take the person who has won a number of obedience titles and make that person the class instructor. Unfortunately, that person may be a very good dog trainer but that has absolutely no bearing on whether or not that person is a good teacher.

A trainer is someone who can train dogs. A trainer can communicate with dogs, knows how to change their behavior and how to teach dogs. A teacher is someone who can teach people. A teacher

227

knows how to get peoples' interest, how to keep a class interesting and the students motivated. Most of all, a teacher knows how to communicate with people effectively. An obedience class instructor must think of herself as a teacher first and a dog trainer second.

Teaching

The essence of teaching is communication. A teacher must be able to impart knowledge to a student. Imparting that knowledge requires more than simply telling or lecturing. Students who attend lectures have a tendency to become dazed and although some of the information may register, a great deal of material is usually lost.

The average adult retains only about 10 percent of what he hears in a straight lecture situation. If the teacher adds visual demonstrations, that retention increases to about 20 percent. If there is reading material or handouts that can be looked at later, the retention will be greatly increased—provided the student actually looks at the material.

Retention increases with practice. While it is impossible to force students to practice their new skills at home, a teacher can make sure they practice in class. By watching them try out their new skills, the teacher can make sure the student is working properly and that Fido is responding as he should.

If an obedience instructor uses a well-trained demonstration dog, the retention is increased significantly because the visual impact of a well-trained dog is very strong. If the instructor goes back and forth between demonstrating with an untrained class dog and a well-trained demonstration dog, the retention will be about as high as it can get, considering the other factors mentioned. However, the untrained dog must be successful in the exercise being demonstrated so the instructor must choose the dog to be used wisely.

Teachers fail for a number of reasons. First of all, the teacher must be able to tailor the approach to the subject depending upon the class. Students in a first-week beginners' class have absolutely no knowledge of what a "High in Trial" award is, so if the instructor tells them that Fido must sit straight so that he can eventually earn a High in Trial, the instructor has lost every student in class. First-week students want to know how these things can help them now and that is how the instructor should tailor the approach.

Some teachers use negative reinforcement to try to teach. They embarrass their students, demean them or compare one student with another. Some teachers use group punishment to try to motivate the class. A few teachers yell and scream while others simply bore the class to tears.

A teacher is failing when class attrition is high. Nationally, the attrition rate for dog obedience classes is close to 50 percent. That is totally unacceptable. Every teacher's goal should be a zero attrition rate; however a rate that stays between 5 and 10 percent is perfectly acceptable.

A Better Way

Nature teaches with negative reinforcement. A bee sting teaches us to avoid those pretty little insects. A snake bite makes us move away from even the suggestion of a snake and a reaction to poison ivy teaches us to be more observant.

However, nature also teaches with positive reinforcement. The smell of a beautiful flower rewards us for paying attention. The taste of a bright red strawberry, the sight of an inviting green meadow and the smell of pine trees are all rewards for enjoying nature.

A good teacher can use positive reinforcement to create her students' success. The subject matter must be broken down into small learning steps, as we have done throughout this book, and each of those steps can and should be rewarded. The reward can be verbal praise in front of the class, "Good job. I can tell you practiced this week." Or the reward can be a small prize: a gold star, a dog training book or a coupon for an ice cream. (Yes, it works on adults as well as children!)

A good teacher works to keep the class motivated. The positive reinforcement will help but sometimes more than just that is needed. Covering the subject matter that the students need is important to motivation and many times a particular class may need a variation of the normal lesson plan. However, much of the motivation comes directly from the teacher. Enthusiasm is contagious!

Teachers must also be patient. That question your student is asking you may have been asked four hundred times before, but answer it as if it were being asked for the first time. The answer is just as important to this student as it was to the first person who asked it.

Teachers must also be aware of the student with learning disabilities. Not everyone learns at the same rate and the slower students have a right to attend class, too. Be patient and give them as much help as you can without patronizing them.

Don't be afraid to have a sense of humor—not a dry, biting wit but a warm, funny chuckle type sense of humor. People can learn better when they are relaxed and nothing relaxes better than a good laugh.

When a Student Needs Help

Helping people can often be very difficult. Some people take offense very easily when it might be insinuated they are doing something wrong. Other people have such fragile egos that any critique at all is too much. Some people are always sure they are right, even though they are attending your class where you are the expert. People are so varied and diverse that helping them becomes a study in human nature.

When you see a student who is having problems, go up to him or her and preface your suggestion with a bit of praise: "Mrs. Smith, you are praising Muffy well, but I think we can get better results if your timing is a little better. Let's try this...." By using this approach, Mrs. Smith's ego isn't damaged and she doesn't feel threatened. You have told her that her praise is good and you have given her some suggestions for improving her training. Painless! And very effective.

"John, you are doing a good job of shaping Tigger into a sit and your voice is good. But I think it will be a little easier if Tigger is paying more attention to you. Let's work on the watch me some more and see if that helps."

Always explain why you want the student to do something, understanding the how's and why's makes learning easy. Praise the students' little successes, offer constructive help instead of critiques and praise their persistence.

The Demonstration Dog

I have had several dogs that were excellent demo dogs. Each dog was very different from the others but they were each very effective in their own way. Michi was an imposing dog. A 90-pound, black and red German Shepherd Dog, Michi was a marshmallow at heart. He would happily ignore rowdy, first week students and heel, sit, down and stay. And he did it over and over and over again, for many years. He was so impressive that people would ask about him years later.

We, as a species, respond very well to visual stimuli. What we see is much more important to us than what we hear. A teacher may explain something, but if we can hear it and also see it, we will retain and understand that information much better.

Explaining the heel position to someone whose dog pulls him down the street is hard. That student will have a difficult time visualizing what the heel is. A good demo dog will allow you to demonstrate so that the student can have a picture in his mind of what the exercise looks like.

The demo dog must be well socialized to both people and other dogs. He must ignore challenges from students' dogs and he must be able to accept handling from strangers. He must be clean and neat at all classes.

Most of all, the demo dog must have presence. When you are

demonstrating with him, all eyes must be glued to you and your dog. Michi had that presence.

Goals of a Training Program

Your first goal as an obedience class instructor should be to provide a means of educating the dog owner so that he or she has a well-controlled, well-mannered companion. You should provide that education in a manner that the dog owner can accept. If your training methods are unusually harsh, or off the wall, or don't fill the needs of the dog owner, or your teaching skills are ineffective, you will be failing as a teacher.

You should also provide opportunities for the dog owner who wishes to go on to advanced training. If you don't offer advanced training, be prepared to refer your students to someone who does. Explain to your students what is available and what these things are. A beginner doesn't know what utility means, so explain it.

Looking at the Long View

Most people that teach obedience classes do so because they love dogs and want to share that joy. Most teachers get a thrill out of watching their students learn, grow and progress. But many teachers also want to make a difference in the world, in dogs' lives. Many unfortunate dogs live short, cruel lives often due to the negligence of uncaring or uneducated owners.

Dog training creates its own legacy. The parents that we see in class now will treat their dog differently after class is over. We hope to have instilled in them a knowledge of what their dog is, why he does what he does and what their responsibilities are to this animal. Later, their children will be raised in a household in which the dog is respected as a member of the family and is treated as such. And it is our greatest hope that those children will continue the legacy.

This nine-week-old puppy is learning to trust his owner, to coordinate his legs and to navigate an agility obstacle too! (Australian Shepherd)

Chapter Fifteen

There's More You and Fido Can Do

When the dog was created, it licked the hand of God and God stroked its head, saying What do you want, dog? *It replied,* My Lord, I want to stay with you, in heaven, on a mat in front of the gate...

Marie Neal

The More You Do

If you enjoy training your dog, there are a number of other activities that you can take part in. Some require some training; a few require extensive training. Others are strictly for fun and a few are to demonstrate the dog's natural instincts. Look over the list and decide which activities might suit you and your dog. Then contact the organization listed and find out if there is a local club that might be having a meeting soon or hosting an event. Go meet some of the people and see what's going on with the group. If it looks interesting to you, join. And have fun!

Agility

Agility is an active sport that is a combination of grand prix jumping (like that for horses), a kid's playground and a military obstacle course. Dogs must run a specified course, jumping jumps of different sizes and shapes, crawling through tunnels, climbing obstacles and at the same time, race the clock.

Agility competition requires a physically fit dog and handler and good, reliable off-lead control of the dog. All sizes of dogs may participate in agility although the naturally athletic dog has an advantage.

Agility can also be enjoyed without competition. Many obedience classes include agility because it has a number of benefits to the dog and the dog/owner relationship. Agility helps build body awareness in young dogs, and it helps the dog develop confidence in himself and his abilities and also builds trust in his owner.

For more information, look for: *Enjoying Dog Agility,* by Julie Daniels, 1991, Doral Publishing, 2619 Industrial Street NW, Portland OR 97210.

Or write to:

National Committee for Dog Agility, 401 Bluemont

Gracie navigates the teeter-totter obstacle in an agility class.
(Basset Hound)

Circle, Manhattan, KS 66502.

U. S. Dog Agility Assoc., Inc., PO Box 850955, Richardson, TX 75085-0955.

Carting

Carting is a practical skill and can also be a competitive sport. Many dog owners teach their medium-, large- and giant-size dogs to pull a wagon because it can be tremendously useful. Several national breed clubs have capitalized on those skills and instituted a carting program.

Write:

Collie Carting Program, PO Box 1379, Saratoga Springs, NY 12866.

Newfoundland Club of America, 6765 West Platz Rd, RD 1, Fairview, PA 16415.

Conformation Competition

Conformation competition or, as it is commonly known, breed showing was originally designed to pick from a group of dogs the dog that most closely demonstrated the written standard for the breed. The standard describes, in great detail, exactly how that particular breed should look. The standard details the coat, color, head shape, tail, gait, expression and much, much more. The breed standard is what ensures that a Greyhound will continue to look like a Greyhound and not a Rottweiler.

By selecting these dogs, in competition with the other dogs entered and against the judge's vision of the *perfect* dog of that breed, the dog owners and breeders can continue to improve the breed. Ideally, only the best dogs, of proper breed type, sound physical conformation and good temperament would be bred.

The American Kennel Club provides the largest governing body for conformation dog shows in the United States. Shows are held all over the country every weekend of the year, somewhere.

Write:

AKC, 51 Madison Ave., New York, New York, 10010.

The United Kennel Club is the country's second oldest and

Conformation competition can be very challenging and very exciting. Chocho finishes his Championship. (Papillon)

largest registry for purebred dogs. The UKC emphasizes the working qualities of various breeds, but it also sponsors conformation shows.

Write:

UKC, 100 East Kilgore Rd., Kalamazoo, MI 49001.

The States Kennel Club, Rare Breed Club of America, Australian Shepherd Club of America and a number of other smaller registries and rare-breed clubs all sponsor, support or govern conformation shows. A list of those registries and others like them may be found in the book, *Everything You Always Wanted to Know About Dogs,* by Susan Bulanda, Doral Publishing, 2619 Industrial St. NW, Portland OR 97210.

Field Trials

A variety of different types of field trials are available for the different sporting dog breeds. Both the AKC and UKC have field trial programs. The AKC has programs for: Basset Hounds, Beagles, Dachshunds, pointing breeds, retrieving breeds and spaniels. The UKC publishes a magazine called *Hunting Retriever.* The UKC also has a program for Coonhounds and publishes the magazine, *Coonhound Bloodlines*.

For additional information, contact both the AKC and the UKC, addresses above.

Flyball

Flyball is a team relay sport. Each team consists of four dog/owner teams. The dogs, one at a time, in a relay format, run a series of four hurdles and step on the lever of a box that tosses a tennis ball. When the ball is thrown, the dog much catch the ball and then run the series of jumps back to the owner. The team that finishes first, wins.

Write:

North American Flyball Assoc., 1342 Jeff St., Ypsilanti, MI 48198.

Frisbee

It's amazing to think that flying discs, or Frisbees, were not originally invented for dogs. Frisbee competition was begun when Ashley Whippet's owner invaded a nationally televised baseball game in New York and began throwing Frisbees for his talented Whippet. Ashley Whippet was lost in New York for several days while his owner languished in jail, but the two were reunited and a new sport was born.

Write:

Even if you don't own sheep, herding can be an interesting sport for dogs with herding instincts. (Australian Shepherd)

Flyball is an enjoyable sport for dogs that love tennis balls. (Australian Shepherd)

Friskies Ashley Whippet Frisbee Championships, PO
Box 725, Encino, CA 91426.

Gaines Flying Disc Booklet, *Teach Your Dog to Catch
a Flying Disc*, PO Box 8177, Kankakee, IL 60902.

Herding

One of the oldest jobs that dogs can do for man is herding.
The herding instinct is very strong, strong enough so that dogs will
herd children, the family cats and will run circles around their owners if given half a chance. The stories abound about dogs raised in the
city, never seeing livestock and then arriving at a herding instinct test
and passing in their first introduction to stock.

Write:

American Herding Breed Assoc., 1548 Victoria Way,
Pacifica, CA 94044.

The AKC also has a herding program, as does the Australian
Shepherd Club of America. Most states have individual clubs, both for
specific breeds and for all herding breeds.

Check with your local breed club or see the list in *Everything
You Always Wanted to Know About Dogs*.

Lure Coursing

Lure coursing is another sport based on instinct. Sighthounds

*One of Jupiter's best motivators is a Frisbee.
(Golden Retriever)*

Tracking is a fun activity to pursue, as well as a needed skill for working or search and rescue dogs, and tracking titles are available. (German Shepherd Dog)

chasing an artificial lure are a beautiful sight to see. These are the fastest dogs on earth who seem to fly above the ground effortlessly.

Write:

The American Sighthound Field Assoc., PO Box 1293-M, Woodstock, GA 30188.

Scent Hurdles

Scent hurdles is another team sport very similar to Flyball, except that after running the hurdles, the dog must find his owners pre-scented dumbbell from a group of other dumbbells.

Many local training clubs sponsor teams.

Schutzhund

Schutzhund originated in Germany as a means of testing and preserving the working instincts of dogs. It combines protection work with obedience and tracking, with additional tests for endurance, traffic safe dogs, drafting, companion dogs and watch dogs. The Canadian Kennel Club recognizes Schutzhund titles although the AKC does not.

Write:

Landersverband DVG America, PO Box 160399, Miami, FL 33116.

North American Working Dog Assoc., 1677 N. Alisar Ave., Monterey Park, CA 91754.

United Schutzhund Clubs of America, 3704 Lemoy
Ferry Rd., St. Louis, MO 63125.

Search and Rescue

Search and rescue work is very rewarding but requires a great
deal of time for training both the dog and the owner. The dog learns
air scenting, tracking, working a scent, alerting the owner and more.
The owner must learn radio communications, emergency first aid, base
camp strategy, search tactics, victim psychology and more.

Write:

National Association for Search and Rescue, PO Box
3709, Fairfax, VA 22308.

SAR Dog Alert, PO Box 39, Somerset, CA 95684.

Sledding

Sled dog racing has become a very popular sport, due much
to the publicity surrounding the annual Iditarod race in Alaska. Although most northern breeds are normally associated with sled dog
racing, there are many teams of a variety of breeds. There was one
successful team made up entirely of Standard Poodles. Another not
quite so successful team (that still had fun even if they didn't win) was

*Therapy Dogs provide unconditional love and affectioin. (Toy
Poodle)*

240

made up of Irish Setters.

Write:

Arctic Sled Dog Club of America, RD 1, Box 191, Middle Grove, NY 12850.

International Federation of Sled Dog Sports, 7118 N. Beehive Rd., Pocatello, ID 83201.

International Sled Dog Racing Assoc., PO Box 446, Norman, ID 83848-0446.

Weight Pulling

Weight Pulling probably originated with Jack London's story of Buck, his faithful canine lead dog that moved tremendous loads, simply for the love of his owner. Weight pulling today is much more humane and is divided into weight groups based on the dog's size so that even small dogs can participate.

Write:

International Weight Pulling Assoc., PO Box 994, Greeley, CO 80632.

Have Fun!

There are other sports that you and your dog can do, such as trick training, water rescue, French Ring Sport, temperament testing and more. You can find out about the sports listed above and any others known to dog and man by getting a copy of *Everything You Always Wanted to Know About Dogs*, listed earlier in this chapter, or *201 Ways to Enjoy Your Dog* by Ellie Milon, Alpine Publications.

Most of all, enjoy your dog and have fun.

PART IV. REFERENCE MATERIAL

Appendix A

Explanation of Commonly Used Initials

Registries

AKC	American Kennel Club
UKC	United Kennel Club
MBDCA	Mixed Breed Dog Clubs of America
ASCA	Australian Shepherd Club of America
NDR	National Dog Registry (tatto registration)
SKC	States Kennel Club

Obedience

CD	Companion Dog (Novice)
CDX	Companion Dog Excellent (Open)
UD	Utility Dog (Utility)
TD	Tracking Dog
TDX	Tracking Dog Excellent
OTCH	Obedience Trial Champion
CGC	Canine Good Citizen
HIT	High in Trial
U-CD, CDX, UD UKC	Obedience Titles

Conformation

BIS	Best in Show
BOB	Best of Breed
BOS	Best Opposite Sex to Best of Breed
BOW	Best of Winners
WD	Winners Dog
WB	Winners Bitch
RWD	Reserve Winners Dog
RWB	Reserve Winners Bitch
EDM	Entry Day of Match
EDS	Entry Day of Show
PEO	Pre Entry Only

Working

HIC	Herding Instinct Certified
AATD	Animal Assisted Therapy Dog
TDI	Therapy Dog International
ASFA	American Sighthound Field Association
TT	Temperament Tested
SCHI,II, III	Schutzhund Dog, degrees I, II or III

For example, Ch Elmac's Watachie Chocho des CDX, TT, CGC, AATD is a Papillon that is a breed champion (CH), has earned his Companion Dog Excellent title (CDX), has passed the temperament test (TT), passed the AKC Canine Good Citizen test (CGC) and is a registered therapy dog with Therapy Dog International (AATD).

Appendix B

Sample Vocabulary for a Well-Educated Companion Dog

Word	What we want Fido to understand
Acck!	Interruption, stop what you're doing
Bath	Time to get a bath
Bring it back (here)	Bring me what you are retrieving
Car	Identification of your car
Come	Stop what you're doing and come to me
Cookie	Identification of a food treat
Down	Lay down and be still
Drop	Emergency down, do it very quickly
Easy	Be careful you're too rough
Get Off	As in get off the sofa
Give	Drop what you have in your mouth
Good Boy (or girl)	Praise, whatever you did was right
Heel	Walk with me, paying attention to me
In	Go into whatever I'm pointing at; car
Kennel	Identification of a crate, get in kennel
Let's Go	Go with me but not at a heel
Move	Get out of the way
No Jump	Don't jump up and put your feet on me
Okay	Good job but not as good as good boy!
Over	Jump over this obstacle
Out	Go through this door
Quiet	Don't bark or whine right now
Release	Relax and play for a minute
Roll Over	Trick training, lay down and roll over
Shake	Give me your paw and allow me to shake
Speak	Bark on my command to speak
Sit	Lower your hips to the ground, be still

Stand	Stand on all four feet, upright
Stay	Don't move from position
Take it	Pick up whatever I'm directing you to
That's enough	Stop whatever you're doing
Through	Go through what I'm directing you to
Tub	Tub is where a bath happens
Turn around	Change directions, as for grooming
Wait	Like a stay but something else follows

Appendix C

A Layman's Glossary of Training and Behavior Terms

Aggression - Fido's hostile reaction to outside stimuli. It could be in defense of you or your property, or it could be in self-defense or a reaction to a real or perceived threat. Aggression is the *fight* portion of the fight-or-flight instinct.

Anticipation - Fido does something before you give the command. Shy, fearful, insecure or overeager dogs should be allowed to anticipate during the learning stages to help build confidence. However, it should be stopped after Fido learns the exercise.

Avoidance - Fido's defensive reaction to a threat, real or imaginary. Avoidance is the *flight* portion of the fight-or-flight instinct.

Behavior Chain - A series of actions or behaviors that are then combined into one complicated routine. For example: The retrieve over the high jump is a behavior chain, as are many of the advanced obedience exercises.

Competition - 1) The sport of dog obedience or other aspects of dog sports that pit one dog/owner team against another or against the clock. 2) Two or more dogs being trained together can bring competition into play and you can use it to your advantage. One dog in a down/stay while another works can cause the dog not working to anticipate training more favorably.

Compulsive training - A type of training in which the dog is given no choice as to his actions. He is not allowed to make a mistake. This type of training is often called *force* training.

Conditioning, classical or Pavlovian - Pavlovian conditioning is the most famous; the dog salivates at the sound of a bell, knowing that food is then coming. This is an unconscious process, the animal is reacting to a stimulus.

Conditioning, operant - This is when the dog learns that he can produce a stimulus, food or reward, by his own actions. He is the initiator or the operator.

249

Extinction - Putting a behavior under control and then eliminating it. For example, telling Fido "Speak" each time he barks and then teaching him "No speak."

Force - Making the dog do what we want, using a leash and collar or hands. Not allowing the dog a choice. Compulsive training.

Habituation - Typically known as *horse training* methods, it means getting an animal used to something so that there is no more fear. With a horse it might be flicking it all over with a saddle blanket. With a dog it might be running a brush all over it, or a leash, something similar.

Imprinting - A type of learning that occurs very early in life and is vitally important for the animal's recognition of what it is. Often seen in baby ducks hatched and fed by people. They often will not breed with other ducks as adults.

Inducive training - To use an object of attraction, a motivator, to elicit a movement or action from Fido, voluntarily. Example: Fido follows a treat to the floor to lay down.

Jackpot - A term Karen Pryor uses in her book, *Lads Before the Wind*, to signify a reward that is larger than normal. For example: Ending a training session on a high note with a jackpot reward takes the sting out of ending the training session.

Mimic - Many dogs can learn by watching each other or even watching their owner. Many dogs will attempt a new agility obstacle after they have seen another dog go over it.

Shaping - Using a motivator or training tool to cause the dog to do something. That effort is then rewarded.

Time Out - A time out or free time period away from training gives Fido time to absorb the new information. It is especially useful if the dog is confused. Time outs can vary from a few hours to overnight or even a few days.

Bibliography

Bauman, Diane, *Beyond Basic Dog Training*. Howell Books: New York, 1986.

Beck, Alan, ScD and Aaron Katcher, MD, *Between Pets and People*. Perigee Books, 1983.

Benjamin, Carol Lea, *Mother Knows Best*. Howell Books: New York, 1985.

Bulanda, Susan, *Everything You Always Wanted to Know About Dogs*. Doral Publishing: Wilsonville, OR, 1992.

Campbell, William, *Behavior Problems in Dogs*. American Veterinary Publications: Goleta, CA, 1992

Caras, Roger, *A Dog is Listening*. Summit Books: New York, 1992.

Colflesh, Linda, *Making Friends*. Howell Books: New York, 1990.

Daniels, Julie, *Enjoying Dog Agility*. Doral Publishing: Wilsonville, OR, 1991.

Fisher, John, *Think Dog!* Trafalgar Square Publishing: North Pomfret, VT, 1990.

Flaherty, Charles, *Animal Learning and Cognition*. Alfred Knopf: New York, 1985.

Fogle, Bruce, *Pets and Their People*. Viking Press: New York, 1983.

Fox, Dr Michael, *Superdog*. Howell Books: New York, 1990.

Hart, DVM, Benjamin and Lynette Hart, *Canine and Feline Behavioral Therapy*. Lea & Febiger: Philadelphia, 1985.

Hart, DVM, Benjamin and Lynette Hart, *The Perfect Puppy*. Freeman and Co.: New York, 1988.

Milani, DVM, Myrna, *The Body Language and Emotion of Dogs.* Wm Morrow and Co.: New York, 1986.

Milon, Ellie, **201** *Ways to Enjoy Your Dog.* Alpine Publications: Loveland, CO, 1990.

Monk's of New Skete, *How to be Your Dog's Best Friend.* Howell Books: New York, 1978.

Pryor, Karen, *Don't Shoot the Dog.* Bantam New Age Books: New York, 1985.

Pryor, Karen, *How to Teach Your Dog to Play Frisbee.* Simon and Schuster: New York, 1985.

Pryor, Karen, *Lads before the Wind.* Sunshine Books: North Bend, WA, 1975.

Rose, Tom and Gary Patterson, *Training the Competitive Working Dog.* Gilblaut Publishing: Englewood, CO, 1985.

Volhard, Jack and Wendy, *Open and Utility Training.* Howell Books: New York, 1992.

Volhard, Joachim and Gail Thomas Fisher, *Training Your Dog.* Howell Books: New York, 1983.

Volhard, Jack and Melissa Bartlett, *What All Good Dogs Should Know.* Howell Books: New York, 1991.

Index

254